AN INTRODUCTION TO THE STUDY OF FISHES

AN INTRODUCTION TO THE STUDY OF FISHES

Volume I

ALBERT C.L.G. GUNTHER

ATLANTIC PUBLISHERS AND DISTRIBUTORS

Published by
ATLANTIC PUBLISHERS AND DISTRIBUTORS
B-2, Vishal Enclave, New Delhi-27
Phone 5413460

Sales Office
4346/4C, Ansari Road, Darya Ganj,
New Delhi-110 002
Phone 3273880, 3285873
Fax 91-11-3285873

ISBN 81-7156-480-1 (Vol. I)
ISBN 81-7156-482-8 (Set)

Typeset at
APD Computer Graphics
B-2, Vishal Enclave, New Delhi-110 027
Printed in India at
Malhotra Enterprises
New Delhi

PREFACE.

THE scope of the present work is to give in a concise form an account of the principal facts relating to the structure, classification, and life-history of Fishes. It is intended to meet the requirements of those who are desirous of studying the elements of Ichthyology; to serve as a book of reference to zoologists generally; and, finally, to supply those who, like travellers, have frequent opportunities of observing fishes, with a ready means of obtaining information. The article on "Ichthyology," prepared by the late Sir J. Richardson for the eighth edition of the "Encyclopædia Britannica," is the only publication which has hitherto partly satisfied such requirements; and when I undertook, some years ago, to revise, or rather rewrite that article for the new edition of that work, it occurred to me that I might at the same time prepare a Handbook of Ichthyology, whilst reserving for the article an abstract so condensed as to be adapted for the wants of the general reader.

From the general plan of the work I have only departed in those chapters which deal with the Geographical Distribution of Fishes. This is a subject which has never before been treated in a general and comprehensive manner, and seemed to demand particular attention. I have, therefore, thought it right to give nominal lists of the Faunæ, and the other details of fact on which I have based my conclusions, although all the necessary materials may be found in my "Catalogue of Fishes."

A few references only to the numerous sources which were consulted on the subjects of Chapters 1-12, are inserted in the text; more are not required by the beginner; he is introduced to a merely elementary account of facts well known to the advanced student.

With regard to the illustrations, about twenty have been prepared after originals published by Cuvier, J. Müller, Owen, Traquair, Duméril, Cunningham, Hasse, Poey, Siebold, and Gegenbaur, A similar number, representing extinct fishes, have been taken, with the kind permission of the author, from Owen's "Palæontology" My best thanks are due also to the Committee of Publications of the Zoological Society, and to the Editors of the "Annals and Magazine of Natural History," and of the "Journal des Museum Godeffroy," for the loan of woodcuts illustrating some of my papers on South American fishes and on larval forms. The remainder of the illustrations (about three-fourths) are either original figures, or formed part of the article on 'Ichthyology' in the former edition of the "Encyclopædia Britannica."

CONTENTS.

INTRODUCTORY REMARKS.

CHAPTER I.

CHAPTER II.

CHAPTER III.

CHAPTER IV.

CHAPTER V.

CHAPTER VI.

CHAPTER VII.

CHAPTER VIII.

CHAPTER IX.

CHAPTER X.

CHAPTER XI.

CHAPTER XII.

CHAPTER XIII.

CHAPTER XIV.

CHAPTER XV.

CHAPTER XVI.

CHAPTER XVII.

CHAPTER XVIII.

CHAPTER XIX.

CHAPTER XX.

CHAPTER XXI.

INTRODUCTORY REMARKS.

ACCORDING to the views generally adopted at present, all those Vertebrate animals are referred to the Class of Fishes, which living in water, breathe air dissolved in water by means of gills or branchiæ; whose heart consists of a single ventricle and single atrium; whose limbs, if present, are modified into fins, supplemented by unpaired, median fins; and whose skin is either naked, or covered with scales or osseous plates or bucklers. With few exceptions fishes are oviparous. However, there are not a few members of this Class which show a modification of one or more of these characteristics, as we shall see hereafter, and which nevertheless, cannot be separated from it. The distinction between the Class of Fishes and that of Batrachians is very slight indeed.

The branch of Zoology which treats of the internal and external structure of fishes, their mode of life, and their distribution in space and time, is termed Ichthyology.[1]

[1] From ἰχθυς, fish, and λογος, doctrine or treatise.

CHAPTER I.

HISTORY AND LITERATURE.

Aristotle. THE commencement of the history of Ichthyology coincides with that of Zoology generally. ARISTOTLE (384-322 B.C.) had a perfect knowledge of the general structure of fishes, which he clearly discriminates from the Aquatic animals with lungs and mammæ, *i.e.* Cetaceans, and from the various groups of Aquatic Invertebrates. He says that "the special characteristics of the true fishes consist in the branchiæ and fins, the majority having four fins, but those of an elongate form, as the eels, having two only. Some, as the *Muræna*, lack the fins altogether. The Rays swim with their whole body, which is spread out. The branchiæ are sometimes furnished with an opercle, sometimes without one, as is the case in the cartilaginous fishes. . . . No fish has hairs or feathers; most are covered with scales, but some have a rough or smooth skin. The tongue is hard, often toothed; and sometimes so much adherent that it seems to be wanting. The eyes have no lids; nor are any ears or nostrils visible, for what takes the place of nostrils is a blind cavity. Nevertheless they have the senses of tasting, smelling, and hearing. All have blood. All scaly fishes are oviparous, but the cartilaginous fishes (with the exception of the Sea-devil, which Aristotle places along with them) are viviparous. All have a heart, liver, and gall-bladder; but kidneys and urinary bladder are absent. They vary much in the structure of their intestines: for whilst the mullet has a fleshy stomach like a bird, others have no stomachic dilatation. Pyloric coeca are close to the stomach, variable in number; there are even some, like the majority of the cartilaginous fishes, which have none whatever. Two bodies are situated along the spine, which have the function of testicles, and open towards the vent, and which are much enlarged in the spawning season. The scales become harder with age. Not being provided with lungs, they have no voice, but several can emit grunting sounds. They sleep like other animals. In the majority the females exceed the males in size; and in the Rays and Sharks the male is distinguished by an appendage on each side of the vent."

Aristotle's information on the habits of fishes, their migrations, mode and time of propagation, utility, is, as far as it has been tested, surprisingly correct. Unfortunately, only too often we lack the means of recognising the species of which he gives a description. His ideas of specific distinction were as vague as those of the fishermen whose nomenclature he adopted; it never occurred to him that such popular names are subject to change, or may be entirely lost with time, and the difficulty of deciphering his species is further increased by the circumstance that popular names are often applied by him to the same fish, or that different stages of growth are designated by distinct names. The number of fishes known to Aristotle seems to have been about 115, all of which are inhabitants of the Ægean Sea.

That one man should have discovered so many truths, and formed so sure a base for Zoology, is less surprising than the fact that for about eighteen centuries a science which seemed to offer particular attractions to men gifted with power of observation, was no farther advanced. Yet this is the case. Aristotle's disciples, as well as his successors, remained satisfied to be his copiers or commentators, and to collect fabulous stories or vague notions. With very few exceptions (such as *Ausonius*, who wrote a small poem, in which he describes from his own observations the fishes of the Mosel) authors entirely abandoned original research. And it was not until about the middle of the sixteenth century that Ichthyology made a new step in advance by the appearance of *Belon*, *Rondelet*, and *Salviani*, who almost simultaneously published their grand works, by which the idea of species was established definitely and for all times.

Belon. P. BELON travelled in the countries bordering on the eastern part of the Mediterranean, in the years 1547-50; he collected rich stores of positive knowledge, which he deposited in several works. The one most important for the progress of Ichthyology is that entitled "De aquatilibus libri duo" (Paris 1553; small 4to.) Belon knows about 110 fishes; of which he gives rude, but generally recognisable, figures. In his descriptions he pays regard to the classical as well as vernacular nomenclature, and states the outward characteristics, sometimes even the number of fin-rays, frequently also the most conspicuous anatomical peculiarities.

Although Belon but rarely gives definitions of the terms used by him, it is generally not very difficult to ascertain the limits which he intended to assign to each division of aquatic animals. He very properly divides them into such as are provided with blood, and into those without it: two divisions, called in modern language Vertebrate and Invertebrate aquatic animals. The former are classified by him according to sizes, the further subdivisions being based on the structure of the skeleton, mode of propagation, number of limbs, form of the body, and on the physical character of the localities inhabited by fishes. This classification is as follows:—

I. The larger fishes or Cetaceans.

A. Viviparous Cetaceans with bony skeletons (= Cetacea).

B. Viviparous Amphibians.

1. With four limbs: Seals, Hippopotamus, Beaver, Otter, and other aquatic Mammalia.
2. With two limbs: Mermaids, etc.

C. Oviparous Amphibians (= Reptiles and Frogs).

D. Viviparous Cartilaginous fishes.

1. Of an oblong form (= Sharks).
2. Of a flat form (= Rays and Lophius).

E. Oviparous Cartilaginous fishes (= Sturgeons and Silurus).

F. Oviparous Cetaceans, with spines instead of bones (= large marine fishes, like the Thunny, Sword-fish, Sciænoids, Bass, Gadoids, Trachypterus).

II. Spinous Oviparous fishes of a flat form (= Pleuronectidæ).

III. Fishes of a high form, like Zeus.

IV. Fishes of a snake-like form (= Eels, Belone, Sphyræna).

V. Small Oviparous, spinous, scaly, marine fishes.

1. Pelagic kinds.
2. Littoral kinds.
3. Kinds inhabiting rocky localities.

VI. Fluviatile and Lacustrine fishes.

The work of the Roman ichthyologist, H. SALVIANI (1514-72), is characteristic of the high social position which the author held as the physician of three popes. Its title is "Aquatilium animalium historia" (Rom. 1554-57, fol.) It treats exclusively of the fishes of Italy. Ninety-two species are figured on seventy-six plates which, as regards artistic execution, are masterpieces of that period, although those specific characteristics which now-a-days constitute the value of a zoological drawing, were entirely overlooked by the author or artist. No attempt is made at a natural classification, but the allied forms generally are placed in close proximity. The descriptions are quite equal to those given by Belon, entering much into the details of the economy and usefulness of the several species, and were evidently composed with the view of collecting in a readable form all that might

Salviani.

prove of interest to the class of society in which the author moved. Salviani's work is of a high standard, most remarkable for the age in which he lived. It could not fail to convey valuable instruction, and to render Ichthyology popular in the country to the fauna of which it was devoted, but it would not have advanced Ichthyology as science generally; and in this respect Salviani is not to be compared with Rondelet or Belon.

Rondelet. G. RONDELET (1507-1557) had the great advantage over Belon in having received a medical education at Paris, and more especially in having gone through a complete course of instruction in anatomy as a pupil of Guentherus of Andernach. This is conspicuous throughout his works—"Libri de Piscibus marinis" (Lugd. 1554, fol.); and "Universæ aquatilium historiæ pars altera" (Lugd. 1555, fol.) Nevertheless they cannot be regarded as more than considerably enlarged editions of Belon's work. For although he worked independently of the latter, and differs from him in numerous details, the system adopted by him is characterised by the same absence of the true principles of classification. Rondelet had a much more extensive knowledge of details. His work is almost entirely limited to European, and chiefly Mediterranean, forms, and comprises not less than 197 marine and 47 freshwater fishes. His descriptions are more complete and his figures much more accurate than those of Belon; and the specific account is preceded by introductory chapters in which he treats in a general manner on the distinctions, the external and internal parts, and on the economy of fishes. Like Belon, he had no conception of the various categories of classification—for instance, confounding throughout his work the terms "genus" and "species;" but he had intuitively a notion of what his successors called a "species," and his principal object was to collect and give as much information as possible of such species.

For nearly a century the works of Belon and Rondelet remained the standard works of Ichthyology; but this science did not remain stationary during this period. The attention of naturalists was now directed to the products of foreign countries, especially the Spanish and Dutch possessions in the New World; and in Europe the establishment of anatomical schools and academies led to the careful investigation of the internal anatomy of the most remarkable European forms. Limited as these efforts were as to their scope, being directed either only to the fauna of some district, or to the dissection of a single species, they were sufficiently numerous to enlarge the views of naturalists, and to destroy that fatal dependency on preceding authorities which had continued to keep in bonds the minds of even such men as Rondelet and Belon.

W. Piso G. Margrav.

The most noteworthy of those who were active in tropical countries are W. PISO and G. MARGRAV. They accompanied as physicians the Dutch Governor, Prince Moritz of Nassau, to Brazil (1637-44). Margrav especially studied the fauna of the country, and although he died before his return to Europe, his observations were published by his colleague, and embodied in a work "Historia naturalis Braziliæ" (Lugd. 1648, fol.), in which the fourth book treats of the fishes. He describes about 100 species, all of which had been previously unknown, in a manner far superior to that of his predecessors. The accompanying figures are not good, but nearly always recognisable, and giving a fair idea of the form of the fish. Margrav himself, with the aid of an artist, had made a most valuable collection of coloured drawings of the objects observed and described by him, but many years were allowed to pass before it was scientifically utilised by Bloch and others.

Anatomists, 1600-1700.

Of the men who left records of their anatomical researches, we may mention BORELLI (1608-79), who wrote a work "De motu animalium" (Rom. 1680, 4to), in which he explained the mechanism of swimming, and the function of the air-bladder; M. MALPIGHI (1628-94), who examined the optic nerve of the sword-fish; the celebrated J. SWAMMERDAM (1637-80), who described the intestines of numerous fishes; and J. DUVERNEY (1648-1730), who entered into detailed researches of the organs of respiration.

A new era in the history of Ichthyology commences with *Ray*, *Willughby*, and *Artedi*, who were the first to recognise the true principles by which the natural affinities of animals should be determined. Their labours stand in so intimate a connection with each other that they represent only one stride in the progress of this science.

Ray and Willughby J. RAY (born 1628 in Essex, died 1705), was the friend and guide of F. WILLUGHBY (1635-72). They had recognised that a thorough reform of the treatment of the vegetable and animal kingdoms had become necessary; that the only way of bringing order into the existing chaos was that of arranging the various forms with regard to their structure; that they must cease to be burdened with inapplicable passages and quotations of the ancient writers, and to perpetuate the erroneous or vague notions of their predecessors. They abandoned speculation, and adhered to facts only. One of the first results, and perhaps the most important, of their method was, that having recognised the "species" as such, they defined this term, and fixed it as the base, from which all sound zoological knowledge has to start.

Although they had divided their work thus that Ray attended to the plants principally, and Willughby to the animals, the "Historia piscium" (Oxford, 1686, fol.), which bears Willughby's name on the titlepage, and was edited by Ray, is clearly their joint production. A great part of the observations contained in it were collected during their common journeys in Great Britain and on the Continent, and it is no exaggeration to say that at that time these two Englishmen knew the fishes of the Continent, especially those of Germany, better than any other Continental zoologist.

By the definition of fishes as animals with blood, breathing by gills, provided with a single ventricle of the heart, covered with scales or naked; the Cetaceans are excluded. Yet, at a later period Ray appears to have been afraid of so great an innovation as the separation of whales from fishes, and, therefore, he invented a definition of fish which comprises both. The fishes proper are then arranged in the first place according to the cartilaginous or osseous nature of the skeleton; further subdivisions being formed with regard to the general form of the body, the presence or absence of ventral fins, the soft or spinous structure of the dorsal rays, the number of dorsal fins, etc. Not less than 420 species are thus arranged and described, of which about 180 were known to the authors from autopsy: a comparatively small proportion, descriptions and figures still forming at that time in a great measure a substitute for collections and museums. With the increasing accumulation of forms the want of a fixed nomenclature is now more and more felt.

PETER ARTEDI would have been a great ichthyologist if Ray or Willughby had never preceded him. But he was fully conscious of the fact that both had prepared the way for him, and therefore he derived all possible advantages from their works. Born in 1705 in Sweden, he studied with Linnæus at Upsala; from an early period he devoted himself entirely to the study of fishes, and was engaged in the arrangement and description of the ichthyological collection of *Seba*, a wealthy Dutchman who had formed the then perhaps richest museum, when he was accidentally drowned in one of the canals of Amsterdam in the year 1734, at an age of twenty-nine years. His manuscripts were fortunately rescued by an Englishman, Cliffort, and edited by his early friend Linnæus.

P. Artedi.

The work is divided into the following parts :—

1. In the "Bibliotheca Ichthyologica" Artedi gives a very complete list of all preceding authors who have written on fishes, with a critical analysis of their works.

2. The "Philosophia Ichthyologica" is devoted to a description of the external and internal parts of fishes; Artedi fixes a precise terminology of all the various modifications of the organs, distinguishes between those characters which determine a genus and such as indicate a species or merely a variety; in fact he establishes the method and principles which subsequently have guided every systematic ichthyologist.

3. The "Genera Piscium" contains well-defined diagnoses of forty-five genera, for which he fixes an unchangeable nomenclature.

4. In the "Species Piscium" descriptions of seventy-two species, examined by himself, are given; descriptions which even now are models of exactitude and method.

5. Finally, in the "Synonymia Piscium" references to all previous authors are arranged for every species, very much in the same manner which is adopted in the systematic works of the present day.

Artedi has been justly called the Father of Ichthyology.

Linnæus.

So perfect was his treatment of the subject, that even LINNÆUS could no more improve it, only modify and add to it; and as far as Ichthyology is concerned, Linnæus has scarcely done anything beyond applying binominal terms to the species properly described and classified by Artedi.

Artedi had divided the fishes proper into four orders, viz. *Malacopterygii*, *Acanthopterygii*, *Branchiostegi*, and *Chondropterygii*, of which the third only, according to our present knowledge, appears to be singularly heterogeneous, as it comprises *Balistes*, *Ostracion*, *Cyclopterus*, and *Lophius*. Linnæus, besides separating the Cetaceans entirely from the class of fishes (at least since the 10th edition of the "Systema Naturæ") abandoned Artedi's order of Branchiostegi, but substituted a scarcely more natural combination by joining it with Artedi's Chondropterygians, under the name of "Amphibia nantes."

His classification of the genera appears in the 12th edition of the "Systema," thus—

Amphibia Nantes.

Spiraculis compositis.

- Petromyzon.
- Raia.
- Squalus.
- Chimæra.

Spiraculis solitariis.

- Lophius.
- Acipenser.
- Cyclopterus.
- Balistes.
- Ostracion.
- Tetrodon.
- Diodon.
- Centriscus.
- Syngnathus.
- Pegasus.

Pisces Apodes.

- Muræna.
- Gymnotus.
- Trichiurus.
- Anarhichas.
- Ammodytes.
- Ophidium.
- Stromateus.
- Xiphias.

Pisces Jugulares.

- Callionymus.
- Uranoscopus.
- Trachinus.
- Gadus.
- Blennius.

Pisces Thoracici.

- Cepola.
- Echeneis.
- Coryphæna.
- Gobius.
- Cottus.
- Scorpæna.
- Zeus.
- Pleuronectes.
- Chætodon.
- Sparus.
- Labrus.
- Sciæna.
- Perca.
- Gasterosteus.
- Scomber.
- Mullus.
- Trigla.

Pisces Abdominales.

- Cobitis.
- Amia.
- Silurus.
- Teuthis.
- Loricaria.
- Salmo.
- Fistularia.
- Esox.
- Elops.
- Argentina.
- Atherina.
- Mugil.
- Mormyrus.
- Exocœtus.
- Polynemus.
- Clupea.
- Cyprinus.

Gronow and Klein. Two contemporaries of *Linnæus* attempted a systematic arrangement of fishes; both had considerable opportunities for their study, especially in possessing extensive collections; but neither exercised any influence on the progress of Ichthyology. The one, L. T. GRONOW, a German who resided in Holland, closely followed the arrangements proposed by Artedi and Linnæus, and increased the number of genera and species from the contents of his own museum. He published two works, "Museum Ichthyologicum" (Lugd. 1754-6, fol.), and "Zoophylacium" (Lugd. 1763-81, fol.); a posthumous work, containing numerous excellent descriptions of new forms was published by J. E. Gray in 1854 under the title of "Systema Ichthyologicum." To Gronow also is due the invention of preparing flat skins of fishes in a dry state, and preserving them in the manner of a herbarium. The specimens thus prepared by him belong to the oldest which have been preserved down to our time.

Much less important are the ichthyological labours of J. T. KLEIN (1685-1759). They are embodied in five parts (*Missus*) of a work entitled "Historia naturalis piscium" (Sedæ, 1740-9, 4to.) He regarded a system merely as the means of recognising the various forms of animals, not as the expression of their natural affinities; and that method seemed to him to be the most perfect by which an animal could be most readily determined. He eschewed all reference to minute or anatomical characters. Hence his system is a series of the most unnatural combinations, and we cannot be surprised that Linnæus passed in silence over Klein's labours.

Pupils and Successors of Linnæus The works of Artedi and Linnæus excited fresh activity, more especially in Scandinavia, Holland, Germany, and England, such as has not been equalled in the history of biological science either before or after. Whilst some of the pupils and followers of Linnæus devoted themselves to an examination and study of the fauna of their native countries, others proceeded on voyages of discovery to foreign and distant countries. Of these latter the following may be specially mentioned:—*O. Fabricius* worked out the Fauna of Greenland, *Kalm* collected in North America, *Hasselquist* in Egypt and Palestine, *Brünnich* in the Mediterranean, *Osbeck* in Java and China, *Thunberg* in Japan; *Forskal* examined and described the fishes of the Red Sea; *Steller, Pallas, S. T. Gmelin,* and *Güldenstedt* traversed nearly the whole of the Russian Empire in Europe and Asia. Others attached themselves as naturalists to the celebrated circumnavigators of the last century, like the two *Forsters* (father and son), and *Solander*, who accompanied Cook; *Commerson*, who travelled with Bougainville; and *Sonnerat*. Numerous new and startling forms were discovered by those men, and the foundation was laid of the knowledge of the geographical distribution of animals.

Of those who studied the fishes of their native country the most celebrated are *Pennant* (Great Britain), *O. F. Müller* (Denmark), *Duhamel* (France), *Meidinger* (Austria), *Cornide* (Spain), *Parra* (Cuba).

The materials brought together by those and other zoologists were so numerous that, not long after the death of Linnæus, the necessity was felt of collecting them in a compendious form. Several compilators undertook this task; they embodied the recent discoveries in new editions of Artedi's and Linné's classical works, but not possessing either a knowledge of the subject or any critical discernment, they only succeeded in covering those noble monuments under a mass of confused rubbish. For Ichthyology it was fortunate that two men at least, Bloch and Lacépède, made it a subject of long and original research.

MARK ELIEZER BLOCH, born in the year 1723 at Anspach in Germany, practised as a physician in Berlin; he had reached M. E. Bloch.

an age of fifty-six years when he commenced to write on ichthyological subjects. To commence at his age a work in which he intended not only to give full descriptions of the species known to him from specimens or drawings, but also to illustrate every species in a style truly magnificent for his time, was an undertaking of the execution of which an ordinary man would have despaired. Yet he accomplished not only this task, but even more, as we shall see hereafter.

His work consists of two divisions:—

1. "Oeconomische Naturgeschichte der Fische Deutschlands" (Berl. 1782-4, 4to. Plates in fol.)

2. "Naturgeschichte der auslændischen Fische" (Berl. 1785-95, 4to. Plates in fol.)

Bloch's work is unique, and probably will for ever remain so. Although Cuvier fifty years later undertook a similar general work on fishes, the subject had then become too extensive to allow of an attempt of giving illustrations of all the species, or illustrations of a similar size and costliness.

The first division of the work, which is devoted to a description of the fishes of Germany, is entirely original, and based upon Bloch's own observations. His descriptions as well as figures were made from nature, and are, with but few exceptions, still serviceable; many continue to be the best existing in literature.

Bloch was less fortunate and is much less reliable in his natural history of foreign fishes. For many of the species he had to rely on more or less incorrect drawings and descriptions of travellers; frequently, also, he was deceived as to the origin of specimens which he acquired by purchase. Hence his accounts contain numerous confusing errors which it would have been difficult to correct, if not nearly the whole of the materials on which his work is based had been preserved in the collections at Berlin.

After the completion of his Ichthyology Bloch occupied

himself with systematic work. He prepared a general system of fishes, in which he arranged not only those described in his great work, but also those with which he had become acquainted afterwards from the descriptions of others. The work was ably edited and published after Bloch's death by a philologist, *J. G. Schneider*, under the title "M. E. Blochii Systema ichthyologiæ iconibus ex. illustratum" (Berl. 1801, 8vo.) The number of species enumerated in it amounts to 1519. The system is based upon the number of the fins, the various orders being termed *Hendecapterygii*, *Decapterygii*, etc. We need not add that an artificial method like this led to the most unnatural combinations or severances.

Bloch's Ichthyology remained for many years the standard work, and, by the great number of excellent illustrations, proved a most useful guide to the student. But as regards originality of thought, Bloch was far surpassed by his contemporary, B. G. E. DE LACÉPÈDE, born at Agen, in France, in 1756, a man of great and general erudition, who died as Professor of the Museum of Natural History of Paris in 1826. **Lacépède.**

Lacépède had to contend with great difficulties in the preparation of his "Histoire des Poissons" (Paris, 1798-1803, 4to, in 5 vols.), which was written during the most disturbed period of the French Revolution. A great part of it was composed whilst the author was separated from collections and books, and had to rely on his notes and manuscripts only. Even the works of Bloch and other contemporaneous authors remained unknown, or at least inaccessible, to him for a long time. Therefore we cannot be surprised that his work abounds in all those errors to which a compiler is subject. The same species not only appears under two and more distinct specific names, but it sometimes happens that the author understands so little the source from which he derives his information that the description is referred to one genus and the accompanying figure to another. The names of genera are unduly multiplied; and the figures with which the work is illustrated are far inferior to those of Bloch. Thus the influence of Lacépede on the progress of Ichthyology was infinitely less than that of his fellow-labourer; and the labour caused to his successors by correcting the numerous errors into which he has fallen, probably outweighs the assistance which they derived from his work.

Anatomists.

The work of the principal cultivators of Ichthyology in the period between Ray and Lacépède was chiefly systematic and descriptive, but also the internal organisation of fishes received attention from more than one great anatomist. *Haller*, *Camper*, and *Hunter*, examined the nervous system and organs of sense; and more especially *Alexander Monro* (the son) published a classical work, "The Structure and Physiology of Fishes explained and compared with those of Man and other Animals" (Edinb. 1785, fol.) The electric organs of fishes (*Torpedo* and *Gymnotus*) were examined by *Réaumur*, *Allamand*, *Bancroft*, *Walsh*, and still more exactly by *J. Hunter*. The mystery of the propagation of the Eel called forth a large number of essays, and even the artificial propagation of Salmonidæ was known and practised by *Gleditsch* (1764).

Faunists.

Bloch and Lacépède's works were almost immediately succeeded by the labours of *Cuvier*, but his early publications were of necessity tentative, preliminary, and fragmentary, so that a short period elapsed before the spirit infused by this great anatomist into Ichthyology could exercise its influence on all workers in this field. Several of such antecuvierian works must be mentioned on account of their importance to our knowledge of certain Faunas: the "Descriptions and Figures of Two Hundred Fishes collected at Vizagapatam on the coast of Coromandel" (Lond. 1803; 2 vols. in fol.), by *Patrick Russel*; and "An Account of the Fishes found in the River Ganges and its branches" (Edinb. 1822; 2 vols. in

4to), by *F. Hamilton* (formerly *Buchanan*)—works distinguished by a greater accuracy of their drawings (especially in the latter), than was ever attained before. A "Natural History of British Fishes" was published by *E. Donovan* (Lond. 8vo, 1802-8); and the Mediterranean Fauna formed the study of the lifetime of *A. Risso* ("Ichthyologie de Nice." Paris, 1810, 8vo; and "Histoire naturelle de l'Europe Meridionale." Paris, 1827, 8vo). A slight beginning in the description of the fishes of the United States was made by *S. L. Mitchell*, who published, besides various papers, a "Memoir on the Ichthyology of New York," in 1815.[1]

G. Cuvier.

G. Cuvier did not occupy himself with the study of fishes merely because this class formed part of the "Règne animal," but he devoted himself to it with particular predilection. The investigation of their anatomy, and especially of their skeleton, was taken up by him at an early period, and continued until he had succeeded in completing so perfect a framework of the system of the whole class that his immediate successors could content themselves with filling up those details for which their master had no leisure. Indefatigable in examining all the external and internal characters of the fishes of a rich collection, he ascertained the natural affinities of the infinite variety of fishes, and accurately defined the divisions, orders, families, and genera of the class, as they appear in the various editions of the "Règne animal." His industry equalled his genius: he opened connections with almost every accessible part of the globe; not only French travellers and naturalists, but also Germans, Englishmen, Americans, rivalled one another to assist him with collections; and for many years the Museum of the Jardin des Plantes was the centre where all ichthyological treasures were deposited. Thus Cuvier

[1] Down to this period the history of Ichthyology is fully treated in the first volume of Cuvier and Valenciennes' "Hist. nat. d. Poiss."

brought together a collection the like of which had never been seen before, and which, as it contains all the materials on which his labours were based, must still be considered to be the most important. Soon after the year 1820, Cuvier, assisted by one of his pupils, A. VALENCIENNES, commenced his great work on fishes, "Histoire naturelles des Poissons," of which the first volume appeared in 1828. The earlier volumes, in which Cuvier himself took his share, bear evidence of the freshness and love with which both authors devoted themselves to their task. After Cuvier's death in 1832 the work was left entirely in the hands of Valenciennes, whose energy and interest gradually slackened, to rise to the old standard in some parts only, as, for instance, in the treatise on the Herring. He left the work unfinished with the twenty-second volume (1848), which treats of the Salmonoids. Yet, incomplete as it is, it is indispensable to the student.

There exist several editions of the work, which, however, have the same text. One, printed in 8vo, with coloured or plain figures, is the one in common use among ichthyologists. A more luxurious edition in 4to has a different pagination, and therefore is most inconvenient to use.

As mentioned above, the various parts of the work are very unequally worked out. Many of the species are described in so masterly a manner that a greater excellency of method can hardly be conceived. The history of the literature of these species is entered into with minuteness and critical discernment; but in the later volumes, numerous species are introduced into the system without any description, or with a few words only, comparing a species with one or more of its congeners. Cuvier himself, at a late period of his life, seems to have grown indifferent as to the exact definition of his species: a failing commonly observed among Zoologists when attention to descriptive details becomes to them a tedious task. What is more surprising is, that a man of his anatomical and physiological knowledge should have overlooked the fact that secondary sexual characters are developed in fishes as in any other class of animals, and that fishes undergo great changes during growth; and, consequently, that he described almost all such sexual forms and different stages of growth under distinct specific and even generic names

The system finally adopted by Cuvier is the following:—

A. POISSONS OSSEUX.

I.—A BRANCHIES EN PEIGNES OU EN LAMES.

1. A MÂCHOIRE SUPÉRIEURE LIBRE.

a. *Acanthoptérygiens.*

Percoïdes.	Sparoïdes.	Branchies labyrinthiques.
Polynèmes.	Chétodonoïdes.	Lophioïdes.
Mulles.	Scomberoïdes.	Gobioïdes.
Joues cuirassées.	Muges.	Labroïdes.
Scienoïdes.		

b. *Malacoptérygiens.*

Abdominaux	*Subbrachiens.*	*Apodes.*
Cyprinoïdes	Sparoïdes.	Murenoïdes.
Siluroïdes.	Pleuronectes.	
Salmonoïdes.	Discoboles.	
Clupeoïdes.		
Lucioïdes.		

2. A MÂCHOIRE SUPÉRIEURE FIXÉE.

Sclérodermes. Gymnodontes.

II. A BRANCHIES EN FORME DE HOUPPES.

Lophobranches.

B. CARTILAGINEUX OU CHONDROPTÉRYGIENS.

Sturioniens. Plagiostomes. Cyclostomes.

We have to compare this system with that of Linnæus if we wish to measure the gigantic stride Ichthyology has made during the intervening period of seventy years. The various characters employed for classification have been examined throughout the whole class, and their relative importance has been duly weighed and understood. Though Linnæus had formed a category of "Amphibia nantes" for fishes with a cartilaginous skeleton, which should coincide with Cuvier's "Poissons Cartilagineux," he had failed to understand the very nature of cartilage, apparently comprising by this term any skeletal framework of less firmity than ordinary bone. Hence he considered *Lophius*, *Cyclopterus*, *Syngnathus* to be cartilaginous fishes. Adopting the position and development of the ventral fins as a highly important character, he was obliged to associate fishes with rudimentary and inconspicuous ventral fins, like *Trichiurus*, *Xiphias*, etc., with the true Eels. The important category of a "family" appears now in Cuvier's system fully established as that intermediate between genus and order. Important changes in Cuvier's system have been made and proposed by his successors, but in the main it is still that of the present day.

Cuvier had extended his researches beyond the living forms, into the field of palæontology; he was the first to observe the close resemblance of the scales of the fossil *Palæoniscus* to those of the living *Polypterus* and *Lepidosteus*, the prolongation and identity of structure of the upper caudal lobe in *Palæoniscus* and the Sturgeons, the presence of peculiar "fulcra" on the anterior margin of the dorsal fin in *Palæoniscus* and *Lepidosteus:* inferring from these facts that that fossil genus was allied *either* to the Sturgeons *or* to *Lepidosteus*. But it did not occur to him that there was a close relationship between those recent fishes. *Lepidosteus* and, with it, the fossil genus remained in his system a member of the order of *Malacopterygii abdominales*.

It was left to L. Agassiz (born 1807, died 1873) to point out the importance of the character of the structure of the scales, and to open a path towards the knowledge of a whole new sub-class of fishes, the *Ganoidei*.

Impressed with the fact that the peculiar scales of *Polypterus* and *Lepidosteus* are common to all fossil osseous fishes down to the chalk, he takes the structure of the scales generally as the base for an ichthyological system, and distinguishes four orders:—

1. *Placoids.*—Without scales proper, but with scales of enamel, sometimes large, sometimes small and reduced to mere points (Rays, Sharks, and Cyclostomi, with the fossil *Hybodontes*).

2. *Ganoids.*—With angular bony scales, covered with a thick stratum of enamel: to this order belong the fossil Lepidoides, Sauroides, Pycnodontes, and Coelacanthi; the recent Polypterus, Lepidosteus, Sclerodermi, Gymnodontes, Lophobranches, and Siluroides; also the Sturgeons.

3. *Ctenoids.*—With rough scales, which have their free margins denticulated: Chætodontidæ, Pleuronectidæ, Percidæ, Polyacanthi, Sciænidæ, Sparidæ, Scorpænidæ, Aulostomi.

4. *Cycloids.*—With smooth scales, the hind margin of which lacks denticulation: Labridæ, Mugilidæ, Scombridæ, Gadoidei, Gobiidæ, Murænidæ, Lucioidei, Salmonidæ, Clupeidæ, Cyprinidæ.

We have no hesitation in affirming that if Agassiz had had an opportunity of acquiring a more extensive and intimate knowledge of existing fishes before his energies were absorbed in the study of their fossil remains, he himself would have recognised the artificial character of his classification. The distinctions between cycloid and ctenoid scales, between placoid and ganoid fishes are vague, and can hardly be maintained. As far as the living and post-cretacean forms are concerned, the vantage-ground gained by Cuvier was abandoned by him; and therefore his system could never supersede that of his predecessors, and finally shared the fate of every classification based on the modifications of one organ only. But Agassiz has the merit of having opened an immense new field of research by his study of the infinite variety of fossil forms. In his principal work "Recherches sur les Poissons fossiles," (Neuchatel, 1833-43, 4to, atlas in fol.), he placed them before the world arranged in a methodical manner, with excellent descriptions and illustrations. His power of discernment and penetration in determining even the most fragmentary remains is truly astonishing; and if his order of Ganoids is an assemblage of forms very different from that as it is circumscribed now, he was at any rate the first who recognised that such an order of fishes exists.

The discoverer of the *Ganoidei* was succeeded by their

J. Müller. explorer, JOHANNES MÜLLER (born 1801, died 1858). In his classical memoir "Ueber den Bau und die Grenzen der Ganoiden" (Berlin, 1846; 4to), he showed that the Ganoids differed from all the other osseous fishes, and agreed with the Plagiostomes, in the structure of their heart. By this primary character, all heterogeneous elements, as *Siluroids*, *Osteoglossidæ*, etc., were eliminated from the order as understood by Agassiz. On the other hand, he did not recognise the affinity of *Lepidosiren* to the Ganoids, but established for it a distinct sub-class, *Dipnoi*, which he placed at the opposite end of the system. By his researches into the anatomy of the Lampreys and Amphioxus, their typical distinctness from other cartilaginous fishes was proved; they became the types of two other sub-classes, *Cyclostomi* and *Leptocardii*.

Müller proposed several other not unimportant modifications of the Cuvierian system; and although all cannot be maintained as the most natural arrangements, yet his researches have given us a much more complete knowledge of the organisation of the Teleosteous fishes, and later enquiries have shown that, on the whole, the combinations proposed by him require only some further modification and another definition to render them perfectly natural.

Under the name of *Pharyngognathi* he combined fishes with the lower pharyngeals coalesced into one bone, viz. the Labroids, Chromides, and Scombresoces. The association of the third family with the two former seemed to himself a somewhat arbitrary proceeding; and it had to be abandoned again, when a number of fishes which cannot be separated from the Acanthopterygians, were found to possess the same united pharyngeals.

A more natural combination is the union of the Cod-fishes with the Flat-fishes into the order *Anacanthini.* Flat-fishes are in fact nothing but asymmetrical Cod-fishes. Müller separates them from the remaining Malacopterygians by the absence of a connecting duct between the air-bladder and oesophagus. However, it must be admitted that the examination of those fishes, and especially of the young stages, is not complete enough to raise the question beyond every doubt, whether the presence or absence of that duct is an absolutely distinctive character between Anacanths and Malacopterygians.

Many of the families established by Cuvier were re-examined and better defined by Müller, as may be seen from the following outline of his system :—

Sub-classis I.—Dipnoi.

Ordo I.—Sirenoidei.

Fam. 1. Sirenoidei.

Sub-classis II.—Teleostei.

Ordo I.—Acanthopteri.

Fam. 1. Percoidei.
„ 2. Cataphracti.
„ 3. Sparoidei.
„ 4. Sciænoidei.
„ 5. Labyrinthiformes.
„ 6. Mugiloidei.
„ 7. Notacanthini.
„ 8. Scomberoidei.
Fam. 9. Squamipennes.
„ 10. Taenioidei.
„ 11. Gobioidei.
„ 12. Blennioidei.
„ 13. Pediculati.
„ 14. Theutyes.
„ 15. Fistulares.

Ordo II.—Anacanthini.

Sub-ordo I.—Anacanthini sub-brachii.

Fam. 1. Gadoidei.
„ 2. Pleuronectides.

Sub-ordo II.—Anacanthini apodes.

Fam. 1. Ophidini.

Ordo III.—Pharyngognathi.

Sub-ordo I.—Pharyngognathi acanthopterygii.

Fam. 1. Labroidei cycloidei.
„ 2. Labroidei ctenoidei.
„ 3. Chromides.

Sub-ordo II.—Pharyngognathi malacopterygii.

Fam. 1. Scomberesoces.

Ordo IV.—Physostomi.

Sub-ordo I.—Physostomi abdominales.

Fam. 1. Siluroidei.
„ 2. Cyprinoidei.
„ 3. Characini.
„ 4. Cyprinodontes.
„ 5. Mormyri.
„ 6. Esoces.
Fam. 7. Galaxiæ.
„ 8. Salmones.
„ 9. Scopelini.
„ 10. Clupeidæ.
„ 11. Heteropygii.

Sub-ordo II.—Physostomi apodes s. anguillares.

Fam. 12. Muræenoidei.
„ 13. Gymnotini.
„ 14. Symbranchii.

Ordo V.—Plectognathi.

Fam. 1. Balistini.
2. Ostraciones.
„ 3. Gymnodontes.

Ordo VI.—Lophobranchii.

Fam. 1. Lophobranchi.

Sub-classis III.—Ganoidei.

Ordo I.—Holostei.

Fam. 1. Lepidosteini.
„ 2. Polypterini.

Ordo II.—Chondrostei.

Fam. 1. Acipenserini,
„ 2. Spatulariæ.

Sub-classis IV.—Elasmobranchi s. Selachii.

Ordo I.—Plagiostomi.

Sub-ordo I.—Squalidæ.

Fam. 1. Scyllia.
„ 2. Nyctitantes.
„ 3. Lamnoidei.
„ 4. Alopeciæ.
„ 5. Cestraciones.
Fam. 6. Rhinodontes.
„ 7. Notidani.
„ 8. Spinaces.
„ 9. Scymnoidei.
„ 10. Squatinæ.

Sub-ordo II.—Rajidæ.

Fam. 11. Squatinorajæ.
„ 12. Torpedines.
„ 13. Rajæ.
Fam. 14. Trygones.
„ 15. Myliobatides.
„ 16. Cephalopteræ.

Ordo II.—Holocephali.

Fam. 1. Chimaeræ.

Sub-classis V.—Marsipobranchii s. Cyclostomi.

Ordo I.—Hyperoartii.

Fam. 1. Petromyzonini.

Ordo II.—Hyperotreti.

Fam. 1. Myxinoidei.

Sub-classis VI.—Leptocardii.

Ordo I.—Amphioxini.

Fam. 1. Amphioxini.

The discovery (in the year 1871) of a living representative of a genus hitherto believed to be long extinct, *Ceratodus*, Discovery of Ceratodus.

threw a new light on the affinities of Fishes. The author who had the good fortune of examining this fish, was enabled to show that, on the one hand, it was a form most closely allied to *Lepidosiren;* on the other, that it could not be separated from the Ganoid fishes, and therefore that also *Lepidosiren* was a Ganoid: a relation pointed at already by Huxley in a previous paper on "Devonian Fishes." This discovery led to further considerations[1] of the relative characters of Müller's sub-classes, and to the system which is followed in the present work.

Having followed the development of the ichthyological system down to the latest time, we have to retrace our steps to enumerate the most important contributions to Ichthyology which appeared contemporaneously with or subsequently to the publication of Cuvier and Valenciennes's great work. As in other branches of Zoology, activity increased almost with every year; and for convenience's sake we may arrange these works in three rubrics.

Recent Works.

I.—Voyages, containing general Accounts of Zoological Collections.

A. *French.*

1. "Voyage autour du monde sur les Corvettes de S. M. l'Uranie et la Physicienne, sous le commandement de M. Freycinet. Zoologie: Poissons par *Quoy* et *Gaimard.*" (Paris, 1824, 4to, atlas fol.)

2. "Voyage de la Coquille. Zoologie par *Lesson.*" (Paris, 1826-30, 4to, atlas fol.)

3. "Voyage de l'Astrolabe, sous le commandement de M. J. Dumont d'Urville. Poissons par *Quoy* et *Gaimard.*" (Paris, 1834, 8vo, atlas fol.)

[1] Description of Ceratodus. "Phil. Trans.," 1871, ii.

4. "Voyage au Pôle Sud par M. J. Dumont d'Urville. Poissons par *Hombron* et *Jacquinot*." (Paris, 1853-4, 8vo, atlas fol.)

B. *English.*

1. "Voyage of H.M.S. Sulphur. Fishes by *J. Richardson*." (Lond. 1844-5, 4to.)

2. "Voyage of H.M.S.S. Erebus and Terror. Fishes by *J. Richardson*." (Lond. 1846. 4to.)

3. "Voyage of H.M.S. Beagle. Fishes by *L. Jenyns*." (Lond. 1842, 4to.)

4. "Voyage of H.M.S. Challenger. Fishes by *A. Günther*" (in course of publication).

C. *German.*

1. "Reise der österreichischen Fregatte Novara. Fische von *R. Kner*." (Wien. 1865, 4to.)

II.—FAUNAE.

A. *Great Britain.*

1. *R. Parnell*, "The Natural History of the Fishes of the Firth of Forth." (Edinb. 1838, 8vo.)

2. *W. Yarrell*, "A History of British Fishes." (3d edit. Lond. 1859, 8vo.)

3. *J. Couch*, "A History of the Fishes of the British Islands." (Lond. 1862-5, 8vo.)

B. *Denmark and Scandinavia.*

1. *H. Kröyer*, "Danmark's Fiske." (Kjöbnh. 1838-53, 8vo.)

2. *S. Nilsson*, "Skandinavisk Fauna." (Vol. IV. Fiskarna. Lund. 1855, 8vo.)

3. *Fries och Ekström*, "Skandinaviens Fiskar." (Stockh. 1836, 4to, with excellent plates.)

C. *Russia.*

1. *Nordmann,* "Ichthyologie Pontique," in "Voyage dans la Russie méridionale de *Demidoff.*" (Tom. iii. Paris, 1840, 8vo, atlas fol.)

D. *Germany.*

1. *Heckel* and *Kner,* "Die Süsswasser-fische der Oesterreichischen Monarchie." (Leipz. 1858, 8vo.)

2. *C. T. E. Siebold,* "Die Süsswasser-fische von Mitteleuropa." (Leipz. 1863, 8vo.)

E. *Italy and Mediterranean.*

1. *Bonaparte,* "Iconografia della Fauna Italica." Tom. iii. Pesci. (Roma, 1832-41, fol.) (Incomplete.)

2. *Costa,* "Fauna del Regno di Napoli." Pesci. (Napoli, 4to, about 1850.) (Incomplete.)

F. *France.*

1. *E. Blanchard,* "Les Poissons des eaux douces de la France." (Paris, 1866, 8vo.)

G. *Pyrenean Peninsula.*

The freshwater Fish-fauna of Spain and Portugal was almost unknown, until *F. Steindachner* paid some visits to those countries for the purpose of exploring the principal rivers. His discoveries are described in several papers in the "Sitzungsberichte der Akademie zu Wien." *B. du Bocage* and *F. Capello* contributed towards the knowledge of the marine fishes on the coast of Portugal. ("Jorn. Scienc. Acad. Lisb.")

H. *North America.*

1. *J. Richardson,* "Fauna Boreali Americana." Part III. Fishes. (Lond. 1836, 4to.) The species described in this work are nearly all from the British possessions in the North.

2. *Dekay*, "Zoology of New York." Part IV. Fishes. (New York, 1842, 4to.)

3. "Reports of the United States Commission of Fish and Fisheries." (5 vols. Washingt. 1873-79, 8vo. In progress. Contains most valuable information.)

Besides these works, numerous descriptions of North American freshwater fishes have been published in the Reports of the various U. S. Government expeditions, and in North American scientific journals, by *Storer*, *Baird*, *Girard*, *W. O. Ayres*, *Cope*, *Jordan*, *Brown Goode*, etc.; but a good general, and especially critical, account of the fishes of the United States is still a desideratum.

I.—*Japan.*

1. "Fauna Japonica." Poissons par *H. Schlegel.* (Lugd. Bat. 1850, fol.)

J.—*East Indies; Tropical parts of the Indian and Pacific Oceans.*

1. *E. Rüppell*, "Atlas zu der Reise im Nördlichen Afrika." (Frankf. 1828, fol.)

2. *E. Rüppell*, "Neue Wirbelthiere. Fische." (Frankf. 1837, fol.)

These two works form the standard works for the student of the Fishes of the Red Sea, and are distinguished by a rare conscientiousness and faithfulness of the descriptions and figures; so that there is no other part of the tropical seas, with the fishes of which we are so intimately acquainted, as with those of the Red Sea. But these works have a still wider range of usefulness, in as much as only a small proportion of the fishes is limited to that area, the majority being distributed over the Indian Ocean into Polynesia. Ruppell's works were supplemented by the two first of the following works:—

3. *R. L. Playfair* and *A. Günther*, "The Fishes of Zanzibar." (Lond. 1866, 4to); and

4. *C. B. Klunzinger*, "Synopsis der Fische des Rothen Meers." (Wien. 1870-1, 8vo.)

5. *T. Cantor*, "Catalogue of Malayan Fishes." (Calcutta, 1850, 8vo.)

6. *F. Day*, "The Fishes of India" (Lond. 1875, 4to, in progress); contains an account of the freshwater and marine species, and is not yet complete.

7. *A. Günther*, "Die Fische der Südsee." (Hamburg, 4to; from 1873, in progress.)

Unsurpassed in activity, as regards the exploration of the fish fauna of the East Indian Archipelago, is *P. Bleeker*, a surgeon in the service of the Dutch East Indian Government (born 1819, died 1878), who, from the year 1840, for nearly thirty years, amassed immense collections of the fishes of the various islands, and described them in extremely numerous papers, published chiefly in the Journals of the Batavian Society. When his descriptions and the arrangement of his materials evoked some criticism, it must be remembered that, at the time when he commenced his labours, and for many years afterwards, he stood alone, without the aid of a previously named collection on which to base his first researches, and without other works but that of Cuvier and Valenciennes. He had to create for himself a method of distinguishing species and of describing them; and afterwards it would have been difficult for him to abandon his original method and the principles by which he had been guided for so many years. His desire of giving a new name to every individual, to every small assemblage of species wherever practicable, or of changing an old name, detracts not a little from the satisfaction with which his works would be used otherwise. It is also surpri ing that a man with his anatomical knowledge and unusual facilities should have been satisfied with the merely external examination of the specimens. But none of his numerous articles contain anything relating to the anatomy, physiology, or habits of the fishes which came under his notice; hence his attempts at systematic arrangement are very far from indicating an advance in Ichthyology.

Soon after his return to Europe (1860) Bleeker commenced to collect the final results of his labours in a grand work, illustrated by coloured plates, "Atlas Ichthyologique des Indes Orientales Néerlandaises." (Amsterd fol. 1862); the publication of which was interrupted by the author's death in 1878.

K.—*Africa.*

1. *A. Günther,* "The Fishes of the Nile" in Petherick's "Travels in Central Africa." (Lond. 1869, 8vo.)

2. *W. Peters,* "Naturwissenschaftliche Reise nach Mossambique. IV. Flussfische." (Berl. 1868, 4to.)

L.—*West Indies and South America.*

1. *L. Agassiz,* "Selecta genera et species Piscium, quæ in itinere per Brasiliam, collegit J. B. de Spix." (Monach. 1829, fol.)

2. *F. de Castlenau,* "Animaux nouveaux ou rares, recueillis pendant l'expedition dans les parties centrales de l'Amérique du Sud. Poissons." (Paris, 1855, 4to.)

3. *A. Günther,* "An account of the Fishes of the States of Central America." (In Trans. Zool. Soc. 1868.)

4. *L. Vaillant* and *F. Bocourt,* "Mission scientifique au Mexique et dans l'Amérique centrale. Poissons." (Paris, 1874, 4to.) (In progress.)

F. Poey, the celebrated naturalist of Havannah, devoted many years of study to the Fishes of Cuba. His papers and memoirs are published partly in two periodicals, issued by himself, under the title of "Memorias sobre la Historia natural de la Isle de Cuba" (from 1851), and "Repertorio

Fisico-natural de la Isla de Cuba" (from 1865), partly in North American scientific journals. And, finally, *F. Steindachner* has published many contributions, accompanied by excellent figures, to our knowledge of the Fishes of Central and South America.

M.—*New Zealand.*

1. *F. W. Hutton* and *J. Hector*, "Fishes of New Zealand." (Wellingt. 1872, 8vo.)

N.—*Arctic Regions.*

1. *C. Lütken*, "A revised Catalogue of the Fishes of Greenland," in "Manual of the Natural History, Geology, and Physics of Greenland." (Lond. 1875, 8vo.) Although only a nominal list, this catalogue is useful, as it contains references to all the principal works in which Arctic fishes have been described. The fishes of Spitzbergen were examined by *A. J. Malmgren* (1865).

III.—Anatomical Works.

The number of authors who worked on the anatomy of fishes is almost as great as that of faunists; and we should go beyond the limits of the present work if we mentioned more than the most prominent and successful. *M. H. Rathke, J. Müller, J. Hyrtl*, and *H. Stannius* left scarcely any organ unexamined, and their researches had a direct bearing either on the relation of the class of fishes to the other vertebrates, or on the systematic arrangement of the fishes themselves. *E. E. von Baer, F. de Filippi, C. Vogt, W. His, W. K. Parker*, and *F. M. Balfour* worked at their embryology; *A. Kölliker* and *G. Pouchet* at their histology. The osteology was specially treated by *G. Bakker, F. C. Rosenthal, L. Agassiz*, and *C. Gegenbaur*; the nervous system by *Gottsche, Philipeaux, Stannius, L. de Sanctis, L. Stieda, Baudelot* and *Miclucho-Maclay*; the organ of hearing by *E. H. Weber, C. Hasse*, and *G. Retzius*. The electric fishes were examined by *E. Geoffroy*,

C. Matteuci, P. Pacini, T. Bilharz, and *Max Schultze.* The development and metamorphosis of the Lamperns was made the subject of research by *H. Müller, M. Schultze,* and *P. Owsjannikow;* Müller's examination of *Branchiostoma* was continued by *J. Marcusen, A. Kovalevsky, L. Stieda, W. Müller, C. Hasse, T. Huxley,* and *F. M. Balfour.* The most comprehensive accounts of the anatomy of fishes are contained in the following works:—

1. *H. Stannius,* "Zootomie der Fische," 2d edit. (Berl. 1854, 8vo.)

2. *R. Owen,* "Anatomy of Vertebrates," vol. i. (Lond. 1866, 8vo.)

3. *R. Owen,* "Lectures on the Comparative Anatomy and Physiology of the Vertebrate Animals." Part I. Fishes. (Lond. 1846, 8vo.)

4. *T. Huxley,* "A Manual of the Anatomy of Vertebrated Animals." (Lond. 1871, 16mo.)

It has been mentioned above that the great work of Cuvier and Valenciennes had been left incomplete. Several authors, therefore, supplied detailed accounts of the orders omitted in that work. *Müller* and *Henle* published an account of the Plagiostomes, and *Kaup* of the Murænidæ and Lophobranchii. *A. Duméril,* finally, commenced an "Histoire naturelle des Poissons ou Ichthyologie générale," of which, however, two volumes only appeared, containing a complete account of the "Plagiostomes" (Paris, 1865, 8vo), and of the "Ganoids and Lophobranchs." (Paris, 1870, 8vo.) Latest Systematic Works.

So great an activity had prevailed in Ichthyology since the publication of the "Histoire naturelle" by Cuvier and Valenciennes, and the results of the manifold enquiries were scattered over such a multitude of publications, that it became imperative to collect again all these materials in one comprehensive work. This was done in the "Catalogue of Fishes," published by the Trustees of the British Museum, in eight volumes (Lond. 1859-70). Beside the species previously described many new forms were added, the number total of species referred to in those volumes amounting to 8525. As regards the systematic arrangement—Müller's system was adopted in the main, but the definition of the families is much modified. This, however, need not be further entered into here, and will become sufficiently apparent in the subsequent parts of the present work.

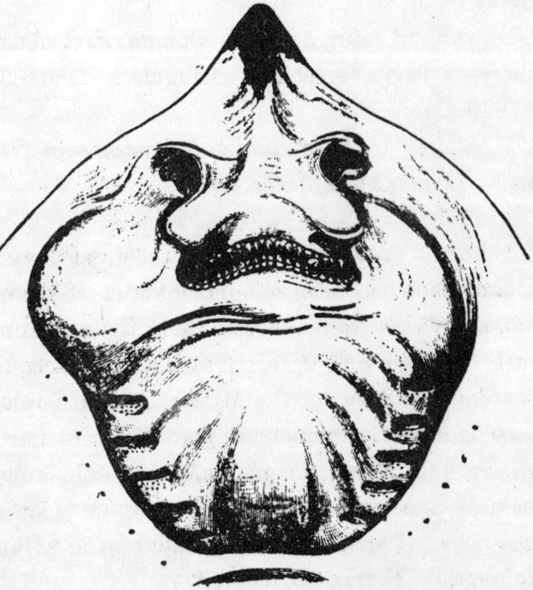

Fig. 1.—Lower aspect of head of *Raia lemprieri*.

CHAPTER II.

TOPOGRAPHICAL DESCRIPTION OF THE EXTERNAL PARTS OF FISHES.

In the body of a fish four parts are distinguished: the *head, trunk, tail,* and the *fins;* the boundary between the first and second being generally indicated by the *gill-opening,* and that between the second and third by the *vent.* The form of the body and the relative proportions of those principal parts are subject to much variation, such as is not found in any other class of Vertebrates. In fishes which are endowed with the power of steady and more or less rapid locomotion, a deviation from that form of body, which we observe in a perch, carp, or mackerel, is never excessive. The body forms a simple, equally-formed wedge, compressed or slightly rounded, well fitted for cleaving the water. In fishes which are in the habit of moving on the bottom, the whole body, or at least the head, is *vertically depressed* and flattened; the head may be so enormously enlarged that the trunk and tail appear merely as an appendage. In one family of fishes, the *Pleuronectidæ* or Flat-fishes, the body is compressed into a thin disk; they swim and move on one side only, which remains constantly directed towards the bottom, a peculiarity by which the symmetry of all parts of the body has been affected. A *lateral compression* of the body, in conjunction with a lengthening of the vertical and a shortening of the longitudinal axis, we find in fishes moving comparatively slowly through

Form of the body.

the water, and able to remain (as it were) suspended in it. This deviation from the typical form may proceed so far that the vertical axis greatly exceeds the longitudinal in length; generally all the parts of the body participate in this form, but in one kind of fish (the Sun-fish or *Orthagoriscus*) it is chiefly the tail which has been shortened, and reduced so much as to present the appearance of being cut off. An excessive lengthening of the longitudinal axis, with a shortening of the vertical, occurs in Eels and eel-like fishes, and in the so-called Band-fishes. They are bottom-fish, capable of insinuating themselves into narrow crevices and holes. The form of the body of these long-fish is either cylindrical, snake-like, as in the Eels and many Codfishes, or strongly compressed as in the Band-fishes (*Trichiurus*, *Regalecus*, etc.) It is chiefly the tail which is lengthened, but frequently the head and trunk participate more or less in this form. Every possible variation occurs between these and other principal types of form. The old ichthyologists, even down to Linnæus, depended in great measure on them for classification; but although often the same form of body obtains in the same group of fishes, similarity of form by no means indicates natural affinity; it only indicates similitude of habits and mode of life.

Eye. *The external parts of the Head.*—The *Eye* divides the head into the *ante-orbital* and *post-orbital* portion. In most fishes, especially in those with a compressed head, it is situated on the side and in the anterior half of the length of the head; in many, chiefly those with a depressed head, it is directed upwards, and sometimes situated quite at the upper side; in very few, the eyes look obliquely downwards. In the Flat-fishes both eyes are on the same side of the head, either the right or the left, always on that which is directed towards the light, and coloured.

Fishes in general, compared with other Vertebrata, have large eyes. Sometimes these organs are enormously enlarged, their great size indicating that the fish is either nocturnal, or lives at a depth to which only a part of the sun's rays penetrate. On the other hand, small eyes occur in fishes inhabiting muddy places, or great depths to which scarcely any light descends, or in fishes in which the want of an organ of sight is compensated by the development of other organs of sense. In a few fishes, more particularly in those inhabiting caves or the greatest depths of the ocean, the eyes have become quite rudimentary and hidden under the skin.

In the *ante-orbital* portion of the head, or the *Snout*, are situated the mouth and the nostrils. **Snout.**

The *Mouth* is formed by the intermaxillary and maxillary bones, or by the intermaxillary only in the upper jaw, and by the mandibulary bone in the lower. These bones are either bare or covered by integument, to which frequently labial folds or lips are added. As regards form, the mouth offers as many variations as the body itself, in accordance with the nature of the food, and the mode of feeding. It may be narrow, or extremely wide and cleft to nearly the hind margin of the head; it may be semi-elliptical, semicircular, or straight in a transverse line; it may be quite in front of the snout (*anterior*), or at its upper surface (*superior*), or at its lower (*inferior*), or extending along each side (*lateral*); sometimes it is sub-circular, organised for sucking. The jaws of some fishes are modified into a special weapon of attack (Sword-fish, Saw-fish); in fact, throughout the whole class of fishes the jaws are the only organ specialised for the purpose of attacking; weapons on other parts of the body are purely defensive. **Mouth.**

Both jaws may be provided with skinny appendages, *barbels*, which, if developed and movable, are sensitive organs of touch.

In the majority of fishes the *Nostrils* are a double opening on each side of the upper surface of the snout; the openings **Nostrils.**

of each side being more or less close together. They lead into a shallow groove; and only in one family (the Myxinoids) perforate the palate. In this family, as well as in the Lampreys, the nasal aperture is single. In many Eels the openings are lateral, the lower perforating the upper lip. In the Sharks and Rays (Fig. 1, p. 34) they are at the lower surface of the snout, and more or less confluent; and, finally, in the Dipnoi and other Ganoids, one at least is within the labial boundary of the mouth.

The space across the forehead, between the orbits, is called the *inter-orbital* space; that below the orbit, the *infra-orbital* or *sub-orbital* region.

Gill-cover. In the *post-orbital* part of the head there are distinguished, at least in most Teleosteous Fishes and many Ganoids, (Fig. 24) the *præoperculum*, a sub-semicircular bone, generally with a free and often serrated or variously-armed margin; the *operculum*, forming the posterior margin of the gill-opening, and the *suboperculum* and *inter-operculum* along its inferior margin. All these bones, collectively called *opercles*, form the *gill-cover*, a thin bony lamella covering the cavity containing the gills. Sometimes they are covered with so thin a membrane that the single bones may be readily distinguished; sometimes they are hidden under a thick integument. In some cases the inter-operculum is rudimentary or entirely absent (Siluroids).

Gill-opening. The *Gill-opening* is a foramen, or a slit behind or below the head, by which the water which has been taken up through the mouth for the purpose of breathing is again expelled. This slit may extend from the upper end of the operculum all round the side of the head to the symphysis of the lower jaw; or it may be shortened and finally reduced to a small opening on any part of the margin of the gill-cover. Sometimes (*Symbranchus*) the two openings, thus reduced, coalesce, and form what externally appears as a single opening only. The margin of the gill-cover is provided with a cutaneous fringe, in order to more effectually close the gill-opening; and this fringe is supported by one or several or many bony rays, the *branchiostegals.* The space on the chest between the two rami of the lower jaw and between the gill-openings is called the *isthmus.*

The Sharks and Rays differ from the Teleosteous and Ganoid fishes in having five branchial slits (six or seven in *Hexanchus* and *Heptanchus*), which are lateral in the Sharks, and at the lower surface of the head in the Rays (Fig. 1, p. 34). In Myxine only the gill-opening is at a great distance from

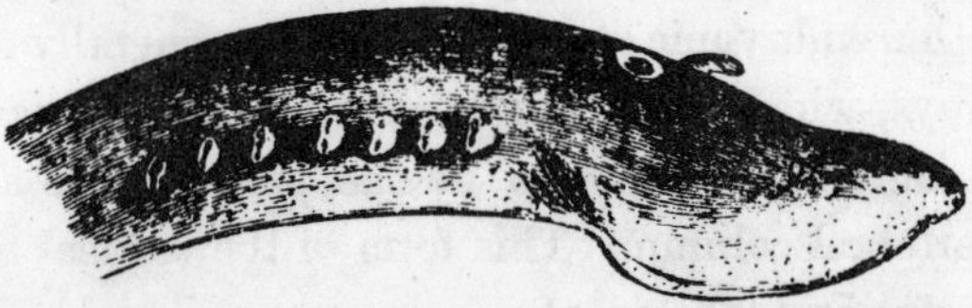

Fig. 2.—Head of *Mordacia mordax*, showing the single nostril, and seven branchial openings.

the head; it is either single in this family (Cyclostomi), or there are six and more on each side (Fig. 2).

In the *Trunk* are distinguished the *back*, the *sides*, and the *abdomen.* It gradually passes in all fishes into the *Tail;* the termination of the abdominal cavity and the commencement of the tail being generally indicated by the position of the vent. The exceptions are numerous: not only certain abdominal organs, like the sexual, may extend to between the muscles of the tail, but the intestinal tract itself may pass far backwards, or, singularly, it may be reflected forwards, so that the position of the vent may be either close to the extremity of the tail or to the foremost part of the trunk.

In many fishes the greater part of the tail is surrounded by the fins, leaving only a small portion (between dorsal, caudal, and anal fins) finless; this part is called the *free portion* or the *peduncle* of the tail.

Fins. The *Fins* are divided into *vertical* or *unpaired*, and into *horizontal* or *paired fins*. Any of them may be present or absent; and their position, number, and form are most important guides in determining the affinities of fishes.

The *vertical* fins are situated in the median dorsal line, from the head to the extremity of the tail, and in the ventral line of the tail. In fishes in which they are least developed or most embryonic, the vertical fin appears as a simple fold of the skin surrounding the extremity of the tail. In its further progress of development in the series of fishes, it gradually extends more forwards, and may reach even the head and vent. Even in this embryonic condition the fin is generally supported by fine rays, which are the continuations of, or articulated to, other stronger rays supported by the processes or apophyses of the vertebral column. This form of the vertical fin is very common, for instance in the Eels, many Gadoid, Blennioid and Ganoid fishes in which, besides, the rays have ceased to be simple rods, showing more or less numerous joints (simple *articulated* rays; Fig. 3). *Branched* rays are dichotomically split, the joints increasing in number towards the extremity.

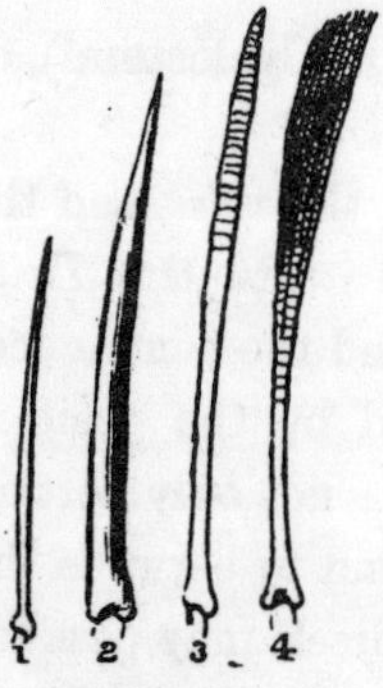

Fig. 3.

1. Simple ray.
2. Spine.
3. Simple articulated ray (soft).
4. Branched ray (soft).

The continuity of the vertical fin, however, is interrupted in the majority of fishes; and three fins then are distinguished: one in the dorsal line—the *dorsal* fin; one in the ventral line behind the anus—the *anal* fin; and one confined to the extremity of the tail—the *caudal* fin.

The *caudal* fin is rarely symmetrical, so that its upper half would be equal to its lower; the greatest degree of asymmetry obtains in fishes with heterocercal termination of the vertebral column (see subsequently, Figs. 31, 41). In fishes in which it is nearly symmetrical it is frequently prolonged into an upper and lower *lobe*, its hind margin being concave or more or less deeply excised; in others the hind margin is rounded, and when the middle rays greatly exceed in length the outer ones the fin assumes a pointed form.

Many and systematically important differences are observed in the *dorsal* fin, which is either spiny-rayed (spinous) (*Acanthopterygian*), or soft-rayed (*Malacopterygian*). In the former, a smaller or greater number of the rays are simple and without transverse joints; they may be flexible, or so much osseous matter is deposited in them that they appear hard and truly spinous (Fig. 3); these spines form always the anterior portion of the fin, which is detached from, or continuous

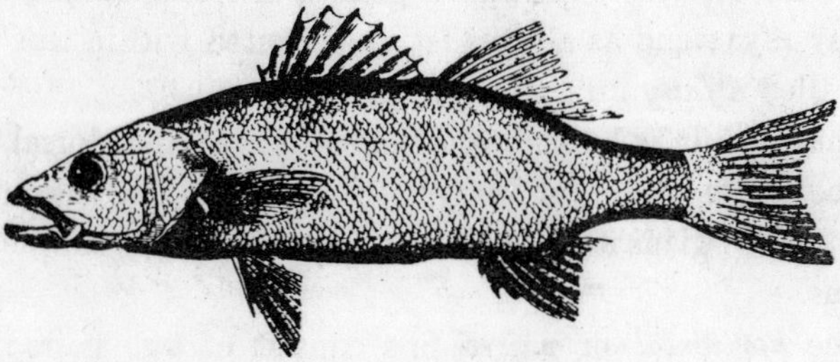

Fig. 4.—Labrax lupus (Bass), an Acanthopterygian with anterior spinous, and posterior soft dorsal fin.

with, the remaining jointed rays. The spines can be erected or depressed at the will of the fish; if in the depressed position the spines cover one another completely, their points lying in the same line, the fish is called *homacanth;* but if the spines are asymmetrical, alternately broader on one side than on the other, the fish is called *heteracanth.* The spinous division, as well as the one consisting of jointed rays, may again be subdivided. In the *Malacopterygian* type all the rays remain jointed; indeed, sometimes the foremost ray, with its preceding short supports, is likewise ossified, and a hard spine, but the articulations can nearly always be distinctly traced. Sometimes the dorsal fin of Malacopterygian fishes is very long, extending from the head to the end of the tail, sometimes it is reduced to a few rays only, and in a few cases it is

Fig. 5.—Saurus undosquamis, a Malacopterygian with anterior soft dorsal, and additional adipose fin.

entirely absent. In addition to the rayed dorsal fin, many Malacopterygian fishes (as the Salmonoids, many Siluroids, Scopeloids, etc.) have another of greater or lesser extent, without any rays; and as always fat is deposited within this fold, it is called a *fatty* fin (*pinna adiposa*).

The *anal* fin is built on the same plan as the dorsal, and may be single or plural, long or short, or entirely absent; in Acanthopterygians its foremost rays are frequently simple and spinous.

The *horizontal* or *paired* fins consist of two pairs: the pectorals and ventrals.

The *pectoral* fins (with their osseous supports) are the homologues of the anterior limbs of the higher Vertebrata. They are always inserted immediately behind the gill-opening; either symmetrical with a rounded posterior margin, or asymmetrical, with the upper rays longest and strongest; in Malacopterygians with a dorsal spine the upper pectoral ray is frequently developed into a similar defensive weapon.

The *ventral* fins are the homologues of the hind-limbs, and inserted on the abdominal surface, either behind the pectorals (*Pisces* s. *Pinnæ abdominales*), or below them (*Pisces* s. *Pinnæ thoracicæ*), or in advance of them (*Pisces* s. *Pinnæ jugulares*). They are generally narrow, composed of a small number of rays, the outer of which is frequently osseous. In some small groups of fishes, like the Gobies, the fins coalesce and form a suctorial disk.

Fig. 6.—Salmo salar (Salmon), with abdominal ventral fins.

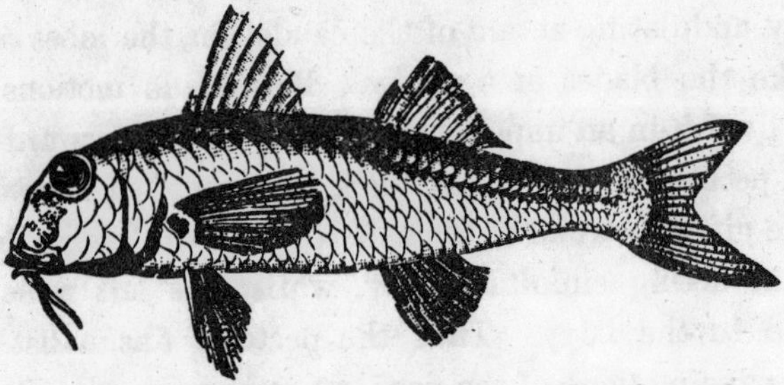

Fig. 7.—Mullus barbatus (Red Mullet), with thoracic ventral fins.

Fig. 8.—Burbot (Lota vulgaris), with jugular ventral fins.

For the definition of the smaller systematic groups, and the determination of species, the numbers of the spines and rays are generally of the greatest importance. This holds good, especially for the ventral rays, by the number of which the Acanthopterygian affinities of a fish can nearly always be determined. The numbers of the dorsal and anal rays generally correspond to the number of vertebræ in a certain portion of the spine, and are therefore constant specific, generic, or even family characters; but when their number is very great, a proportionally wide margin must be allowed for variation, and the taxinomic value of this character becomes uncertain. The numbers of the pectoral and caudal rays are rarely of any account.

Function of the Fins. The fins are organs of motion; but it is chiefly the tail and the caudal fin by which the fish impels itself forward. To execute energetic locomotion the tail and caudal fin are strongly bent, with rapidity, alternately towards the right and left; whilst a gentle motion forwards is effected by a simply undulating action of the caudal fin, the lobes of which act like the blades of a screw. Retrograde motions can be made by fish in an imperfect manner only, by forward-strokes of the pectoral fins. When the fish wants to turn towards the left, he gives a stroke of the tail towards the right, the right pectoral acting simultaneously, whilst the left remains adpressed to the body. Thus the pectoral fins assist in the progressive motions of the fish, but rather directing its course than acting as powerful propellers. The chief function of the paired fins is to maintain the balance of the fish in the water, which is always the most unsteady where there is no weight to sink it: when the pectoral of one side, or the pectoral and ventral of the same side are removed, the fish loses its balance and falls on the side opposite; when both pectorals are removed, the fish's head sinks; on removal of the dorsal and anal fins the motion of the fish assumes a zig-zag course. A fish deprived of all fins, as well as a dead fish, floats with the belly upwards, the back being the heavier part of the body.

In numerous groups of fishes which live in mud, or are enabled to pass a longer or shorter time in soil periodically dried and hardened during the hot season, forms occur entirely devoid of, or with only rudimentary, ventral fins (Cyprinodon, Ophiocephalidæ, Galaxiidæ, Siluridæ). The chief function of these fins being to balance the body of the fish whilst swimming, it is evident that in fishes moving during a great part of their life over swampy ground, or through more or less consistent mud, this function of the ventral fins ceases, and that nature can readily dispense with these organs altogether.

In certain fishes the shape and function of the fins are considerably modified: thus, in the Rays, locomotion is almost entirely effected and regulated by the broad and expanded pectoral fins acting with an undulatory motion of their margins, similar to the undulations of the long vertical fins of the Flat-fishes; in many Blennies the ventral fins are adapted for walking on the sea-bottom; in some Gobioids (*Periophthalmus*), Trigloids, Scorpænioids, and Pediculati the pectoral fins are perfect organs of walking; in the Gobies, Cyclopteri, and Discoboli the ventral fins are transformed into an adhesive disk, and finally in the Flying-fish, in which the pectorals act as a parachute. In the Eels and other snake-like fishes, the swimming as well as the gliding motions are effected by several curvatures of the body, alternate towards the right and left, resembling the locomotion of Snakes.

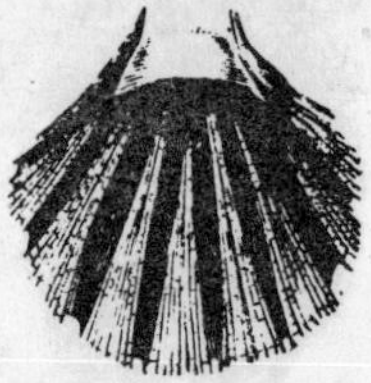

Fig. 9.—Ventrals of *Gobius*.

In the *Syngnathi* (Pipe-fishes) and *Hippocampi*, whose body admits of but a slight degree of lateral curvature, and whose caudal fin is generally small, if present at all, locomotion is very limited, and almost wholly dependent on the action of the dorsal fin, which consists of a rapid undulating movement.

Skin and Scales.

The *skin* of fishes is either covered with scales, or naked, or provided with more or less numerous scutes of various forms and sizes. Some parts, like the head and fins, are more frequently naked than scaly. All fishes provided with electric organs, the majority of Eels, and the Lampreys, are naked. *Scales* of fishes are very different from those of Reptiles; the latter being merely folds of the cutis, whilst the scales of fishes are distinct horny elements, developed in grooves or pockets of the skin, like hairs, nails, or feathers. Very small or rudimentary scales are extremely thin, homogeneous in structure, and more or less imbedded in the skin, and do not cover each other. When more developed, they are imbricated (arranged in the manner of tiles), with the posterior part extruded and free, the surface of the anterior portion being usually covered by the skin to a greater or less extent. On their surface (Figs. 10 and 11) may be observed a very fine striation concentric and parallel to the margin, and coarser striæ radiating from a central point towards the hind margin. Scales without a covering of enamel, with an entire (not denticulated) posterior margin, and with a concentric striation, are called *Cycloid* scales. *Ctenoid* scales (Figs. 12-15) are generally thicker, and provided with spinous teeth on the posterior edges of the layers of which the scale consists. In some species only the layer nearest to the margin is provided with denticulations (Fig. 14). Scales, the free surface of which is spiny, and which have no denticulation on the margin, have been termed *Sparoid* scales; but their distinction from ctenoid scales is by no means sharp, and there are even intermediate

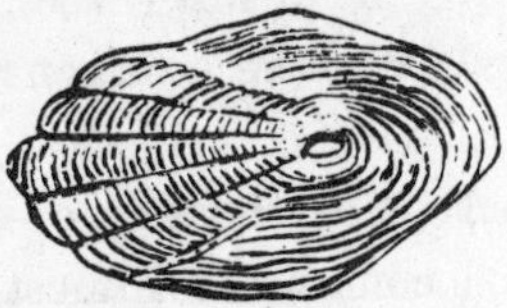

Fig. 10.—Cycloid scale of Gadopsis marmoratus (magn.)

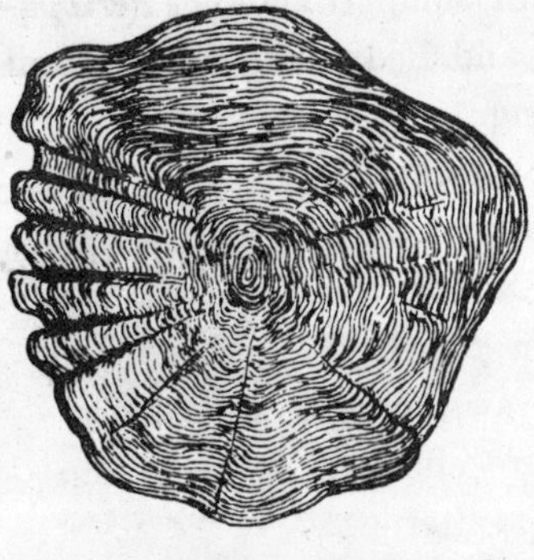

Fig. 11.—Cycloid scale of Scopelus resplendens (magn.)

forms between the cycloid and ctenoid types. Both kinds of

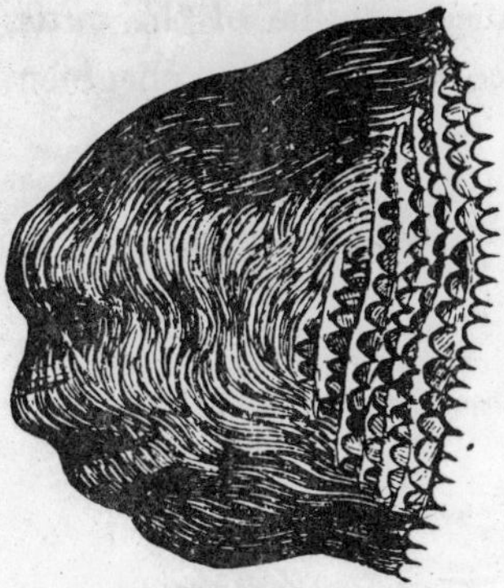

Fig. 12.—Ctenoid scale of Scatophagus multifasciatus (magn.)

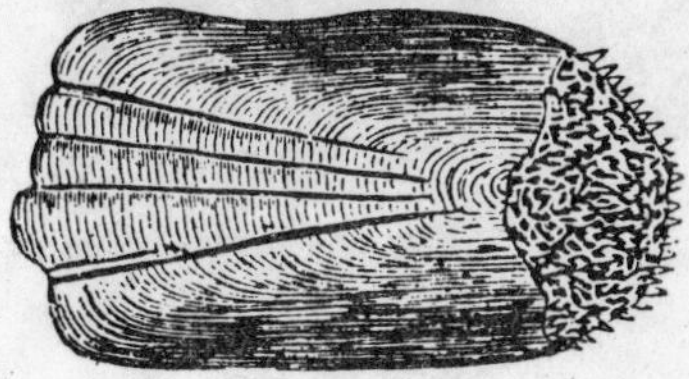

Fig. 13.—Ctenoid scale of Platycephalus cirrhonasus (magn.)

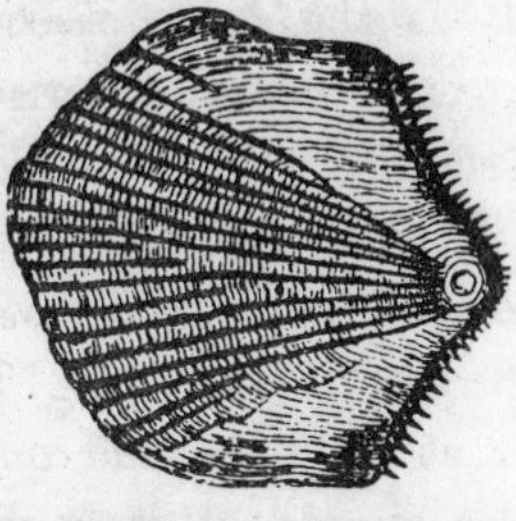

Fig. 14.—Ctenoid scale of Gobius ommaturus (magn.)

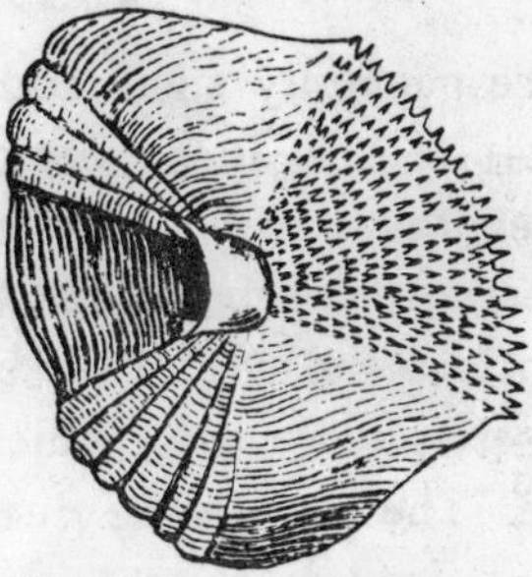

Fig. 15.—Ctenoid scale of Lethrinus (magn.)

scales may occur not only in species of the same genus of fishes, but in the same fish.

Fig. 16. Ganoid Scales.

Ganoid scales are hard and bony, covered with a layer of enamel; they are generally rhombic or quadrangular, rarely rounded and imbricate; and arranged in oblique rows, those of one row being linked together by an articulary process. This type of scales, common in fossil Ganoid fishes, occurs among recent fishes in *Lepidosteus* and *Polypterus* only.

Finally, in Sharks, the Balistidæ, and others, true scales are absent and replaced by the ossified papillæ of the cutis, which give the surface the appearance of fine-grained chagreen.

Fig. 17.—Dermal papillæ of Monacanthus trossulus.

Fig. 18.—Dermal papillæ of Monacanthus hippocrepis (magn.)

These generally small bodies, as well as the large osseous scutes of the Rays, Sturgeons, etc., have been comprised under the common name *Placoid* scales; a term which deservedly is being abandoned.

Along the side of the body of osseous fishes runs a series of perforated scales, which is called the *lateral line* (Fig. 21). The perforating duct is simple at its base, and may be also simple at its outer opening (Fig. 19), or (and this is frequently the case) the portion on the free surface of the scale is ramified (Fig. 20). The lateral line runs from the head to the tail, sometimes reaching the caudal fin, sometimes stopping in front of it, sometimes advancing over its rays. It is nearer to the dorsal profile in some fishes than in others. Some species have several lateral lines, the upper one coasting the dorsal, the lower the abdominal outline, one running along the middle as usual.

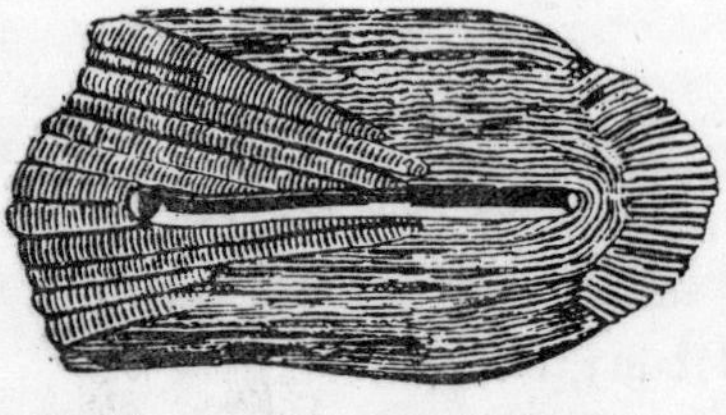

Fig. 19.—Cycloid scale from the lateral line of Odax lineatus (magn.)

The scales of the lateral line are sometimes larger than the others, sometimes smaller, sometimes modified into scutes,

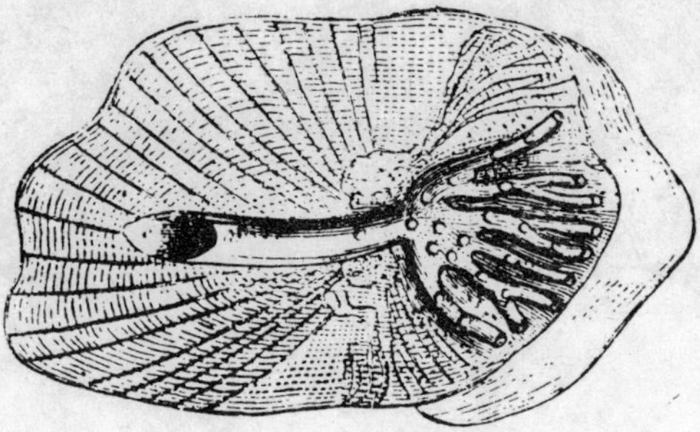

Fig. 20.—Cycloid scale from the lateral line of Labrichthys laticlavius (magn.)

sometimes there are no other scales beside them, the rest of the body being naked. The foramina of the lateral line are the outlets of a muciferous duct which is continued on to the head, running along the infraorbital bones, and sending off a branch into the præopercular margin and mandible. In many fishes, as in many Sciænoids, Gadoids, and in numerous deep-sea fishes, the ducts of this muciferous system are extraordinarily wide, and generally filled with mucus, which is congealed or contracted in specimens preserved in spirits, but swells again when the specimens are immersed in water. This system is abundantly provided with nerves, and, therefore, has been considered to be the seat of a sense peculiar to fishes, but there cannot be any doubt that its function is the excretion of mucus, although probably mucus is excreted also from the entire surface of the fish.

The scales, their structure, number and arrangement, are an important character for the determination of fishes; in most scaly fishes they are arranged in oblique transverse series; and as the number of scales in the lateral line generally corresponds to the number of transverse series, it is usual to count the scales in that line. To ascertain the number of longitudinal series of scales, the scales are counted in one of the transverse series, generally in that running from the commencement of the dorsal fin, or the middle of the back to the

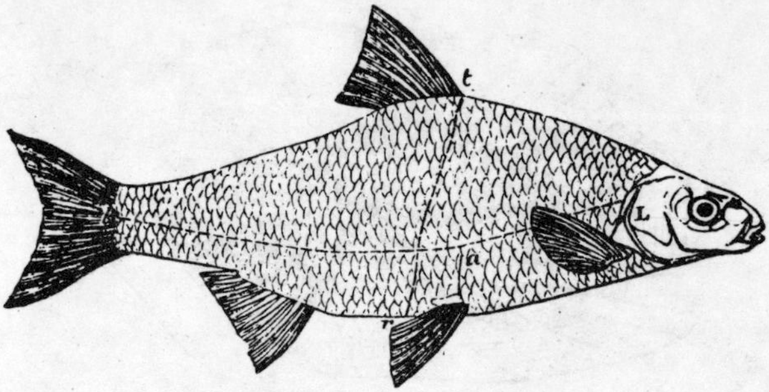

Fig. 21.—Arrangement of scales in the Roach (Leuciscus ratilus): *L l* = Lateral line; *t r* = Transverse line. *a*, Transverse line from lateral line to ventral fin.

lateral line, and from the lateral line down to the vent or ventral fin, or middle of the abdomen.[1]

The scales of many fishes are modified for special purposes, especially to form weapons of defence or a protective armour, but the details of such modifications are better mentioned under the several families in which they occur. All scales are continually growing and wasting away on the surface, and it seems that some fish, at least,—for instance, Salmonoids—"shed" them periodically; during the progress of this shedding the outlines of the scales are singularly irregular.

[1] In the formula generally preceding the description of a fish, "L. lat. 40," would express that the scales between the head and caudal fin are arranged in 40 transverse series; and probably, that the lateral line is composed of the same number of scales. "L. transv. $\frac{8}{5}$" would express that there are eight longitudinal series of scales between the median line of the back and the lateral line, and five between the lateral line and the middle of the abdomen.

CHAPTER III.

TERMINOLOGY AND TOPOGRAPHY OF THE SKELETON.

IN order to readily comprehend the subsequent account of the modifications of the skeleton in the various sub-classes and groups of Fishes, the student has to acquaint himself with the terms used for the numerous bones of the fish skeleton, as well as with their relative position. The skeleton of any of the more common kinds of osseous fish may serve for this purpose; that of the Perch is chosen here.

The series of bones constituting the axis of the body, and destined to protect the spinal chord and some large longitudinal blood-vessels, is called the *vertebral* or *spinal column*; the single bones are the *vertebræ*. The *skull* consists of the bones surrounding the brain and organs of sense, and of a number of arches suspended from it, to support the commencement of the alimentary canal and the respiratory organs.

The *vertebra* (Fig. 22) consists of a body or *centrum* (*c*), with a concave anterior and posterior surface, and generally of several *processes* or *apophyses*, as—1. Two *neurapophyses* (*na*), which, on the dorsal side, rising upwards, form the *neural arch* over the canal, in which the spinal chord is lodged. 2. Two *parapophyses* (*pa*) usually projecting from the lower part of the sides of the body, or two *hæmapophyses* (*ha*) which actually coalesce to form on the ventral side the hæmal canal for a large trunk of the vascular system. 3. A *neural spine* (*ns*), which crowns the neurapophyses, or is interposed between their tips. 4. A *hæmal spine* (*hs*), having the same relation to the hæmapophyses.

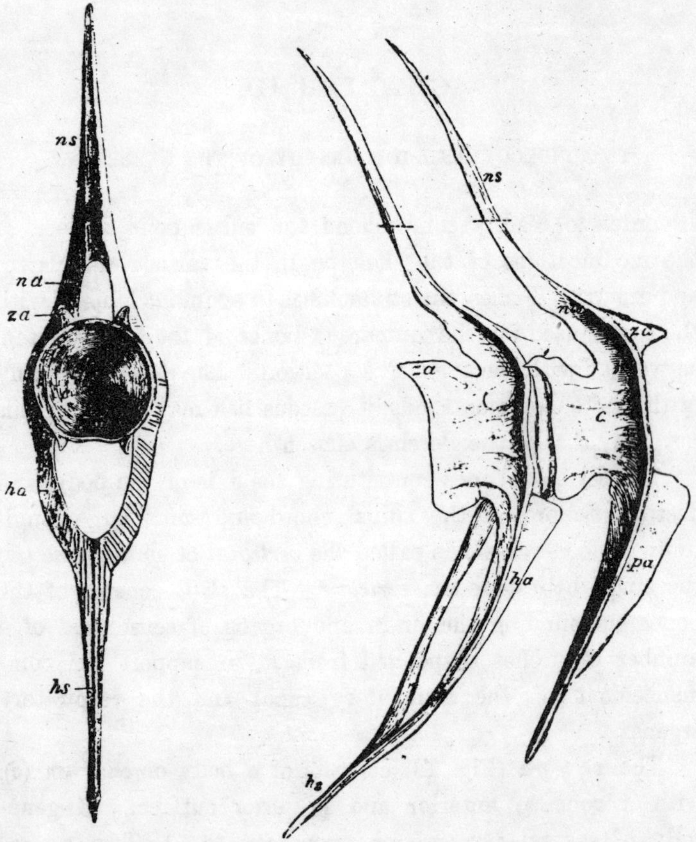

Fig. 22.—Side and Front view of Fish-vertebra.

5. Two *pleurapophyses* or floating *ribs*, suspended from, or from the base of, the parapophyses. 6. In most fishes the neural arches are connected together by articular or oblique processes, *zygapophyses* (*za*), which are developed from the base of each neurapophysis.

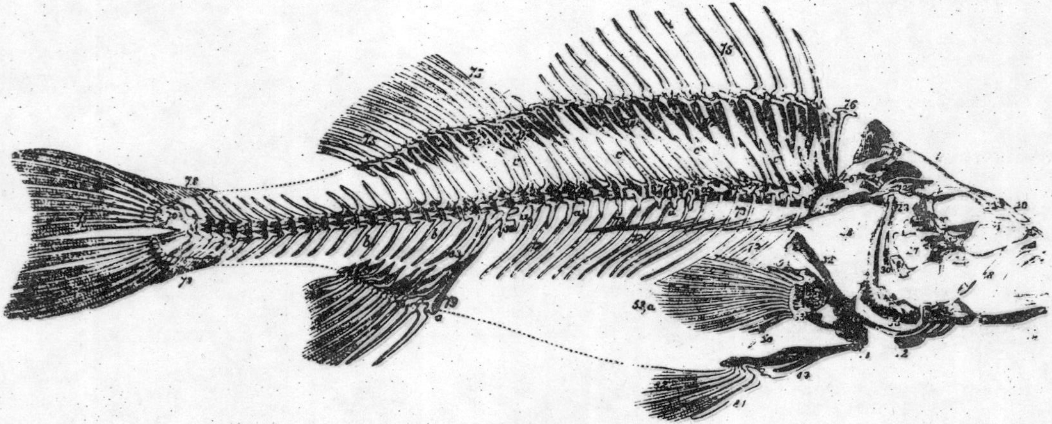

Fig. 23.—Skeleton of the Perch.

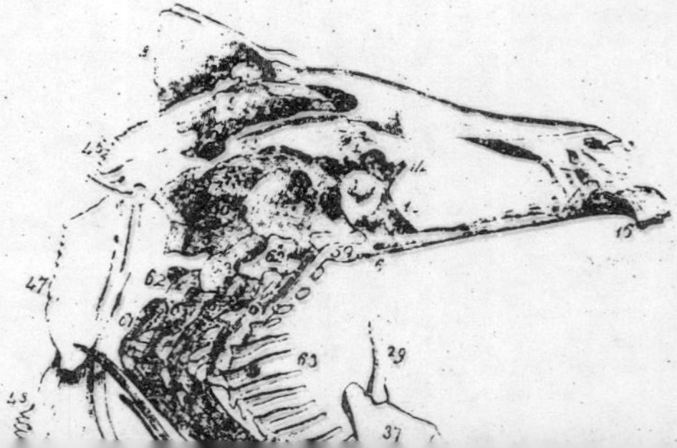

Fig. 24.—Skeleton of a Perch's Skull.

Fig. 25.—Hyoid arch, branchial apparatus, and scapulary arch of the Perch.

Fig. 26.—Lower view of Skull of Perch.

Fig. 27.—Hyoid bone of the Perch

The vertebræ are either *abdominal* or *caudal* vertebræ, the coalescence of the parapophyses into a complete hæmal ring, and the suspension of the anal fin generally forming a sufficiently well-marked boundary between abdominal and caudal regions (Fig. 23). In the Perch there are twenty-one abdominal and as many caudal vertebræ. The centrum of the first vertebra or atlas is very short, with the apophyses scarcely indicated, and lacking ribs like the succeeding vertebra. All the other abdominal vertebræ, with the exception of the last or two last, are provided with ribs, many of which are bifid (72). A series of flat spines (74), called *interneurals*, to which the spines and rays of the dorsal fins are articulated, are supported by the neural spines, the strength of the neurals and interneurals corresponding to that of the *dermal* spines (75). The caudal vertebræ differ from the abdominal in having the hæmapophyseal elements converted into spines similar to the neurals, the anterior being likewise destined to support a series of *interhæmals* (79), to which the anal rays are articulated. The last and smallest caudal vertebra articulates with the *hypural* (70), a fan-like bone, which, together with the dilated hindmost neural and hæmal elements, supports the caudal rays.

Looking at a perch's *skull* from the side (Fig. 24), the most superficial bones will be found to be those of the jaws, a chain of thin bones round the lower half of the eye, and the opercles.

The anterior margin of the upper jaw is formed by the *intermaxillary* or *premaxillary* (17) which bears teeth, terminates in a pedicle above, to allow of a forward sliding motion of the jaw, and is dilated into a flat triangular process behind, on which leans the second bone of the upper jaw, the *maxillary* (18). This bone is toothless, articulates with the vomer and palatine bone, and is greatly dilated towards its distal extremity. Both the maxillary and intermaxillary lie and move parallel to each other, being connected by a narrow membrane; in many other fishes their relative position is very different.

The *mandible* or lower jaw consists of a right and left ramus; their union by a ligament in front is called *symphysis.* Each ramus is formed of several pieces; that which, by a sigmoid concavity articulates with the quadrate, is the *articulary* bone (35); it sends upwards a coronoid process, to which a ligament from the maxillary and the masticatory muscles are attached; and forwards a long-pointed process, to be sheathed in the deep notch of the anterior piece. A small separate piece (36) at the lower posterior angle of the mandible is termed *angular.* The largest piece (34) is tooth-bearing, and hence termed *dentary;* at its inner surface it is always deeply excavated, to receive a cylindrical cartilage, called *Meckel's cartilage,* the remains of an embryonic condition of the jaw, the articulary and angular being but ossified parts of it. In other *Teleostei* this number is still more increased by a *splenial* and other bones.

The *infraorbital* ring of bones (Fig. 23, ^{19}) consists of several (four) pieces, of which the anterior is the largest, and distinguished as *præorbital.*

The so-called *præoperculum* (30) belongs rather to the bones of the suspensorium of the mandible, presently to be described, than to the opercles proper. It is narrow, strong, angularly bent, so as to consist of a vertical and horizontal limb, with an incompletely closed canal running along both limbs. As it is quite a superficial bone, and frequently armed with various spines, its form and configuration form an important item in the descriptive details of many fishes.

The principal piece of the gill-cover is the *operculum* (28), triangular in shape, situated behind, and movably united with, the vertical limb of the præoperculum. There is an articulary cavity at its upper anterior angle for its junction with the hyomandibular. The oblong lamella below the operculum is the *suboperculum* (32), and the one in front of this latter, below the horizontal limb of the præoperculum, is the *interoperculum* (33), which is connected by ligament with the angular piece of the lower jaw, and is also attached to the outer face of the hyoid, so that the gill-covers cannot open or shut without the hyoid apparatus executing a corresponding movement.

The chain of flat bones which, after the removal of the temporal muscles, appear arranged within the inner concavity of the præoperculum (Fig. 24), are comprised with the latter under the common name of *mandibulary suspensorium*. They connect the mandible with the cranium. The uppermost, the *epitympanic* or *hyomandibular* (23), is articulated by a double articulary head with the mastoid and posterior frontal. Another articulary head is destined for the opercular joint. The *mesotympanic* or *symplectic* (31) appears as a styliform prolongation of the lower part of the hyomandibular; is entirely cartilaginous in the young, but nearly entirely ossified in the adult. The position of this bone is noteworthy, because, directly inwards of its cartilaginous junction with the hyomandibular, there is situated the uppermost piece of the hyoid arch, the stylo-hyal. The next bone of the series is the *pretympanic* or *metapterygoid* (27), a flat bone forming a bridge towards the pterygoid, and not rarely absent in the teleosteous sub-class. Finally, the large triangular *hypotympanic* or *quadrate* (26) has a large condyle for the mandibulary joint.

The palatine arch (Fig. 26) connects the suspensorium with the anterior extremity of the skull, and is formed by three bones: the *entopterygoid* (25), an oblong and thin bone attached to the inner border of the palatine and pterygoid, and increasing the surface of the bony roof of the mouth towards the median line; it constitutes also the floor of the orbit. The *pterygoid* (24) (or *os transversum*) starts from the quadrate, and is joined by suture to the *palatine*, which is toothed, and reaches to the vomer and anterior frontal.

In the occipital region there are distinguished the *basioccipital* (5), readily recognised by the conical excavation corresponding and similar to that of the atlas, with which it is articulated through the intervention of a capsule filled with a gelatinous substance (the remains of the notochord); the *exoccipitals* (10) articulated, one on each side, to the basioccipital, and expanding on the upper surface of that bone, so as to meet and support the spinal column; a superficial thin lamella (13), suturally connected with the exoccipitals, not constant in fishes, and erroneously believed by Cuvier to be the *petrosal* (*os petrosum*) of higher animals; further, the *paroccipitals* (9), which are wedged in between the exoccipitals and *supraoccipital*. This last bone (8) forms the key of the arch over the occipital foramen, and raises a strong high crest from the whole length of its mesial line; a transverse supraoccipital ridge, coming from each side of the base of this spine runs outwards laterally to the external angles of the bone. The supraoccipital separates the parietals, and forms a suture with the frontals.

In front of the basioccipital the base of the skull is formed by the *basisphenoid* (*parasphenoid* of Huxley) (6). This very long and narrow bone extends from the basioccipital beyond the brain-capsule to between the orbits, where it forms the support of the fibro-membranous interorbital septum. Anteriorly it is connate with another long hammer-shaped bone (16), the *vomer*, the head of which marks the anterior end of the palate, and is beset with teeth. The *alisphenoids* (11) are short broad bones, rising from the basisphenoid; their posterior margins are suturally connected with the anterior of the basi- and ex-occipitals.

The formation of the posterior part of the side of the skull is completed by the *mastoid* and *parietal* bones. The former (12) projects outwards and backwards farther than the paroccipital, forming the outer strong process of the side of the cranium. This process lodges on its upper surface one of the main ducts of the muciferous system, and affords the base of articulation to a part of the hyomandibular. Its extremity gives attachment to the strong tendon of the dorso-lateral muscles of the trunk. The *parietals* (7) are flat bones, of comparatively much smaller extent than in higher Vertebrates, and separated from each other by the anterior prolongation of the supra-occipital.

The anterior wall of the brain-capsule (or the posterior of the orbit) is formed by the *orbitosphenoids* (14), between which, superiorly, the olfactory nerves, and inferiorly, the optic, pass out of the cranium. In addition to this paired bone, the Perch and many other fishes possess another single bone (15),—the *os sphenoideum anterius* of Cuvier, *ethmoid* of Owen, and *basisphenoid* of Huxley; it is Y-shaped, each lateral branch being connected with an orbitosphenoid, whilst the lower branch rests upon the long basal bone.

A cartilage, the substance of which is thickest above the vomer, and which extends as a narrow stripe along the inter-orbital septum, represents the *ethmoid* of higher Vertebrata; the olfactory nerves run along, and finally perforate it.

There remain, finally, the bones distinguishable on the upper surface of the skull; the largest, extending from the nasal cavities to the occipital, are the *frontal* bones (1), which also form the upper margin of the orbit. The *postfrontals* (4) are small bones placed on the supero-posterior angle of the orbit, and serving as the point from which the infraorbital ring is suspended. The *prefrontals* (2), also small, occupy the anterior margin of the orbit. A pair of small tubiform bones (20), the *turbinals*, occupy the foremost part of the snout, in front of the frontals, and are separated from each other by intervening cartilage.

After removal of the gill-cover and mandibulary suspensorium, the hyoid arch, which encloses the branchial apparatus, and farther behind, the humeral arch are laid open to view (Fig. 25). These parts can be readily separated from the cranium proper.

The *hyoid arch* is suspended by a slender styliform bone, the *stylohyal* (29), from the hyomandibulars; it consists of three segments, the *epihyal* (37), *ceratohyal* (38), which is the longest and strongest piece, and the *basihyal*, which is formed by two juxtaposed pieces (39, 40). Between the latter there is a median styliform ossicle (41), extending forwards into the substance of the tongue, called *glossohyal* or *os linguale;* and below the junction of the two hyoid branches there is a vertical single bone (42), expanded along its lower edge, which, connected by ligament with the anterior extremity of the humeral arch, forms the *isthmus* separating the two gill-openings. This bone is called the *urohyal*. Articulated or attached by ligaments to the epihyal and ceratohyal are a number of sword-shaped bones or rays (43), the *branchiostegals*, between which the branchiostegal membrane is extended.

The *branchial arches* (Figs. 25 and 27) are enclosed within the hyoid arch, with which they are closely connected at the base. They are five in number, of which four bear gills, whilst the fifth (56) remains dwarfed, is beset with teeth, and called the *lower pharyngeal* bone. The arches adhere by their lower extremities to a chain of ossicles (53, 54, 55), *basibranchials*, and, curving as they ascend, nearly meet at the base of the cranium, to which they are attached by a layer of ligamentous and cellular tissue. Each of the first three branchial arches consists of four pieces movably connected with one another. The lowest is the *hypobranchial* (57), the next much longer one (58) the *ceratobranchial*, and, above this, a slender and a short irregularly-shaped *epibranchial* (61). In the fourth arch the hypobranchial is absent. The uppermost of these segments (62), especially of the fourth arch, are dilated, and more or less confluent; they are beset with fine teeth, and generally distinguished as the *upper pharyngeal bones.* Only the ceratobranchial is represented in the fifth arch or lower pharyngeal. On their outer convex side the branchial segments are grooved for the reception of large blood-vessels and nerves; on the inner side they support horny processes (63), called the *gill-rakers,* which do not form part of the skeleton.

The *scapular* or *humeral arch* is suspended from the skull by the (*suprascapula*) *post-temporal* (46), which, in the Perch, is attached by a triple prong to the occipital and mastoid bones. Then follows the (*scapula*) *supraclavicula* (47), and the arch is completed below by the union of the large (*coracoid*) *clavicula* (48) with its fellow. Two flat bones (51, 52), each with a vacuity, attached to the clavicle have been determined as the (*radius* and *ulna*) *coracoid* and *scapula* of higher vertebrates, and the two series of small bones (53) intervening between the forearm and the fin as *carpals* and *metacarpals.* A two-jointed appendage the (*epicoracoid*) *post-clavicula,* is attached to the clavicle: its upper piece (49) is broad and lamelliform, its lower (50) styliform and pointed.

The ventral fins are articulated to a pair of flat triangular bones, the *pubic* bones (80).

The bones of the skull of the fish have received so many different interpretations that no two accounts agree in their nomenclature, so that their study is a matter of considerable difficulty to the beginner. The following synonymic table will tend to overcome difficulties arising from this cause; it contains the terms used by Cuvier, those introduced by Owen, and finally the nomenclature of Stannius, Huxley, and Parker. Those adopted in the present work are printed in italics. The numbers refer to the figures in the accompanying woodcuts (Figs. 23-27).

	Cuvier.	*Owen.*	*Stannius.*	*Huxley, Parker, etc.*
1.	Frontal principal	*Frontal*	Os frontale	
2.	Frontal antérieur	*Prefrontal*	Os frontale anterius	Lateral ethmoid (Parker)
3.	*Ethmoid*	Nasal	Os ethmoideum	
4.	Frontal postérieur	*Postfrontal*	Os frontale posterius	Sphenotic (Parker)
5.	Basilaire	*Basioccipital*	Os basilare	
6.	Sphénoide	*Basisphenoid*	Os sphenoideum basilare	Sometimes referred to as "*Basal*"
7.	Pariétal	*Parietal*	Os parietale	
8.	Interpariétal or occipital supérieure	*Supraoccipital*	Os occipitale superius	
9.	Occipital externe	*Paroccipital*	Os occipitale externum	Epioticum (Huxley)
10.	Occipital lateral	*Exoccipital*	Os occipitale laterale	
11.	Grande aile du sphénoide	*Alisphenoid*	Ala temporalis	Prooticum (*Huxley*)
12.	Mastoidien	*Mastoid*	Os mastoideum + os extrascapulare	Opisthoticum[1] + *Squamosal* (Huxley)
13.	Rocher	Petrosal and Otosteal	Oberflächliche Knochen-lamelle	
14.	Aile orbitaire	*Orbitosphenoid*	Ala orbitalis	Alisphenoid (Huxley)
15.	Sphenoide antérieur	Ethmoid and Ethmoturbinal	Os sphenoideum anterius	*Basisphenoid* (Huxley)
16.	*Vomer*	Vomer	Vomer	
17.	Intermaxillaire	*Inter- or Pre-maxillary*	Os intermaxillare	
18.	Maxillaire supérieur	*Maxillary*	Os maxillare	
19.	Sousorbitaires	*Infraorbital ring*	Ossa infraorbitalia	
20.	Nasal	*Turbinal*	Os terminale	
22.	Palatine	*Palatin*	Os palatinum	
23.	Temporal	Epitympanic	Os temporale	*Hyomandibular* (Huxley)
24.	Transverse	*Pterygoid*	Os transversum s. pterygoideum externum	
25.	Ptérygoidien interne	*Entopterygoid*	Os pterygoideum	Mesopterygoid (Parker)
26.	Jugal	Hypotympanic	Os quadratojugale	*Quadrate* (Huxley)
27.	Tympanal	Pretympanic	Os tympanicum	*Metapterygoid* (Huxley)

[1] Pterotic of Parker.

	Cuvier.	*Owen.*	*Stannius.*	*Huxley, Parker, etc.*
28.	Operculaire	*Operculum*	Operculum	
29.	Styloide	*Stylohyal*	Os styloideum	
30.	Préopercule	*Præoperculum*	Præoperculum	
31.	Symplectique	Mesotympanic	*Os symplecticum*	
32.	Sousopercule	*Suboperculum*	Suboperculum	
33.	Interopercule	*Interoperculum*	Interoperculum	
34.	Dentaire	*Dentary*	Os dentale	
35.	Articulaire	*Articulary*	Os articulare	
36.	Angulaire	*Angular*	Os angulare	
37. 38.	Grandes pièces latérales	*Epihyal*	Segmente der Zungenbein-Schenkel	
		Ceratohyal		
39. 40.	Petites pièces laterales	*Basihyal*		
41.	Os lingual	*Glossohyal*	Os linguale s. entoglossum	
42.	Queue de l'os hyoide	*Urohyal*		Basibranchiostegal (Parker)
43.	Rayon branchiostège	*Branchiostegal*	Radii branchiostegi	
46.	Surscapulaire	Suprascapula	Omolita	*Post-temporal* (Parker)
47.	Scapulaire	Scapula	Scapula	*Supraclavicula* (Parker)
48.	Humeral	Coracoid	Clavicula	*Clavicula* (Parker)
49. 50.	Coracoid	Epicoracoid		*Postclavicula* (Parker)
51.	Cubital	Radius	Ossa carpi	*Coracoid* (Parker)
52.	Radial	Ulna		*Scapula* (Parker)
53.	Os du carpe	*Carpals*	Ossa metacarpi	*Basalia* (Huxley), Brachials (Parker)
53 bis. 54. 55.	Chaine intermédiaire	*Basibranchials*	Copula	
56.	Pharyngiens inférieurs	*Lower Pharyngeals*	Ossa pharyngea inferiora	
57.	Pièce interne de partie inférieure de l'arceau branchiale	*Hypobranchial*	Segmente der Kiemenbogen-Schenkel	
58.	Pièce externe ,,	*Ceratobranchial*		
59.	Stylet de prémière arceau branchiale	*Upper epibranchial of first branchial arch*		
61.	Partie supérieure de l'arceau branchiale	*Epibranchials*		
62.	Os pharyngian supérieur	Pharyngo-branchial	Os pharyngeum superius	*Upper pharyngeals*
63.		*Gill-rakers*		
65.	Rayons de la pectorale	*Pectoral rays*	Brustflossen-Strahlen	

	Cuvier.	*Owen.*	*Stannius.*	*Huxley, Parker, etc.*
67, 68.	Vertèbres abdominales	*Abdominal vertebræ*	Bauchwirbel	
69.	Vertèbres caudales	*Caudal vertebræ*	Schwanzwirbel	
70.	Plaque triangulaire et verticale	[Aggregated interhæmals]	Verticale Platte	*Hypural* (Huxley)
71.		*Caudal rays*	Schwanzflossen Strahlen	
72.	Côte	*Rib*	Rippen	
73.	Appendices or stylets	*Epipleural spines*	Muskel-Gräthen	
74.	Interépineux	*Interneural spines*	Ossa interspinalia s. obere Flossentræger	
75.	Épines et rayons dorsales	*Dorsal rays and spines*	Rückenflossen-Strahlen u. Stacheln	
76.		*First interneural*		
78.		*Rudimentary caudal rays*		
79.	Apophyses épineuses inférieures	*Interhæmal spines*	Untere Flossentræger	
80.		*Pubic*	Becken	
81.		*Ventral spine*	Bauchflossen-Stachel	

CHAPTER IV.

MODIFICATIONS OF THE SKELETON.

THE lowermost sub-class of fishes, which comprises one form only, the Lancelet (*Branchiostoma* [s. *Amphioxus*] *lanceolatum*, possesses the skeleton of the most primitive type.

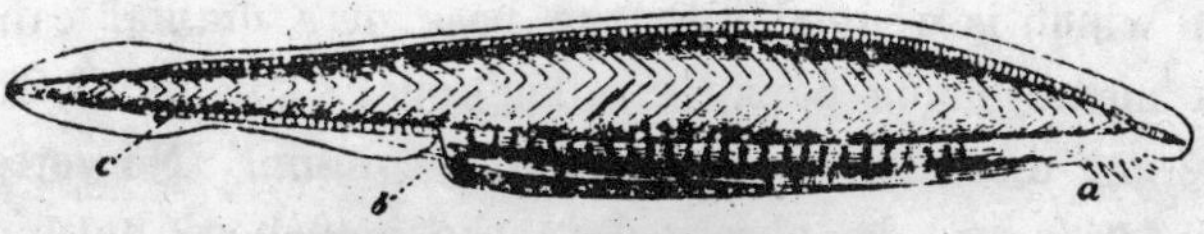

Fig. 28.—Branchiostoma lanceolatum.
a, Mouth ; *b*, Vent ; *c*, abdominal porus.

The vertebral column is represented by a simple *chorda*

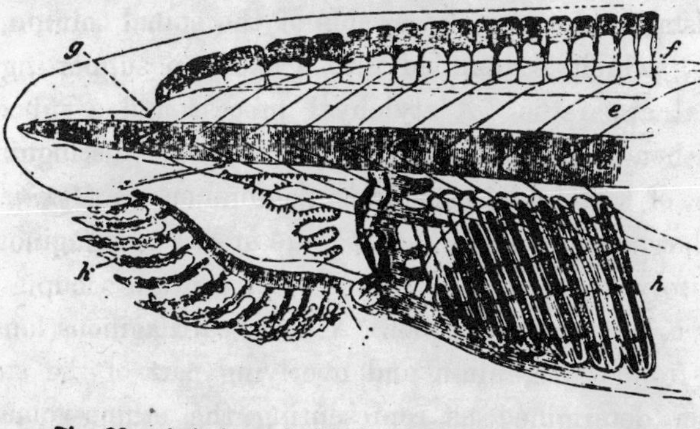

Fig. 29.—Anterior end of body of Branchiostoma (magn.)
d, Chorda dorsalis ; *e*, Spinal chord ; *f*, Cartilaginous rods ; *g*, Eye ; *h*, Branchial rods ; *i*, Labial cartilage ; *k*, Oral cirrhi.

dorsalis or *notochord* only, which extends from one extremity of the fish to the other, and, so far from being expanded into a cranial cavity, it is pointed at its anterior end as well as at its posterior. It is enveloped in a simple membrane like the spinal chord and the abdominal organs, and there is no trace of vertebral segments or ribs; however, a series of short cartilaginous rods above the spine evidently represent apophyses. A maxillary or hyoid apparatus, or elements representing limbs, are entirely absent.

[J. Müller, Ueber den Bau und die Lebenserscheinungen des *Branchiostoma lubricum*, in Abhandl. Ak. Wiss. Berlin, 1844.]

The skeleton of the *Cyclostomata* (or Marsipobranchii) (Lampreys and Sea-hags) shows a considerable advance of development. It consists of a notochord, the anterior pointed end of which is wedged into the base of a cranial capsule, partly membranous partly cartilaginous. This skull, therefore, is not movable upon the spinal column. No vertebral segmentation can be observed in the notochord, but neural arches are represented by a series of cartilages on each side of the spinal chord. In *Petromyzon* (Fig. 30) the basis cranii emits two prolongations on each side: an inferior, extending for some distance along the lower side of the spinal column, and a lateral, which is ramified into a skeleton supporting the branchial apparatus. A stylohyal process and a subocular arch with a palato-pterygoid portion may be distinguished. The roof of the cranial capsule is membranous in *Myxine* and in the larvæ of *Petromyzon*, but more or less cartilaginous in the auditory organ, whilst the olfactory capsule occupies the anterior upper part of the roof. A broad cartilaginous lamina, starting from the cranium and overlying part of the snout, has been determined as representing the ethmo-vomerine elements, whilst the oral organs are supported by large, very peculiar cartilages (*labials*), greatly differing in general configuration and arrangement in the various Cyclostomes. There are three in the Sea-lamprey, of which the middle one is joined to the palate by an intermediate smaller one; the fore-

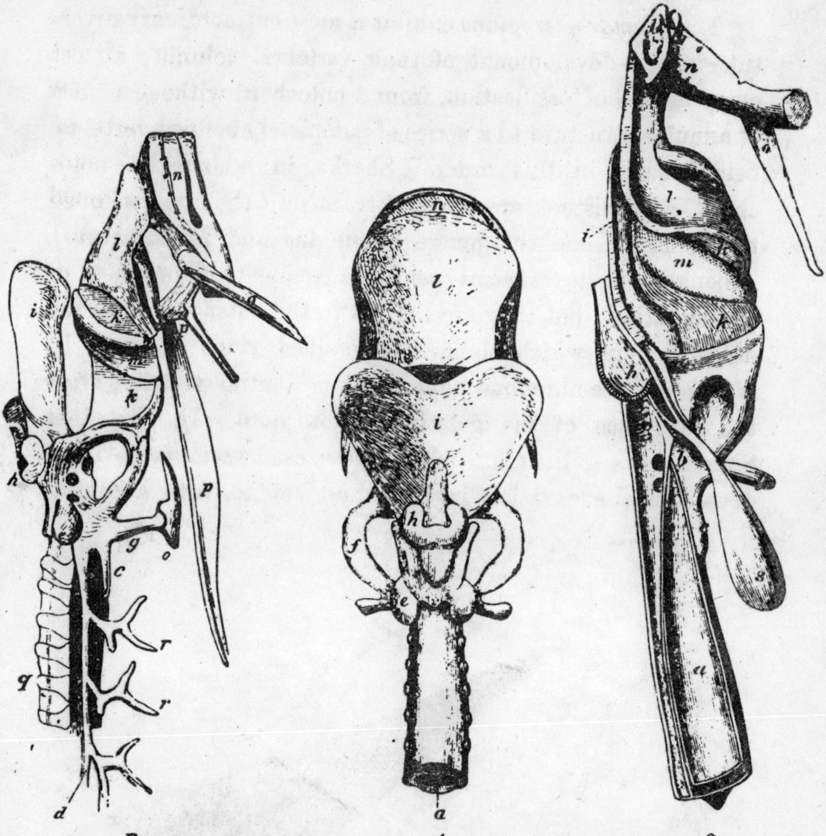

Fig. 30.—Upper (A) and side (B) views, and vertical section (C) of the skull of *Petromyzon marinus.*

a, Notochord; *b*, Basis cranii; *c*, Inferior, and *d*, Lateral process of basis; *e*, Auditory capsule; *f*, Subocular arch; *g*, Stylohyal process; *h*, Olfactory capsule; *i*, Ethmo-vomerine plate; *k*, Palato-pterygoid portion of subocular arch; *l-n*, Accessory labial or rostral cartilages; with *o*, appendage; *p*, lingual cartilage; *q*, neural arches; *r*, Branchial skeleton; *s*, Blind termination of the nasal duct between the notochord and œsophagus.

most is ring-like, tooth-bearing, emitting on each side a styliform process. The lingual cartilage is large in all Cyclostomes.

There is no trace of ribs or limbs.

[J. Müller, Vergleichende Anatomie der Myxinoiden. Erster Theil. Osteologie und Myologie, in Abhandl. Ak. Wiss. Berlin, 1835.]

The *Chondropterygians* exhibit a most extraordinary diversity in the development of their vertebral column; almost every degree of ossification, from a notochord without a trace of annular structure to a series of completely ossified vertebræ being found in this order. Sharks, in which the notochord is persistent, are the *Holocephali* (if they be reckoned to this order, and the genera *Notidanus* and *Echinorhinus*). Among the first, *Chimæra monstrosa* begins to show traces of segmentation; but they are limited to the outer sheath of the notochord, in which slender subossified rings appear. In *Notidanus* membranous septa, with a central vacuity, cross the substance of the gelatinous notochord. In the other Sharks the segmentation is complete, each vertebra having a deep conical excavation in front and behind, with a central

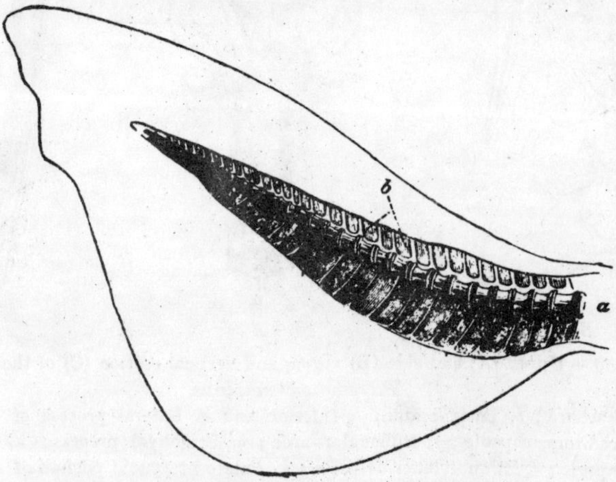

Fig. 31.—Heterocercal Tail of Centrina salviani: *a*, Vertebræ ; *b*, Neurapophyses ; *c*, Hæmapophyses.

canal through which the notochord is continued; but the degree in which the primitive cartilage is replaced by concentric or radiating lamellæ of bone varies greatly in the various genera, and according to the age of the individuals. In the Rays all the vertebræ are completely ossified, and the anterior ones confluent into one continuous mass.

In the majority of Chondropterygians the extremity of the vertebral column shows a decidedly heterocercal condition (Fig. 31), and only a few, like *Squatina* and some Rays, possess a diphycercal tail.

The advance in the development of the skeleton of the Chondropterygians beyond the primitive condition of the previous sub-classes, manifests itself further by the presence of neural and hæmal elements, which extend to the foremost part of the axial column, but of which the hæmal form a closed arch in the caudal region only, whilst on the trunk they appear merely as a lateral longitudinal ridge.

The neural and hæmal apophyses are either merely attached to the axis, as in Chondropterygians with persistent notochord, the Rays and some Sharks; or their basal

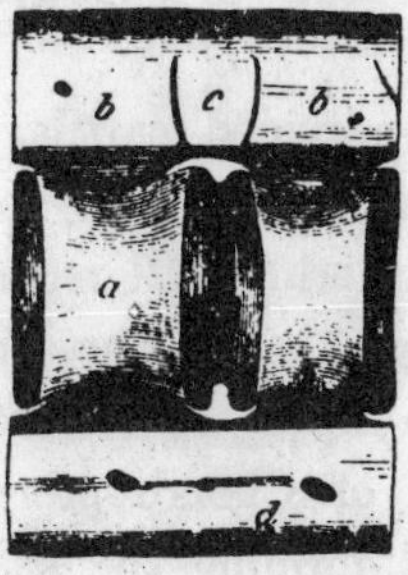

Fig. 32.

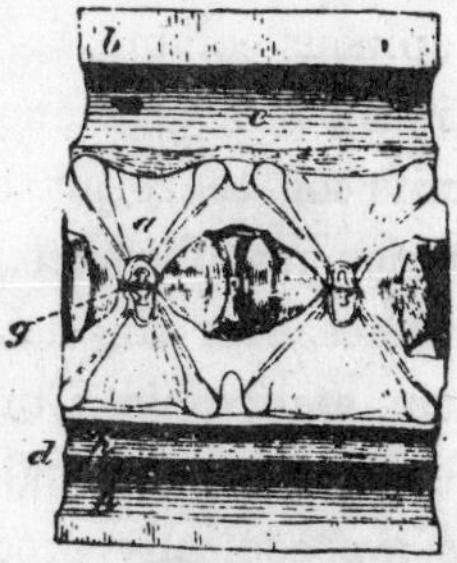

Fig. 33.

Fig. 34.

Fig. 32.—Lateral view. Fig. 33.—Longitudinal section. Fig. 34.—Transverse section of Caudal vertebra of Basking Shark (Selache maxima). (After Hasse.) *a*, Centrum; *b*, Neurapophysis; *c*, Intercrural cartilage; *d*, Hæmapophysis; *e*, Spinal canal; *f*, Intervertebral cavity; *g*, Central canal for persistent portion of notochord; *h*, Hæmal canals for blood-vessels.

portions penetrate like wedges into the substance of the centrum, so that, in a transverse section, in consequence of the difference in their texture, they appear in the form of an X.[1] The interspaces between the neurapophyses of the vertebræ are not filled by fibrous membrane, as in other fishes, but by separate cartilages, *laminæ* or *cartilagines intercrurales*, to which frequently a series of terminal pieces is superadded, which must be regarded as the first appearance of the interneural spines of the Teleostei and many Ganoids. Similar terminal pieces are sometimes observed on the hæmal arches. *Ribs* are either absent or but imperfectly represented (*Carcharias*).

The substance of the *skull* of the Chondropterygians is cartilage, interrupted especially on its upper surface by more or less extensive fibro-membranous fontanelles. Superficially it is covered by a more or less thick chagreen-like osseous deposit. The articulation with the vertebral column is effected by a pair of lateral condyles. In the Sharks, besides, a central conical excavation corresponds to that of the centrum of the foremost vertebral segment, whilst in the Rays this central excavation of the skull receives a condyle of the axis of the spinous column.

The cranium itself is a continuous undivided cartilage, in which the limits of the orbit are well marked by an anterior and posterior protuberance. The ethmoidal region sends horizontal plates over the nasal sacs, the apertures of which retain their embryonic situation upon the under surface of the skull. In the majority of Chondropterygians these plates are conically produced, forming the base of the soft projecting snout; and in some forms, especially in the long-snouted Rays and the Saw-fishes (*Pristis*) this prolongation appears in the form of three or more tubiform rods.

[1] *C. Hasse* has studied the modifications of the texture of the vertebræ and the structure of the Chondropterygian skeleton generally, and shown that they correspond in the main to the natural groups of the system, and, consequently, that they offer a valuable guide in the determination of fossil remains.

As separate cartilages there are appended to the skull a suspensorium, a palatine, mandible, hyoid. and rudimentary maxillary elements.

The suspensorium is movably attached to the side of the skull. It generally consists of one piece only, but in some Rays of two. In the Rays it is articulated with the mandible only, their hyoid possessing a distinct point of attachment to the skull. In the Sharks the hyoid is suspended from the lower end of the suspensorium together with the mandible.

What is generally called the upper jaw of a Shark is, as Cuvier has already stated, not the maxillary, but palatine. It consists of two simple lateral halves, each of which articulates with the corresponding half of the lower jaw, which is formed by the simple representative of Meckel's cartilage.

Some cartilages of various sizes are generally developed on each side of the palatine, and one on each side of the mandible. They are called *labial* cartilages, and seem to represent maxillary elements.

The *hyoid* consists generally of a pair of long and strong lateral pieces, and a single mesial piece. From the former cartilaginous filaments (representing branchiostegals) pass directly outwards. Branchial arches, varying in number, and similar to the hyoid, succeed it. They are suspended from the side of the foremost part of the spinous column, and, like the hyoid, bear a number of filaments.

The vertical fins are supported by interneural and interhæmal cartilages, each of which consists of two and more pieces, and to which the fin-rays are attached without articulation.

The *scapular arch* of the Sharks is formed by a single coracoid cartilage bent from the dorsal region downwards and forwards. In some genera (*Scyllium*, *Squatina*) a small separate scapular cartilage is attached to the dorsal extremities of the coracoid; but in none of the Elasmobranchs is the scapular arch suspended from the skull or vertebral column; it is merely sunk, and fixed in the substance of the muscles. Behind, at the point of its greatest curvature, three carpal cartilages are joined to the coracoid, which Gegenbaur has distinguished as *propterygium*, *mesopterygium*, and *metapterygium*, the former occupying the front, the latter the hind margin of the fin. Several more or less regular transverse series of styliform cartilages follow. They represent the phalanges, to which the horny filaments which are imbedded in the skin of the fin are attached.

In the Rays, with the exception of *Torpedo*, the scapular arch is intimately connected with the confluent anterior portion of the vertebral column. The anterior and posterior carpal cartilages are followed by a series of similar pieces, which extend like an arch forwards to the rostral portion of the skull, and backwards to the pubic region. Extremely numerous phalangeal elements, longest in the middle, are supported by the carpals, and form the skeleton of the lateral expansion of the so-called *disk* of the Ray's body, which thus, in fact, is nothing but the enormously enlarged pectoral fin.

The *pubic* is represented by a single median transverse cartilage, with which a tarsal cartilage articulates. The latter supports the fin-rays. To the end of this cartilage is also attached, in the male Chondropterygians, a peculiar accessory generative organ or clasper.

The *Holocephali* differ from the other Chondropterygians in several important points of the structure of their skeleton, and approach unmistakably certain Ganoids. That their spinal column is persistently notochordal has been mentioned already. Their palatal apparatus, with the suspensorium, coalesces with the skull, the mandible articulating with a short apophysis of the cranial cartilage. The mandible is simple, without anterior symphysis. The spine with which the dorsal fin is armed articulates with a neural apophysis, and is not immovably attached to it, as in the Sharks. The pubic consists of two lateral halves, with a short, rounded, arsal cartilage.

The skeleton of the *Ganoid* Fishes offers extreme variations with regard to the degree in which ossifications replace the primordial cartilage. Whilst some exhibit scarcely any advance beyond the Plagiostomes with persistent cartilage, others approach, as regards the development and specialisation of the several parts of their osseous framework, the Teleosteans so closely that their Ganoid nature can be demonstrated by, or inferred from, other considerations only. All Ganoids possess a separate gill-cover.[1]

The diversity in the development of the Ganoid skeleton is well exemplified by the few representatives of the order in the existing Fish-fauna. Lowest in the scale (in this respect) are those with a persistent notochord, and an *autostylic* skull, that is, a skull without separate suspensorium—the fishes constituting the sub-order *Dipnoi*, of which the existing representatives are *Lepidosiren*, *Protopterus*, and *Ceratodus*, and the extinct (as far as demonstrated at present) *Dipterus*, *Chirodus* (and *Phaneropleuron ?*). In these fishes the notochord is persistent, passing uninterruptedly into the cartilaginous base of the skull. Only now and then a distinct vertical segmentation occurs in the caudal portion of the column, but it does not extend to the notochord itself, but indicates only the limits between the superadded apophyseal elements, each neural being confluent with the opposite hæmal. Some *Dipnoi* are diphy-, others hetero-cercal.

[1] The Ganoids formed at former epochs the largest and most important order of fishes, many of the fossil forms being known from very imperfect remains only. It is quite possible that not a few of the latter, in which nothing whatever of the (probably very soft) endoskeleton has been preserved, should have to be assigned to some other order lower in the scale of organisation than the Ganoids (for instance, the *Cephalaspidæ*).

Neural and hæmal elements and ribs are well developed. In *Ceratodus* each neurapophysis consists of a basal cartilaginous portion, forming an arch over the myelon, and of a superadded second portion. The latter is separated from the former by a distinct line of demarcation, and its two branches are more styliform, cartilaginous at the ends and in the centre, but with an osseous sheath, and coalesced at the top, forming a gable over an elastic fibrous band which runs along and parallel to the longitudinal axis of the column (*Ligamentum longitudinale superius*). To the top of this gable is joined a single long cylindrical neural spine. From the eleventh apophyseal segment a distinct interneural spine, of the same structure as the neural, begins to be developed, and farther on a second interneural is superadded. Towards the extremity of the column these various pieces are gradually reduced in size and number, finally only a low cartilaginous band (the rudiments of the neurapophysis) remaining. The *hæmapophyses* are in form, size, and structure, very similar to the neurapophyses; and all these long bones, including the ribs, have that in common, that they consist of a solid rod of cartilage enclosed in a bony sheath, which, after the disappearance or decomposition of the cartilage, appears as a hollow tube. Such bones are extremely common throughout the order of Ganoids, and their remains have led to the designation of a family as *Cœlacanthi* (κοιλος, hollow; and ἀκανθος, spine).

The primordial *cranium* of the *Dipnoi* is cartilaginous, but with more or less extensive ossifications in its occipital, basal, or lateral portions, and with large tegumentary bones, the arrangement of which varies in the different genera. There is no separate suspensorium for the lower jaw A strong process descends from the cranial cartilage, and offers by means of a double condyle (Fig. 35 *s*) attachment to corresponding articulary surfaces of the lower jaw.

Maxillary and intermaxillary elements are not developed, but, perhaps, represented in *Ceratodus* by some inconstant rudimentary labial cartilages situated behind the posterior nasal opening. Facial cartilages and an infraorbital ring are developed at least in *Ceratodus*. The presence of a pair of small teeth in front indicates the vomerine portion (*v*) which remains cartilage, whilst the posterior pair of teeth are implanted in a pterygo-palatine ossification (*l*), which sometimes is paired, sometimes continuous. The base of the skull is constantly covered by a large basal ossification (*o*).

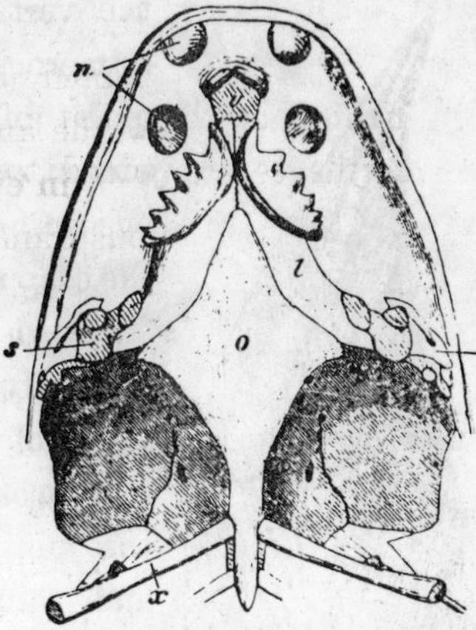

Fig. 35.—Palatal view of Skull of Ceratodus.

The *hyoid* is well developed, sometimes reduced to a pair of ceratohyals, sometimes with a basihyal and glossyhyal. The skeleton of the *branchial apparatus* approaches the Teleosteous type, less so in *Lepidosiren* than in *Ceratodus*, in which five branchial arches are developed, but with the lateral and mesial pieces reduced in number.

A large operculum, and a smaller sub- or inter-operculum are present.

The *scapular* arch consists of a single median transverse cartilage, and a pair of lateral cartilages which bear the articular condyle for the pectoral limb. The latter cartilages form the base of a large membrane-bone, and the whole arch is suspended from the skull by means of an osseous supraclavicle.

The fore-limb of the *Dipnoi* (Fig. 36) differs externally greatly from the pectoral fin of other Ganoid fishes. It is covered with small scales along the middle, from the root to its extremity, and surrounded by a rayed fringe similar to the vertical fin. A muscle split into numerous fascicles extends all the length of the fin, which is flexible in every part and in every direction. The cartilaginous framework supporting it is joined to the scapular arch by an oblong cartilage, followed by a broad basal cartilage (*a*), generally single, sometimes showing traces of a triple division. Along the middle of the fin runs a jointed axis (*b*), the joints gradually becoming smaller and thinner towards the extremity; each joint bears on each side a three, two, or one-jointed branch (*c*, *d*). This *axial* arrangement of the pectoral skeleton, which evidently represents one of its first and lowest conditions, has been termed *Archipterygium* by Gegenbaur. It is found in *Ceratodus* and other genera, but in *Lepidosiren* the jointed axis only has been preserved, with the addition of rudimentary rays in *Protopterus*.

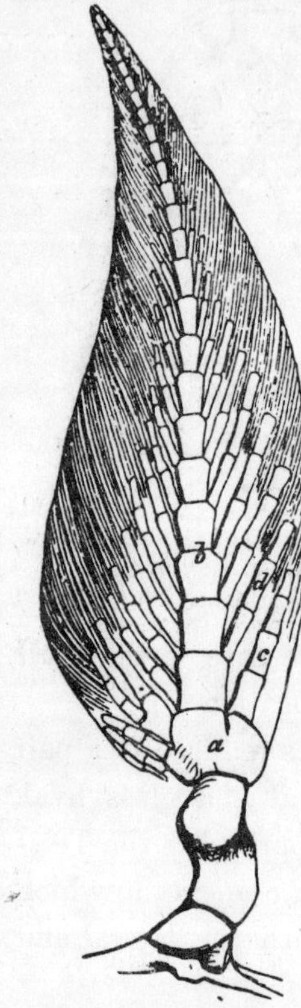

Fig. 36.—Fore-limb of Ceratodus.

The *pubic* consists of a single flattened subquadrangular cartilage, produced into a long single anterior process. Posteriorly it terminates on each side in a condyle, to which the basal cartilage of the ventral paddle is joined. The endoskeleton of the paddle is almost identical with that of the pectoral.

The Ganoid fishes with persistent notochord, but with a *hyostylic* skull (that is, a skull with a separate suspensorium) consist of the sub-order *Chondrostei*, of which the existing representatives are the Sturgeons (*Acipenser*, *Scaphirhynchus*,

Polyodon), and the extinct the *Chondrosteidæ*, *Palæoniscidæ*, and (according to Traquair) *Platysomidæ*.

Their spinal column does not differ essentially from that of the Dipnoi. Segmentation is represented only as far as the neural and hæmal elements are concerned. All are eminently heterocercal. Ribs are present in most, but replaced by ligaments in *Polyodon*.

The primordial cranium of the Sturgeons consists of persistent cartilage without ossifications in its substance, but superficial bones are still more developed and specialised than in the Dipnoi; so it is, at least, in the true Sturgeons, but less so in *Polyodon* (Fig. 37). The upper and lateral parts of the skull are covered by well-developed *membrane bones*, which,

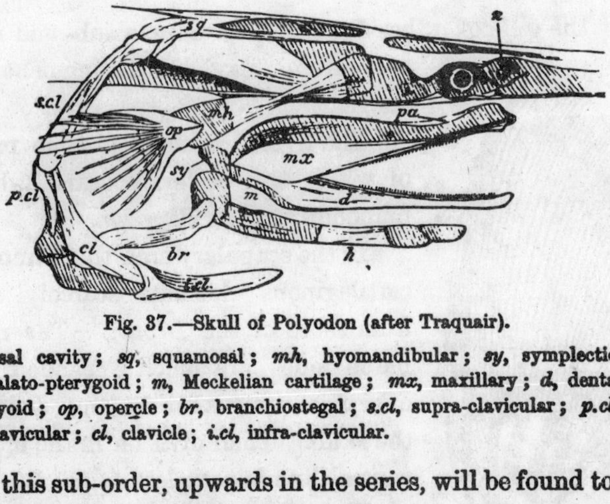

Fig. 37.—Skull of Polyodon (after Traquair).

Nasal cavity; *sq*, squamosal; *mh*, hyomandibular; *sy*, symplectic; *pa*, palato-pterygoid; *m*, Meckelian cartilage; *mx*, maxillary; *d*, dentary; *h*, hyoid; *op*, opercle; *br*, branchiostegal; *s.cl*, supra-clavicular; *p.cl*, post-clavicular; *cl*, clavicle; *i.cl*, infra-clavicular.

from this sub-order, upwards in the series, will be found to exist throughout the remaining forms of fishes. They are bones, the origin of which is not in cartilage but in membranous connective tissue. The lower surface of the skull is covered by an extremely large basal bone, which extends from the vomerine region on to the anterior part of the spinal column. The nasal excavation in the skull is rather lateral than inferior. The ethmoidal region is generally much produced, forming the base of the long projecting snout. The suspensorium is movably attached to the side of the skull, and consists of two pieces, a hyomandibular and a symplectic, which now appears for the first time as a separate piece, and to which the hyoid is attached. The palato-maxillary apparatus is more complex than in the Sharks and Dipnoi; a palato-pterygoid consists of two mesially-connected rami in *Polyodon*, and of a complex cartilaginous disk in *Acipenser*, being articulated in both to the Meckelian cartilage. In addition, the Sturgeons possess one or two pairs of osseous rods, which, in *Polyodon* at least, represent the maxillary, and therefore must be the representatives of the labial cartilages of the Sharks. The Meckelian cartilage is more or less covered by tegumentary bones.

In the gill-cover, besides the operculum, a sub- and interoperculum may be distinguished in *Acipenser*.

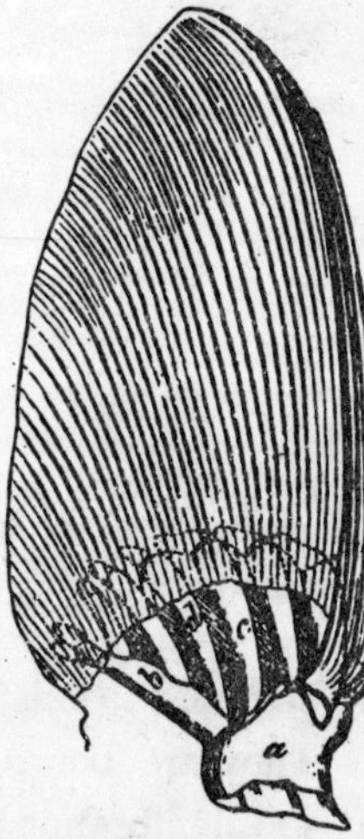

Fig. 38.—Fore-limb of *Acipenser*.

The hyoid consists of three pieces, of which the posterior bears a broad branchiostegal in *Polyodon*.

In the scapulary arch the primordial cartilaginous elements scarcely differ from those of the *Dipnoi*. The membrane-bones are much expanded, and offer a continuous series suspended from the skull. Their division in the median ventral line is complete.

The pectoral is supported by a cartilaginous framework (Fig. 38) similar to that of *Ceratodus*, but much more shortened and reduced in its periphery, the branches being absent altogether on one side of the axis. This modification of the fin is analogous to the heterocercal condition of the end of the spinous column. To the inner corner of a basal cartilage (*a*) a short axis (*b*) is joined, which on its outer side bears a few branches (*d*) only, the remaining branches (*c*) being fixed to the basal cartilage. The dermal fin-rays are opposed to the extremities of the branches, as in the *Dipnoi*.

The *pubic* consists of a paired cartilage, to which tarsal pieces supporting the fin-rays are attached.

The other living Ganoid fishes have the spinous column entirely or nearly entirely ossified, and have been comprised under the common name *Holostei*. However, they form three very distinct types; several attempts have been made to coordinate with them the fossil forms, but this task is beset with extreme difficulties, and its solution hitherto has not proved to be satisfactory.

The *Polypteroidei* have their spinous column formed by distinct osseous *amphicœlous* vertebræ, that is, vertebræ with concave anterior and posterior surfaces. It is nearly diphycercal; a slight degree of heterocercy obtains, inasmuch as the last vertebra is succeeded by a very thin cartilaginous filament which penetrates between the halves of one of the middle rays of the terminal fin. The rays above this cartilaginous filament are articulated to interneurals, those below lack interhæmals, and are attached either to the hæmals or vertebral centres. The neural arches, though ossified, do not coalesce with the centrum, and form one canal only, for the myelon. There are no intermediate elements between the neural spines. Interneurals developed, but simple, articulating with the dermoneurals. The abdominal vertebræ have parapophyses developed with epipleural spines. Only the caudal vertebræ have hæmal spines, which, like the interhæmals, agree in every essential respect with the opposite neurals. *Ribs* are inserted, not on the parapophyses, but on the centre, immediately below the parapophyses.

The *skull* of *Polypterus* (Fig. 39) shows a great advance

towards the Teleosteous type, the number of separable bones

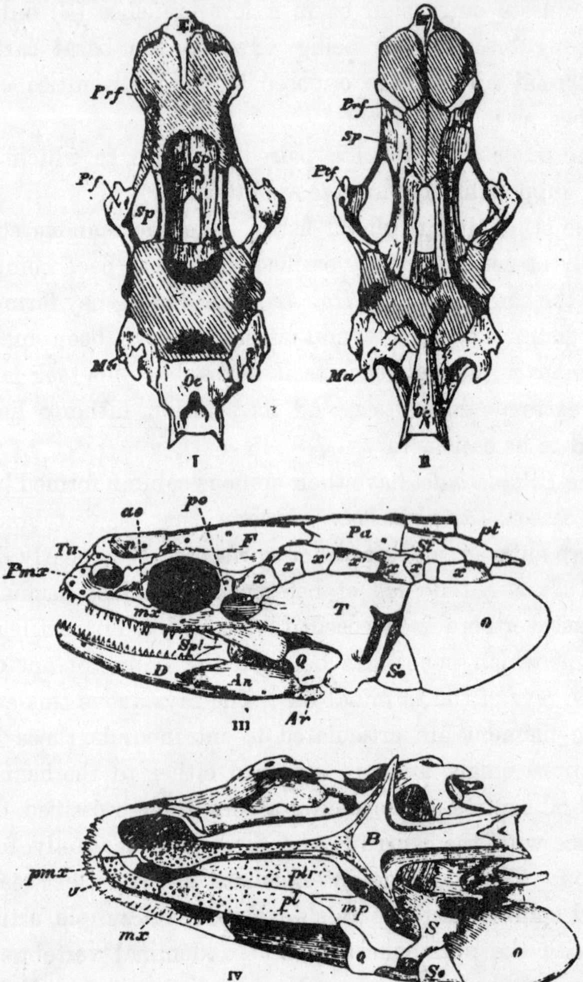

Fig. 39.—Skull of Polypterus. (After Traquair.)

Fig. I. Upper aspect of the Primordial Cranium, with the membrane-bones removed. Fig. II. Lower aspect of the same. Fig. III. Side view, with the membrane-bones. Fig. IV. Lower aspect of the Skull, part of the bones being removed on one side. The parts shaded with oblique lines are cartilage of the primordial skull.

***An*, Angular; *ao*, anteorbital; *Ar*, articulary; *B*, basal; *D*, dentary; *E*,**

ethmoid; *F*, frontal; *Ma*, mastoid; *Mp*, metapterygoid; *Mx*, maxillary; *N*, nasal; *O*, operculum; *Oc*, occipital; *Pa*, parietal; *Pl*, palatine; *Pmx*, præmaxillary; *po*, postorbital; *Prf*, prefrontal; *Pt*, post-temporals; *Ptf*, postfrontal; *Ptr*, pterygoid; *Q*, quadrate; *S*, suspensorium; *So*, suboperculum; *Sp*, sphenoid; *Spl*, splenial; *St*, supratemporals; *T*, tympanic lamina; *Tu*, turbinal; *v*, vomer; *x x*, small ossicles; *x' x'*, spiraculars.

being greatly increased. They are arranged much in the same fashion as in Teleostei. But a great portion of the primordial cranium remains cartilaginous. The membrane-bones which cover the upper and lower surfaces of the brain-case are so much developed as to cause the underlying cartilage to disappear, so that a large vacuity or fontanelle exists in the substance of the upper as well as lower cartilaginous wall. Of ossifications belonging to the primordial skull must be noticed the single occipital with a mastoid on each side. They are separated by persistent cartilage from the sphenoids and postfrontals; the former, which are the largest ossification of the primordial cranium, enclose the anterior half of the brain cavity. Finally, the nasal portion contains a median ethmoid and a pair of præfrontal bones.

Only a very small portion of the bones described are visible externally, nearly the whole of the primordial cranium being covered by the membrane-bones. Of these are seen on the upper surface a pair of parietals, frontals, "nasals," and turbinals; on the lower surface a large cross-shaped basal, anteriorly bordered on each side by a pterygoid, parallel to a palatine which forms a suture with the double vomer. The suspensorium has in front a metapterygoid and quadrate bone, and an operculum and suboperculum are attached to it behind.

Præmaxillaries and maxillaries are now fully developed, but immovably attached to the skull. The lower jaw is ossified, and consists of an articulary, angular, dentary, and splenial. Of labial cartilages a rudiment at the angle of the mouth has remained persistent.

The side of the skull, in front of the operculum, is covered by a large irregularly-shaped bone (*T*) (corresponding to the "tympanic lamina" of *Ceratodus*, Fig. 35, *q*), held by some to be the præoperculum; along its upper circumference lies a series of small ossicles, of which two may be distinguished as spiraculars, as they form a valve for the protection of the spiracular orifice of these fishes. An infraorbital ring is represented by a præ- and post-orbital only.

Each *hyoid* consists of three pieces, none of which bear branchiostegals, the single median piece being osseous in front and cartilaginous behind. Four branchial arches are developed, the foremost consisting of three, the second and third of two, and the last of a single piece. There is no lower pharyngeal. Between the rami of the lower jaw the throat is protected by a pair of large osseous laminæ (*gular plates*), which have been considered to represent the urohyal of osseous fishes.

The scapulary arch is almost entirely formed by the well-developed membrane-bones, which in the ventral line are suturally united. The pectoral fin is supported by three bones, pro-, meso-, and metapterygium, of which the dilated middle one alone bears rays, and is excluded from the articulation with the shoulder-girdle.

The pubic consists of paired bone, to which tarsal bones supporting the fin-rays are attached.

In the *Lepidosteoidei* the vertebræ are completely ossified, and *opisthocœlous*, having a convexity in front and a concavity behind, as in some Amphibians. Though the end of the body externally appears nearly diphycercal, the termination of the vertebral column is, in fact, distinctly heterocercal (Fig. 40). Its extremity remains cartilaginous, is turned upwards, and lies immediately below the scutes which cover the upper margin of the caudal fin. It is preceded by a few rudimentary vertebræ which gradually pass into the fully developed normal vertebræ. The caudal fin is suspended from hæmapophyses only, and does not extend to the neural side of the vertebral

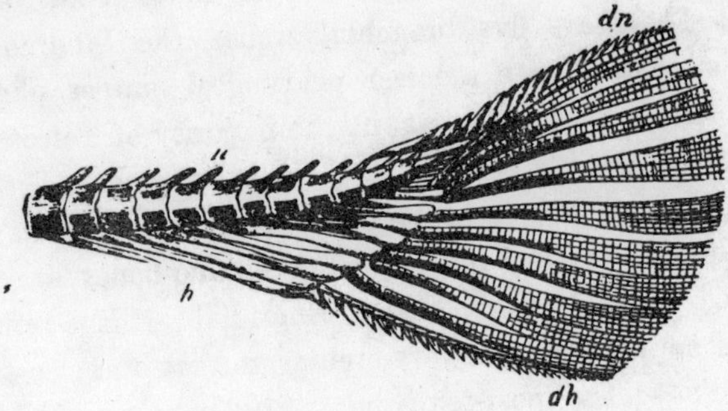

Fig. 40.—Heterocercal Tail of Lepidosteus.

n, Vertebral column; *h*, hæmal spines; *dn*, fulcra; *dh*, lower fulcra.

column. The neural arches coalesce with the centrum; interneurals simple. The abdominal vertebræ have parapophyses, to which the ribs are attached. Only the caudal vertebræ have hæmal spines.

In the skull of *Lepidosteus* the cartilage of the endocranium is still more replaced by ossifications than in *Polypterus;* those ossifications, moreover, being represented by a greater number of discrete bones; especially the membrane-bones are greatly multiplied: the occipital, for instance, consists of three pieces; the vomer is double as in *Polypterus;* the maxillary consists of a series of pieces firmly united by suture. The symplectic reaches the lower jaw, so that the articulary is provided with a double joint, viz. for the symplectic and quadrate; the component parts of the lower jaw are as numerous as in reptiles, a dentary, splenial, articulary, angular, supra-angular, and coronary being distinct. The sides of the head are covered with numerous bones, and a præoperculum is developed in front of the gill-cover which, again, consists of an operculum and suboperculum.

Each hyoid consists of three pieces, of which the middle is the longest, the upper bearing the largest of the three branchiostegals which *Lepidosteus* possesses; a long and large glossohyal is intercalated between the lower ends of the hyoids. There are five branchial arches, the hindmost of which is modified into a lower pharyngeal; upper pharyngeals are likewise present as in the majority of Teleosteous fishes. No gular plate.

Of the scapulary arch the two halves are separated by a suture in the median line; the membrane-bones are well developed, only a remnant of the primordial cartilage remaining; the supraclavicle is very similar to that of Teleosteous fishes, less so the post-temporal. The base to which the limb is attached is a single osseous plate, supporting on its posterior margin semi-ossified rods in small number, which bear the pectoral rays.

The pubic consists of paired bone, the anterior ends of which overlap each other, the extremity of the right pubis being dorsad to that of the left. The elements representing a tarsus are quite rudimentary and reduced in number (two or three).

The vertebral column of the *Amioidei* shows unmistakable characters of the Palæichthyic type. The arrangement of its component parts is extremely simple. The centra of the amphicœlous vertebræ are well ossified, but the neural and hæmal arches do not coalesce with the centra, from which they are separated by a thin layer of cartilage. Singularly, not every vertebra has apophyses: in the caudal portion of *Amia* the vertebræ are alternately provided with them and lack them. The heterocercal condition of the spinous column is well marked: as in the other Holostei the hindmost vertebræ are turned upwards, become smaller and smaller in size, and lose their neural arches, the hæmals remaining developed to the end. Finally, the column terminates in a thin cartilaginous band, which is received between the lateral halves of the fifth or sixth upper caudal ray. Interneurals and interhæmals simple. Only the abdominal vertebræ have parapophyses, with which the ribs are articulated.

The configuration of the skull, and the development and arrangement of its component parts, approaches so much the Teleosteous type that, perhaps, there are greater differences in skulls of truly Teleosteous fishes than between the skulls of *Amia* and many *Physostomi.* Externally the cranium is entirely ossified; and the remains of the cartilaginous primordial cranium (which, however, has no vacuity in its roof) can only be seen in a section, and are of much less extent than in many Physostomous fishes. The immovable intermaxillary, the double vomer, the plurality of ossifications representing the articulary, the double articulary cavity of the mandible for junction with the quadrate and symplectic bones, remind us still of similar conditions in the skull of *Lepidosteus*, but the mobility and formation of the maxillary, the arrangement of the gill-covers, the development of the opercles, the suspensorium, the palate, the insertion of a number of branchiostegals on the long middle hyoid piece, the composition of the branchial framework (with upper and lower pharyngeals), are as in the Teleosteous type. A gular plate replaces the urohyal.

The scapular arch is composed entirely of the membrane-bones found in the *Teleostei,* and the two sides are loosely united by ligament. The base to which the limb is attached is cartilaginous; short semi-ossified rods are arranged along its hinder margin and bear the pectoral rays.

The skeleton of the hind-limb agrees entirely with that of *Lepidosteus.*

[T. W. Bridge, The Cranial Osteology of *Amia calva;* in Journ. Anat. and Physiol. vol. xi.]

In the *Teleosteous* fishes the spinous column consists of completely ossified amphicœlous vertebræ; its termination is *homocercal*—that is, the caudal fin appears to be more or less symmetrical, the last vertebra occupying a central position in the base of the fin, and being coalesced with a flat osseous lamella, the *hypural* (Fig. 23, 70), on the hind margin of which the fin-rays are fixed. The hypural is but a union of modified hæmapophyses which are directed backwards, and the actual termination of the notochord is bent upwards, and lies along the upper edge of the hypural, hidden below the last rudimentary neural elements. In some Teleosteans, as the *Salmonidæ*, the last vertebræ are conspicuously bent upwards: in fact, strictly speaking, this homocercal condition is but one of the various degrees of heterocercy, different from that of many Ganoids in this respect only, that the caudal fin itself has assumed a higher degree of symmetry.

The neural and hæmal arches generally coalesce with the centrum, but there are many exceptions, inasmuch as some portion of the arches of a species, or all of them, show the original division.

The vertebræ are generally united with one another by zygapophyses, and frequently similar additional articulations exist at the lower parts of the centra. Parapophyses and ribs are very general, but the latter are inserted on the centra and the base of the processes, and never on their extremities. The point of insertion of the rib, more especially on the anterior vertebræ, may be still higher—viz. at the base of the neural arch, as in *Cotylis* and allied genera, and even on the top of the neurapophysis, as in *Batrachus*.

There is a great amount of variation as regards the degree in which the primordial cranium persists; it is always more or less replaced by bone; frequently it disappears entirely, but in some fishes, like the *Salmonidæ* or *Esocidæ*, the cartilage persists to the same or even to a greater extent than in the Ganoidei holostei. Added to the bones preformed in cartilage are a great number of *membrane-bones*. The different kinds of these membrane-bones occur with greater or less constancy throughout this sub-class; they often coalesce with, and are no more separable from, the neighbouring or underlying cartilage-bones. All these bones have been topographically enumerated in Chapter IV.

Many attempts have been made to classify the bones of the Teleosteous skull, according to their supposed relation to each other, or with the view to demonstrate the unity of plan on which the skull has been built; but in all either the one or the other of the following two principles has been followed:—

A. The "vertebral doctrine" starts from the undeniable fact that the skull is originally composed of several segments, each of which is merely the modification of a vertebra. The component parts of such a cranial segment are considered to be homologous to those of a vertebra. Three, four, or five cranial vertebræ have been distinguished, all the various bones of the fully-developed and ossified skull being referred, without distinction as to their origin, to one or the other of those vertebral segments. The idea of the typical unity of the osseous framework of Vertebrates has been worked out with the greatest originality and knowledge of detail, by *Owen*, who demonstrates that the fish-skull is composed of *four* vertebræ.

The bones of the fish-skull are, according to him, primarily divisible into those of the *neuroskeleton*, *splanchnoskeleton*, and *dermoskeleton*.

The bones of the *neuro-* or proper *endo-skeleton* are arranged in a series of four horizontally succeeding segments: the occipital, parietal, frontal, and nasal vertebræ; each segment consisting of an upper (neural) and a lower (hæmal) arch, with a common centre, and with diverging appendages.

The *neural* arches of the four vertebræ, in their succession from the occiput towards the snout, are:—

1. *Epencephalic arch*, composed of the occipitals.

2. *Mesencephalic arch,* composed of basisphenoid, alisphenoid, parietal, and mastoid.

3. *Prosencephalic arch,* composed of presphenoid, orbitosphenoid, frontal, and postfrontal.

4. *Rhinencephalic arch,* composed of vomer, prefrontal, and nasal.

The *hæmal* arches in the same order of succession are :—

1. *Scapular* or *scapulo-coracoid* arch, composed of suprascapula, scapula, and coracoid; its appendage consists of the ulna, radius and carpal.

2. *Hyoid* or *stylo-hyoid* arch, composed of stylo-hyal, epihyal, ceratohyal, basihyal, glossohyal, and urohyal; its appendage is the branchiostegals.

3. *Mandibular* or *tympano-mandibular* arch, composed of epi-, meso-, pre-, and hypo-tympanic, and the bones of the lower jaw; its appendage consists of the præoperculum and the other opercles.

4. *Maxillary* or *palato-maxillary* arch, composed of palatine, maxillary, and premaxillary; its appendage consists of the pterygoid and entopterygoid.

Parts of the *splanchnoskeleton* are held to be the ear-capsule or petrosal and the otolite, the eye-capsule or sclerotic, the nose-capsule or "ethmoid" and turbinal; the branchial arches.

The bones of the *dermoskeleton* are the supratemporals, supraorbitals, suborbitals, and labials.

B. In the second method of classifying the bones of the skull prominence is given to the facts of their different origin as ascertained by a study of their development. The parts developed from the primordial skull, or the cartilaginous case protecting the nervous centre are distinguished from those which enclose and support the commencement of the alimentary canal and the respiratory apparatus, and which, consisting of several arches, are comprised under the common name of *visceral skeleton of the skull.* Further, a distinction is made between the bones preformed in cartilage and those originating in tegumentary or membranous tissue. It is admitted that the primordial cranium is a coalition of several segments, the number of which is determined by that of the visceral arches, these representing the hæmal arches of the vertebral column; but the membrane-bones are excluded from a consideration of the vertebral division of the primordial skull, as elements originally independent of it, although these additions have entered into special relations to the cartilage-bones.

With these views the bones of the Teleosteous skull are classified thus:—

1. *Cartilage-bones of the primordial skull.*—The ***basi-occipital*** (5 in Figs. 23-26) has retained the form of a vertebral centrum; it is generally concave behind, the concavity containing remains of the notochord; rarely a rounded articulary head of the first vertebra fits into it, as in *Symbranchus*, and still more rarely it is provided with such an articulary head (*Fistularia*); frequently it shows two excavations on its inner surface for the reception of the *saccus vestibuli.* The ***exoccipitals*** (10) are situated on the side of the basi-occipital, and contribute the greater portion of the periphery of the foramen magnum; frequently they articulate with the first vertebra, or meet in the upper median line, so as to exclude the supraoccipital from the foramen magnum. The ***supraoccipital*** (8) is intercalated between the exoccipitals, and forms a most prominent part by the median crest, which sometimes extends far forwards on the upper side of the skull, and offers attachment to the dorsal portion of the large lateral muscle of the trunk. When the anterior portions of this bone remain cartilaginous, some part of the semicircular canals may be lodged in it

The region of the skull which succeeds the bones described encloses at least the greater portion of the labyrinth, and its component parts have been named with reference to it by some anatomists.[1] The *alisphenoids* (11) (*Prooticum*) form sutures posteriorly with the basi- and ex-occipitals, and meet each other in the median line at the bottom of the cerebral cavity; they contribute to the formation of a hollow in which the hypophysis cerebri and the saccus vasculosus are received; in conjunction with the exoccipital it forms another hollow for the reception of the vestibulum; generally it is perforated by the Trigeminal and Facial nerves. The *paroccipitals* (9) (*Epioticum*) lodge a portion of the posterior vertical semicircular canal, and form a projection of the skull on each side of the occipital crest, to which a terminal branch of the scapular arch is attached. The *Mastoid* (12 + 13) (*Opisthoticum*) occupies the postero-external projection of the head; it encloses a part of the external semicircular canal; is generally coalesced with a membrane-bone, the superficial *squamosal*, which emits a process for the suspension of the scapular arch, and is frequently, as in the Perch, divided into two separate bones.

The anterior portion of the skull varies greatly as regards form, which is chiefly dependent on the extent of the cerebral cavity; if the latter is advanced far forwards, the lateral walls of the primordial cranium are protected by more developed ossifications than if the cerebral cavity is shortened by the presence of a wide and deep orbit. In the latter case parts which normally form the side of the skull are situated in front of the brain-case, between it and the orbit, and generally reduced in extent, often replaced by membranes; especially the interorbital septum may be reduced to membrane. The most constant ossifications of this part of the skull are the *orbitosphenoids* (14), which join the upper anterior margin of the alisphenoids. They vary much with regard to their development — they are small in Gadoids; larger in the Perch, Pike, Salmonoids, Macrodon, and the Clupeoids; and

[1] As first proposed by Huxley.

very large in Cyprinoids and Siluroids, in which they contribute to the formation of the side of the brain-case. The single Y-shaped *Sphenoideum anterius* (15) is as frequently absent as present; it forms the anterior margin of the fossa for the hypophysis. Finally, the *post-frontal* (4) belongs also to this group of cartilage-bones.

The centre of the foremost part of the skull is occupied by the *ethmoid* (3), which shows great variations as regards its extent and the degree of ossification; it may extend backwards into the interorbital septum, and reach the orbitosphenoids, or may be confined to the extremity of the skull; it may remain entirely cartilaginous, or ossify into a lamina which separates the two orbits and encloses an anterior prolongation of the brain-case, along which the olfactory nerves pass: modifications occurring again in higher vertebrates. A paired ossification attached to the fore-part of the ethmoid is the *prefrontals* (2), which form the base of the nasal fossa.

2. *Membrane-bones attached to the primordial skull.*—To this group belong the *parietals* (7) and *frontals* (1). The *squamosal* (12) has been mentioned above in connection with the mastoid. The *supraorbital* is always small, and frequently absent. The lower surface of the skull is protected by the *basisphenoid* (parasphenoid) (6) and the *vomer* (16), both of which, especially the latter, may be armed with teeth.[1]

3. *Cartilage bones of the alimentary portion of the visceral skeleton of the skull.*—The suspensorium consists of three cartilage-bones, and affords a base for the opercular apparatus as well as a point of attachment to the hyoid, whilst in front it is connected with the palato-pterygo-palatine arch. They are the *hyomandibular* (23), *symplectic* (31), and *quadrate*

[1] Stannius (pp. 60, 65) doubts the pure origin of these two bones from membranous tissue, and is inclined to consider them as "the extreme end of the abortive axial system."

(26), connected by means of the *metapterygoid* (27) with the *ecto-* (24) and *ento-pterygoid* (25), the foremost bone of the arch being the *palatine* (22). All these bones have been sufficiently described above (p. 55), and it remains only to be mentioned that the bones of the palatine arch are but rarely absent, as for instance in *Murænophis;* and that the symplectic does not extend to the articulary of the mandible, as in *Amia* and *Lepidosteus*, though its suspensory relation to the Meckelian cartilage is still indicated by a ligament which connects the two pieces. Of the mandibulary bones the *articulary* (35) is distinctly part of Meckel's cartilage. Frequently another portion of cartilage below the articulary remains persistent, or is replaced by a separate membrane-bone, the angular.

4. *Membrane-bones of the alimentary portion of the visceral skeleton of the skull.*—The suspensorium has one tegumentary bone attached to it, viz. the *præoperculum* (30); it is but rarely absent, for instance in *Murænophis.* The *premaxillary* (17) and *maxillary* (18) of the Teleostei appear to be also membrane-bones, although they are clearly analogous to the upper labial cartilages of the Sharks. The premaxillaries sometimes coalesce into a single piece (as in *Diodon, Mormyrus*), or they are firmly united with the maxillaries (as in all *Gymnodonts, Serrasalmo,* etc.) The relative position and connection of these two bones differs much, and is a valuable character in the discrimination of the various families. In some, the front margin of the jaw is formed by the premaxillary only, the two bones having a parallel position, as it has been described in the Perch (p. 53); in others, the premaxillary is shortened, allowing the maxillary to enter, and to complete, the margin of the upper jaw; and finally, in many no part of the maxillary is situated behind the premaxillary, but the entire bone is attached to the end of the premaxillary, forming its continuation. In

the last case the maxillary may be quite abortive. The mobility of the upper jaw is greatest in those fishes in which the premaxillary alone forms its margin. The form of the premaxillary is subject to great variation : the beak of *Belone, Xiphias* is formed by the prolonged and coalesced premaxillaries. The maxillary consists sometimes of one piece, sometimes of two or three. The principal membrane-bone of the mandible is the *dentary* (34), to which is added the *angular* (36) and rarely a smaller one, the *splenial* or *os operculare*, which is situated at the inside of the articulary.

5. *Cartilage-bones of the respiratory portion of the visceral skeleton of the skull.*—With few exceptions all the ossifications of the hyoid and branchial arches, as described above (p. 58), belong to this group.

6. *Membrane-bones of the respiratory portion of the visceral skeleton of the skull.*—They are the following: the opercular pieces, viz. *operculum* (28), *suboperculum* (32), and *interoperculum* (33). The last of these is the least constant; it may be entirely absent, and represented by a ligament extending from the mandible to the hyoid. The *urohyal* (42) which separates the musculi sternohyoidei, and serves for an increased surface of their insertion; and finally the *branchiostegals* (43), which vary greatly in number, but are always fixed to the cerato- and epi-hyals.

7. *Dermal bones of the skull.*—To this category are referred some bones which are ossifications of, and belong to, the cutis. They are the *turbinals* (20), the *suborbitals* (19), and the *supratemporals.* They vary much with regard to the degree in which they are developed, and are rarely entirely absent. Nearly always they are wholly or partly transformed into tubes or hollows, in which the muciferous canals with their numerous nerves are lodged. Those in the temporal and scapulary regions are not always developed; on the other hand, the series of those ossicles may be continued on

to the trunk, accompanying the lateral line. In many fishes those of the infraorbital ring are much dilated, protecting the entire space between the orbit and the rim of the præoperculum; in others, especially those which have the angle of the præoperculum armed with a powerful spine, the infraorbital ring emits a process towards the spine, which thus serves as a stay or support of this weapon (*Scorpænidæ, Cottidæ*).

The *pectoral* arch of the Teleosteous fishes exhibits but a remnant of a primordial cartilage, which is replaced by two ossifications,[1] the *coracoid* (51) and *scapula* (52); they offer posteriorly attachment to two series of short rods, of which the proximal are nearly always ossified, whilst the distal frequently remain small cartilaginous nodules hidden in the base of the pectoral rays. The bones, by which this portion is connected with the skull, are membrane-bones, viz. the *clavicle* (49), with the *postclavicle* (49 + 50), the *supraclavicle* (47), and *post-temporal* (46). The order of their arrangement in the Perch has been described above (p. 59). However, many Teleosteous fish lack pectoral fins, and in them the pectoral arch is frequently more or less reduced or rudimentary, as in many species of *Murænidæ*. In others the membrane-bones are exceedingly strong, contributing to the outer protective armour of the fish, and then the clavicles are generally suturally connected in the median line. The postclavicula and the supraclavicula may be absent. Only exceptionally the shoulder-girdle is not suspended from the skull, but from the anterior portion of the spinous column (*Symbranchidæ, Murænidæ, Notacanthidæ*). The number of basal elements of each of the two series never exceeds five, but may be less; and the distal series is absent in Siluroids.

The *pubic* bones of the Teleosteous fishes undergo many modifications of form in the various families, but they are essentially of the same simple type as in the Perch.

[1] Parker's nomenclature is adopted here.

CHAPTER V.

MYOLOGY.

In the lowest vertebrate, *Branchiostoma*, the whole of the *muscular* mass is arranged in a longitudinal band running along each side of the body; it is vertically divided into a number of flakes or segments (*myocommas*) by aponeurotic septa, which serve as the surfaces of insertion to the muscular fibres. But this muscular band has no connection with the notochord except in its foremost portion, where some relation has been formed to the visceral skeleton. A very thin muscular layer covers the abdomen.

Also in the *Cyclostomes* the greatest portion of the muscular system is without direct relation to the skeleton, and, again, it is only on the skull and visceral skeleton where distinct muscles have been differentiated for special functions.

To the development of the skeleton in the more highly organised fishes corresponds a similar development of the muscles; and the maxillary and branchial apparatus, the pectoral and ventral fins, the vertical fins, and especially the caudal, possess a separate system of muscles. But the most noteworthy is the muscle covering the sides of the trunk and tail (already noticed in *Branchiostoma*), which Cuvier described as the "great lateral muscle," and which, in the higher fishes, is a compound of many smaller segments, corresponding in number with the vertebræ. Each lateral muscle is divided by a median longitudinal groove into a dorsal and ventral half; the depression in its middle is filled by an embryonal muscular substance which contains a large quantity of fat and blood-vessels, and therefore differs from ordinary muscle by its softer consistency, and by its colour which is reddish or grayish. Superficially the lateral muscle appears crossed by a number of white parallel tendinous zigzag stripes, forming generally three angles, of which the upper and lower point backwards, the middle one forwards. These are the outer edges of the aponeurotic septa between the myocommas. Each septum is attached to the middle and the apophyses of a vertebra, and, in the abdominal region, to its rib; frequently the septa receive additional support by the existence of epipleural spines. The fibres of each myocomma run straight and nearly horizontally from one septum to the next; they are grouped so as to form semiconical masses, of which the upper and lower have their apices turned backwards, whilst the middle cone, formed by the contiguous parts of the preceding, has its apex directed forward; this fits into the interspace between the antecedent upper and lower cones, the apices of which reciprocally enter the depressions in the succeeding segment, whereby all the segments are firmly locked together (*Owen*).

In connection with the muscles reference has to be made to the *Electric organs* with which certain fishes are provided, as it is more than probable, not only from the examination of peculiar muscular organs occurring in the Rays, *Mormyrus*, and *Gymnarchus* (the function of which is still conjectural), but especially from the researches into the development of the electric organ of *Torpedo*, that the electric organs have been developed out of muscular substance. The fishes possessing fully developed electric organs, with the power of accumulating electric force and communicating it in the form of shocks to other animals, are the electric Rays (*Torpedinidæ*), the electric Sheath-fish of tropical Africa (*Malapterurus*), and the electric Eel of tropical America

(*Gymnotus*). The structure and arrangement of the electric organ is very different in these fishes, and will be subsequently described in the special account of the several species.

The phenomena attending the exercise of this extraordinary faculty also closely resemble muscular action. The time and strength of the discharge are entirely under the control of the fish. The power is exhausted after some time, and it needs repose and nourishment to restore it. If the electric nerves are cut and divided from the brain the cerebral action is interrupted, and no irritant to the body has any effect to excite electric discharge; but if their ends be irritated the discharge takes place, just as a muscle is excited to contraction under similar circumstances. And, singularly enough, the application of strychnine causes simultaneously a tetanic state of the muscles and a rapid succession of involuntary electric discharges. The strength of the discharges depends entirely on the size, health, and energy of the fish: an observation entirely agreeing with that made on the efficacy of snake-poison. Like this latter, the property of the electric force serves two ends in the economy of the animals which are endowed with it; it is essential and necessary to them for overpowering, stunning, or killing the creatures on which they feed, whilst incidentally they use it as the means of defending themselves from their enemies.

CHAPTER VI.

NEUROLOGY.

THE most simple condition of the nervous central organ known in Vertebrates is found in *Branchiostoma*. In this fish the spinal chord tapers at both ends, an anterior cerebral swelling, or anything approaching a brain, being absent. It is band-like along its middle third, and groups of darker cells mark the origins of the fifty or sixty pairs of nerves which accompany the intermuscular septa, and divide into a dorsal and ventral branch, as in other fishes. The two anterior pairs pass to the membranous parts above the mouth, and supply with nerve filaments a ciliated depression near the extremity of the fish, which is considered to be an olfactory organ, and two pigment spots, the rudiments of eyes. An auditory organ is absent.

The *spinal chord* of the *Cyclostomes* is flattened in its whole extent, band-like, and elastic; also in *Chimæra* it is elastic, but flattened in its posterior portion only. In all other fishes it is cylindrical, non-ductile, and generally extending along the whole length of the spinal canal. The Plectognaths offer a singular exception in this respect that the spinal chord is much shortened, the posterior portion of the canal being occupied by a long cauda equina; this shortening of the spinal chord has become extreme in the Sun-fish (*Orthagoriscus*), in which it has shrunk into a short and conical appendage of the brain. Also in the Devil-fish (*Lophius*) a long cauda equina partly conceals the chord which terminates on the level of about the twelfth vertebra.

The *brain* of fishes is relatively small; in the Burbot (*Lota*) it has been estimated to be $\frac{1}{720}$th part of the weight of the entire fish, in the Pike the $\frac{1}{1305}$th part, and in the large Sharks it is relatively still smaller. It never fills the entire cavity of the cranium; between the dura mater which adheres to the inner surface of the cranial cavity, and the arachnoidea which envelops the brain, a more or less considerable space remains, which is filled with a soft gelatinous mass generally containing a large quantity of fat. It has been observed that this space is much less in young specimens than in adult, which proves that the brain of fishes does not grow in the same proportion as the rest of the body; and, indeed, its size is nearly the same in individuals of which one is double the bulk of the other.

The brain of *Osseous fishes* (Fig. 41) viewed from above shows three protuberances, respectively termed *prosencephalon*, *mesencephalon*, and *metencephalon*, the two anterior of which are paired, the hindmost being single. The foremost pair are the *hemispheres*, which are solid in their interior, and provided with two swellings in front, the *olfactory lobes.* The second pair are the *optic lobes*, which generally are larger than the hemispheres, and succeeded by the third single portion, *the*

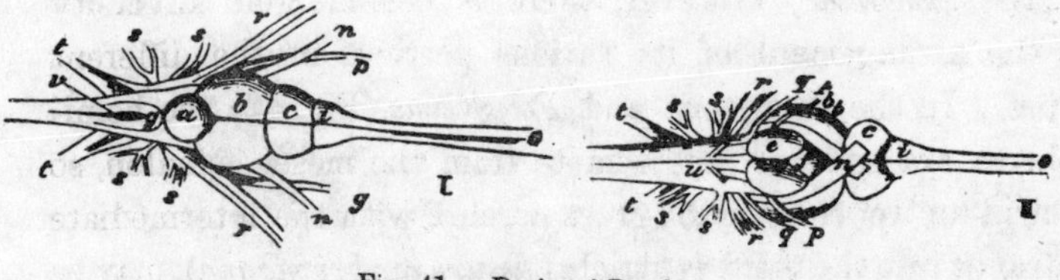

Fig. 41.—Brain of Perch.

I. Upper aspect. II. Lower aspect.

a, cerebellum; *b*, optic lobes; *c*, hemispheres; *e*, lobi inferiores; *f*, hypophysis; *g*, lobi posteriores; *i*, Olfactory lobes; *n*, *N.* opticus; *o*, *N.* olfactorius; *p*, *N.* oculo-motorius; *q*, *N.* trochlearis; *r*, *N.* trigeminus; *s*, *N.* acusticus; *t*, *N.* vagus; *u*, *N.* abducens; *v*, Fourth ventricle.

cerebellum. In the fresh state the hemispheres are of a grayish colour, and often show some shallow depressions on their surface; a narrow commissure of white colour connects them with each other. The optic lobes possess a cavity (*ventriculus lobi optici*), at the bottom of which some protuberances of variable development represent the corpora quadrigemina of higher animals. On the lower surface of the base of the optic lobes, behind the *crura cerebri*, two swellings are observed, the *lobi inferiores*, which slightly diverge in front for the passage of the *infundibulum*, from which a generally large *hypophysis* or *pituitary gland* is suspended. The relative size of the cerebellum varies greatly in the different osseous fishes: in the Tunny and Silurus it is so large as nearly to cover the optic lobes; sometimes distinct transverse grooves and a median longitudinal groove are visible. The cerebellum possesses in its interior a cavity which communicates with the anterior part of the fourth ventricle. The *medulla oblongata* is broader than the spinal chord, and contains the *fourth ventricle*, which forms the continuation of the central canal of the spinal chord. In most fishes a perfect roof is formed over the fourth ventricle by two longitudinal pads, which meet each other in the median line (*lobi posteriores*), and but rarely it remains open along its upper surface.

The brain of *Ganoid fishes* shows great similarity to that of the Teleostei; however, there is considerable diversity of the arrangement of its various portions in the different types. In the Sturgeons and *Polypterus* (Fig. 42) the hemispheres are more or less remote from the mesencephalon, so that in an upper view the crura cerebri, with the intermediate entrance into the third ventricle (*fissura cerebri magna*), may be seen. A vascular membranous sac, containing lymphatic fluid (*epiphysis*), takes its origin from the third ventricle, its base being expanded over the anterior interspace of the optic lobes, and the apex being fixed to the cartilaginous roof of the cranium. This structure is not peculiar to the Ganoids, but found in various stages of development in Teleosteans, marking, when present, the boundary between prosencephalon and mesencephalon. The lobi optici are essentially as in Teleosteans. The cerebellum penetrates into the ventriculus lobi optici, and extends thence into the open sinus rhomboidalis. At its upper surface it is crossed by a commissure formed by the *corpora restiformia* of the medulla.

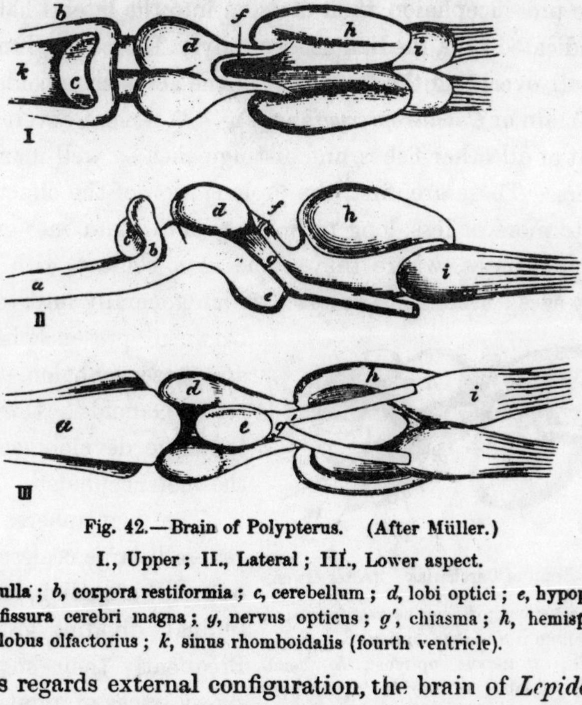

Fig. 42.—Brain of Polypterus. (After Müller.)
I., Upper; II., Lateral; III., Lower aspect.
a, Medulla; *b*, corpora restiformia; *c*, cerebellum; *d*, lobi optici; *e*, hypophysis; *f*, fissura cerebri magna; *g*, nervus opticus; *g'*, chiasma; *h*, hemispheres; *i*, lobus olfactorius; *k*, sinus rhomboidalis (fourth ventricle).

As regards external configuration, the brain of *Lepidosteus* and *Amia* approach still more the Teleosteous type. The prosencephalon, mesencephalon, and metencephalon are contiguous, and the cerebellum lacks the prominent transverse commissure at its upper surface. The sinus rhomboidalis is open.

The brain of the *Dipnoi* shows characters reminding us of that of the Ganoids as well as the Chondropterygians, *Ceratodus* agreeing with *Protopterus* in this respect, as in most other points of its organisation. The hemispheres form the largest part of the brain; they are coalescent, as in Sharks, but possess two lateral ventricles, the separation being externally indicated by a shallow median groove on the upper surface. The olfactory lobes take their origin from the upper anterior end of the hemispheres. Epiphysis and hypophysis well developed. The lobi optici are very small, and remote from the prosencephalon, their division into the lateral halves being indicated by a median groove only. The cerebellum is very small, overlying the front part of the sinus rhomboidalis.

The brain of *Chondropterygians* (Fig. 43) is more developed than that of all other fishes, and distinguished by well-marked characters. These are, first, the prolongation of the olfactory lobes into more or less long pedicles, which dilate into great ganglionic masses, where they come into contact with the olfactory sacs; secondly, the space which generally intervenes between prosencephalon and mesencephalon, as in some Ganoids; thirdly, the large development of the metencephalon.

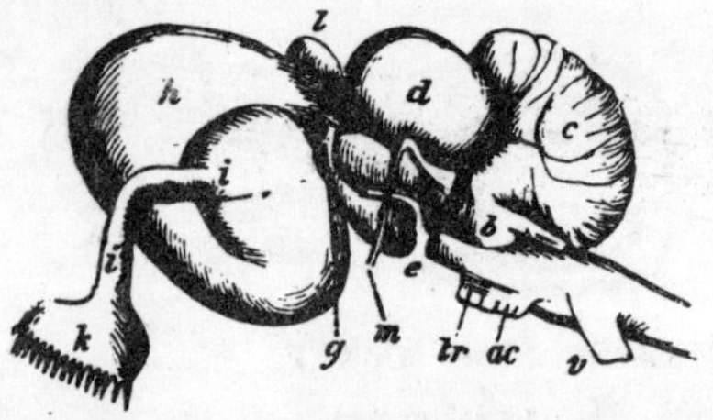

Fig. 43.—Brain of Carcharias. (After Owen.) *ac*, Nerv. acusticus; *b*, corpus restiforme; *c*, cerebellum; *d*, lobus opticus; *e*, hypophysis; *g*, nervus opticus; *h*, hemisphere; *i*, lobus olfactorius; *i'*, olfactory pedicle; *k*, nerv. olfactorius; *l*, epiphysis; *m*, nerv. oculo-motorius; *tr*, nerv. trigeminus; *v*, nerv. vagus.

The hemispheres are generally large, coalescent, but with a median, longitudinal, dividing groove. Frequently their surface shows traces of gyrations, and when they are provided with lateral ventricles, tubercles representing *corpora striata* may be observed. The olfactory pedicles take their origin from the side of the hemispheres, and are frequently hollow, and if so, their cavity communicates with the ventricle of the hemisphere. The optic lobes are generally smaller than the hemispheres, coalescent, and provided with an upper median groove like the prosencephalon. At their base a pair of lobi inferiores are constant, with the hypophysis and *saccus vasculosus* (a conglomeration of vascular loops without medullary substance) between them.

The cerebellum is very large, overlying a portion of the optic lobes and of the sinus rhomboidalis, and is frequently transversely grooved. The side-walls of the fourth ventricle, which are formed by the corpora restiformia, are singularly folded, and appear as two pads, one on each side of the cerebellum (*lobi posteriores* s. *lobi nervi trigemini*).

The brain of the *Cyclostomes* (Figs. 44, 45) represents a type different from that of other fishes, showing at its upper surface

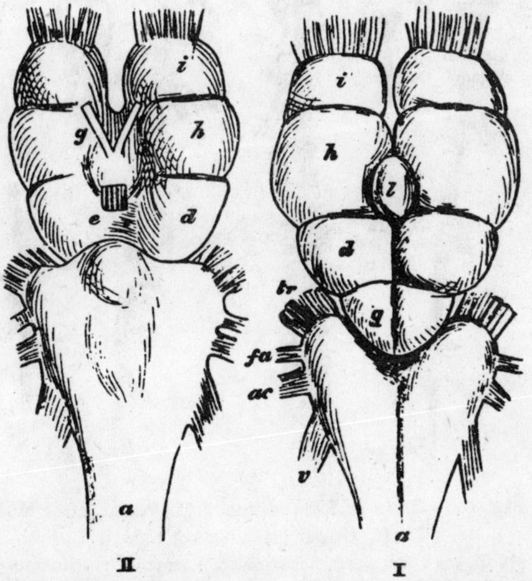

Fig. 44.—Brain of Bdellostoma. (Enlarged, after Müller.)
I., Upper; II., Lower aspect. Letters as in Fig. 45.

three pairs of protuberances in front of the cerebellum; they are all solid. Their homologies are not yet satisfactorily determined, parts of the Myxinoid brain having received by the same observers determinations very different from those given to the corresponding parts of the brain of the Lampreys. The

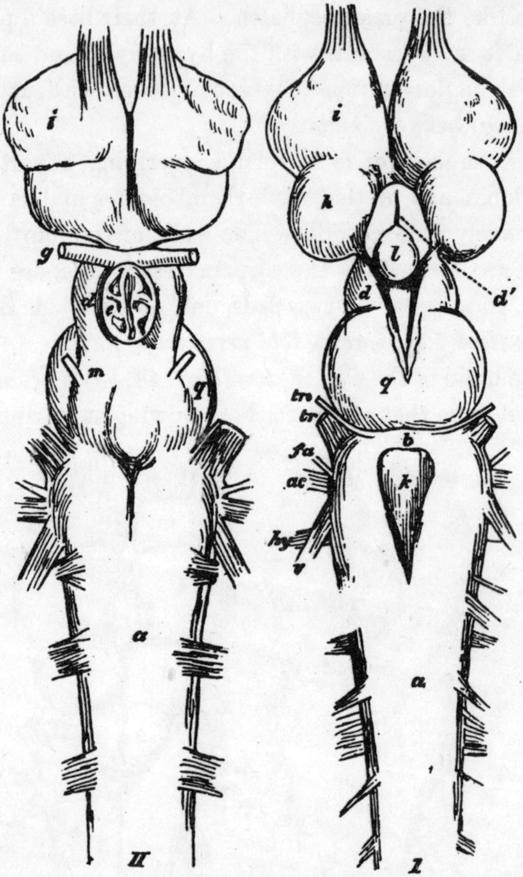

Fig. 45.—Brain of Petromyzon. (Enlarged, after Müller.)
I., Upper; II., Lower aspect.

a, Medulla oblongata; *ac*, nerv. acusticus; *b*, corpus restiforme or rudimentary cerebellum; *d*, lobus ventriculi tertii; *d'*, entrance into the third ventricle; *e*, hypophysis; *fa*, nerv. facialis; *g*, nerv. opticus; *h*, hemisphere; *hy*, nerv. hypoglossus (so named by Müller); *i*, lobus olfactorius; *k*, sinus rhomboidalis; *l*, epiphysis; *m*, nerv. oculo-motorius; *q*, corpora quadrigemina; *tr*, nerv. trigeminus; *tro*, nerv. trochlearis; *v*, nerv. vagus.

foremost pair are the large olfactory tubercles, which are exceedingly large in *Petromyzon*. They are followed by the hemispheres, with a single body wedged in between their posterior half; in *Petromyzon*, at least, the vascular tissue leading to an epiphysis seems to be connected with this body. Then follows the lobus ventriculi tertii, distinctly paired in Myxinoids, less so in *Petromyzon*. The last pair are the *corpora quadrigemina*. According to this interpretation the cerebellum would be absent in Myxinoids, and represented in *Petromyzon* by a narrow commissure only (Fig. 45, *b*), stretching over the foremost part of the sinus rhomboidalis. In the Myxinoids the *medulla oblongata* ends in two divergent swellings, free and obtuse at their extremity, from which most of the cerebral nerves take their origin.

The *Nerves* which supply the organs of the head are either merely continuations or diverticula of the brain-substance, or proper nerves taking their origin from the brain, or receiving their constituent parts from the foremost part of the spinal chord. The number of these spino-cerebral nerves is always less than in the higher vertebrates, and their arrangement varies considerably.

A. *Nerves which are diverticula of the brain* (Figs. 41-45).

The *olfactory* nerves (*first pair*) always retain their intimate relation to the hemispheres, the ventricles of which are not rarely continued into the tubercle or even pedicle of the nerves. The different position of the olfactory tubercle has been already described as characteristic of some of the orders of fishes. In those fishes in which the tubercle is remote from the brain, the nerve which has entered the tubercle as a single stem leaves it split up into several or numerous branches, which are distributed in the nasal organ. In the other fishes it breaks up into branchlets spread into a fan-like expansion at the point, where it enters the nasal cavity. The nerve always passes out of the skull through the ethmoid.

The *optic* nerves (*second pair*) vary in size, their strength corresponding to the size of the eye; they take their origin from the *lobi optici*, the development of which again is proportionate to that of the nerves. The mutual relation of the two nerves immediately after their origin is very characteristic of the sub-classes of fishes. In the *Cyclostomes* they have no further connection with each other, each going to the eye of its own side.[1] In the *Teleostei* they simply cross each other (*decussate*), so that the one starting from the right half of the brain goes to the left eye and *vice versa*. Finally, in *Palæichthyes* the two nerves are fused together, immediately after their origin, into a *chiasma*. The nerve is cylindrical for some portion of its course, but in most fishes gradually changes this form into that of a plaited band, which is capable of separation and expansion. It enters the bulbus generally behind and above its axis. The foramen through which it leaves the skull of Teleostei is generally in a membranous portion of its anterior wall, or, where ossification has taken place, in the orbito-sphenoid.

B. *Nerves proper taking their origin from the brain* (Figs. 41-45).

The *Nervus oculorum motorius* (*third pair*) takes its origin from the Pedunculus cerebri, close behind the lobi inferiores; it escapes through the orbito-sphenoid, or the membrane replacing it, and is distributed to the musculi rectus superior, rectus internus, obliquus inferior, and rectus inferior. Its size corresponds to the development of the muscles of the eye. Consequently it is absent in the blind *Amblyopsis*, and the Myxinoids. In *Lepidosiren* the nerves supplying the muscles of the eye have no independent origin, but are part

[1] According to *Langerhans* "Untersuchungen über Petromyzon planeri" (Freiburg, 1873) an optic chiasma exists in that species.

of the ophthalmic division of the Trigeminus. In *Petromyzon* these muscles are supplied partly from the Trigeminus, partly by a nerve representing the Oculo-motor and Trochlearis, which are fused into a common trunk.

The *Nervus trochlearis* (*fourth pair*), if present with an independent origin, is always thin, taking its origin on the upper surface of the brain from the groove between lobus opticus and cerebellum; it goes to the Musculus obliquus superior of the eye.

C. *Nerves taking their origin from the Medulla oblongata* (Figs. 41-45).

The *Nervus abducens* (*sixth pair*) issues on the lower surface of the brain, taking its origin from the anterior pyramids of the Medulla oblongata, and supplies the Musculus rectus externus of the eye, and the muscle of the nictitating membrane of Sharks.

The *Nervus trigeminus* (*fifth pair*) and the *Nervus facialis* (*seventh pair*) have their origins close together, and enter into intimate connection with each other. In the Chondropterygians and most Teleostei the number of their roots is four, in the Sturgeons five, and in a few Teleostei three. When there are four, the first issues immediately below the cerebellum from the side of the Medulla oblongata; it contains motory and sensory elements for the maxillary and suspensorial muscles, and belongs exclusively to the trigeminal nerve. The second root, which generally becomes free a little above the first, supplies especially the elements for the Ramus palatinus, which sometimes unites with parts of the Trigeminal, sometimes with the Facial nerve. The third root, if present, is very small, and issues immediately in front of the acustic nerve, and supplies part of the motor elements of the facial nerve. The fourth root is much stronger, sometimes double, and its elements pass again partly into the Trigeminal, partly into the Facial nerve. On the passage of these stems through the skull (through a foramen or foramina in the alisphenoid) they form a ganglionic plexus, in which the palatine ramus and the first stem of the Trigeminus generally possess discrete ganglia. The branches which issue from the plexus and belong exclusively to the Trigeminus, supply the organs and integuments of the frontal, ophthalmic, and nasal regions, and the upper and lower jaws with their soft parts. The Facial nerve supplies the muscles of the gill-cover and suspensorium, and emits a strong branch accompanying the Meckelian cartilage to the symphysis, and another for the hyoid apparatus.

The *Nervus acusticus* (*eighth pair*) is strong, and takes its origin immediately behind, and in contact with the last root of the seventh pair.

The *Nervus glosso-pharyngeus* (*ninth pair*) [1] takes its origin between the roots of the eighth and tenth nerves, and issues in Teleostei from the cranial cavity by a foramen of the exoccipital. In the Cyclostomes and Lepidosiren it is part of the Nervus vagus. It is distributed in the pharyngeal and lingual regions, one branch supplying the first branchial arch. After having left the cranial cavity it swells into a ganglion, which in Teleostei is always in communication with the sympathic nerve.

The *Nervus vagus* or *pneumogastricus* (*tenth pair*) rises in all Teleostei and Palæichthyes with two discrete strong roots: the first constantly from the swellings of the corpora restiformia, be they thinner or thicker and overlying the sinus rhomboidalis, or be they developed into lateral plaited pads, as in Acipenser and Chondropterygians. The second much thicker root rises from the lower tracts of the medulla oblongata. Both stems leave the cranial cavity by a common fora-

[1] This nerve is not shown in the figure of the brain of the Perch (Fig. 41), as reproduced above from Cuvier.

men, situated in Teleosteous fishes in the exoccipital; and form ganglionic swellings, of which those of the lower stem are the more conspicuous. The lower stem has mixed elements, motory as well as sensory, and is distributed to the muscles of the branchial arches and pharynx, the œsophagus and stomach; it sends filaments to the heart and to the air-bladder where it exists. The first (upper) stem forms the *Nervus lateralis.* This nerve, which accompanies the lateral mucous system of the trunk and tail, is either a single longitudinal stem, gradually becoming thinner behind, running superficially below the skin (Salmonidæ, Cyclopterus), or deeply between the muscles (Sharks, Chimæra), or divided into two parallel branches (most Teleostei): thus in the Perch there are two branches on each side, the superficial of which supplies the lateral line, whilst the deep-seated branch communicates with the spinal nerves and supplies the septa between the myocommas and the skin. In fishes which lack the lateral muciferous system and possess hard integuments, as the Ostracions, the lateral nerve is more or less rudimentary. It is entirely absent in Myxinoids, but the gastric branches of the Vagus are continued, united as a single nerve, along the intestine to the anus.

No fish possesses a *Nervus accessorius.* Also a separate *Nervus hypoglossus* (*twelfth pair*)[1] is absent, but elements from the first spinal nerve are distributed in the area normally supplied by this nerve in higher vertebrates.

The number of *Spinal* nerves corresponds to that of the vertebræ, through or between which they pass out. Each nerve has two roots, an anterior and posterior, the former of which has no ganglion, and exclusively contains motor elements. The posterior or dorsal has a ganglionic enlarge-

[1] Müller considers a nerve rising jointly with the Vagus in Petromyzon to be this nerve (Fig. 45, *hy*).

ment, and contains sensory elements only. After leaving the vertebral canal each spinal nerve usually divides into a dorsal and ventral branch. The Gadoids show that peculiarity that each of the posterior roots of some or many of the spinal nerves possesses two separate threads, each of which has a ganglion of its own; the one of these threads joins the dorsal and the other the ventral branch. In fishes in which the spinal chord is very short, as in Plectognaths, Lophius, the roots of the nerves are extremely long, forming a thick *Cauda equina.* The additional function which the (five) anterior spinal nerves of *Trigla* have to perform in supplying the sensitive pectoral appendages and their muscles has caused the development of a paired series of globular swellings of the corresponding portion of the spinal chord. A similar structure is found in *Polynemus.*

Fig. 46. Brain and anterior portion of the spinal chord of Trigla (Gurnard), showing the globular swellings at the base of the anterior spinal nerves.

A *Sympathic nervous* system appears to be absent in *Branchiostoma*, and has not yet been clearly made out in *Cyclostomes.* It is well developed in the *Palæichthyes*, but without cephalic portion. This latter is present in all Osseous fishes, in which communication of the Sympathic has been found to exist with all cerebral nerves, except the olfactory, optic, and acustic. The sympathic trunks run along each side of the aorta and the back of the abdomen into the hæmal canal; communicate in their course with the ventral branches of each of the spinal nerves; and, finally, often blend together into a common trunk beneath the tail. At the points of communication with the cerebral and spinal nerves frequently ganglia are developed, from which nerves emerge which are distributed to the various viscera.

CHAPTER VII.

THE ORGANS OF SENSE.

CHARACTERISTIC of the *Organ of Smell* in Fishes is that it has no relation whatever to the respiratory function, with the exception of the *Dipnoi*, in which possibly part of the water received for respiration passes through the nasal sac.

The olfactory organ is single in *Branchiostoma* and the *Cyclostomes*. In the former a small depression on the front end of the body, clothed with a ciliated epithelium, is regarded as a rudimentary organ of smell. In the adult *Petromyzon* a membranous tube leads from the single opening on the top of the head into the cartilaginous olfactory capsule, the inside of which is clothed by membranes prolonged into a posterior blind tube (Fig. 30, *s*), which penetrates the cartilaginous roof of the palate, but not the mucous membrane of the buccal cavity. In the Myxinoids the outer tube is strengthened by cartilaginous rings like a trachea; the capsule is lined by a longitudinally folded pituitary membrane, and the posterior tube opens backwards on the roof of the mouth; the opening is provided with a valve.

In all other Fishes the organ of smell is double, one being on each side; it consists of a sac lined with a pituitary membrane, and without, or with one or two, openings. The position of these openings is very different in the various orders or suborders of Fishes.

In the *Dipnoi* the nasal sac opens downwards by two wide openings which are within the boundaries of the cavity of the mouth. The pituitary membrane is transversely folded, the transverse folds being divided by one longitudinal fold. The walls of the sac are strengthened by sundry small cartilages.

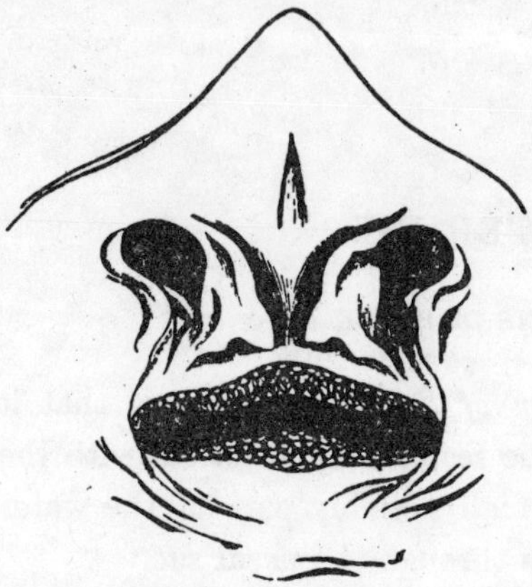

Fig. 47.—Nostrils of *Raia lemprieri*, with nasal flaps reverted.

Also in *Chondropterygians* the openings, of which there is one to each sac, are on the lower part of the snout, and in the Rays, Holocephali, and some Sharks, each extends into the cleft of the mouth. The openings are protected by valvular flaps, supported by small cartilages, and moved by muscles, whence it may be concluded that these fishes are able to scent (actively) as well as to smell (passively).

In the majority of *Teleostei* the olfactory capsules are lateral or superior on the snout, covered externally by the skin, each usually pierced by two openings, which are either close together, or more or less remote from each other; the posterior is generally open, the anterior provided with a valve or tube. In the *Chromides* and *Labroidei ctenoidei* a single opening only exists for each sac. In the *Murænidæ* the two openings of each side are either superior, or lateral, or labial, that is, they are continued downwards and pierce the margin of the upper lip. In many Tetrodonts nasal openings are absent, and replaced by a conical papilla, in which the olfactory nerve terminates.

It is certain that fishes possess the faculty of perceiving odours, and that various scents attract or repel them. A mangled carcase or fresh blood attracts Sharks as well as the voracious Serrasal monoids of the South American rivers. There is no reason to doubt that the seat of that perception is in the olfactory sac; and it may be reasonably conjectured that its strength depends mainly on the degree of development indicated by the number and extent of the interior folds of the pituitary membrane.

Organ of Sight.—The position, direction, and dimensions of the eyes of fishes vary greatly. In some they have an upward aspect, and are often very close together; in others they are lateral, and in a few they are even directed downwards. The Flat-fishes represent the extraordinary anomaly that both eyes are on the same side of the head, and rarely on the same level, one being generally placed more forward than the other. In certain species of marine fishes the eyes are of an extraordinary size, a peculiarity indicating that the fish either lives at a great depth, to which only a small proportion of the rays of light penetrate, or that it is of nocturnal habits. In fishes which have descended to such great depths that no rays whatever can reach them, or in fresh-water fishes living in caves, or in species which grovel and live constantly in mud, the eyes are more or less aborted, sometimes quite rudimentary, and covered by the skin. In very few this organ appears to be entirely absent. In some Gobioids and Trachinoids (*Periophthalmus, Boleophthalmus, Uronoscopus*, etc.) the eyes, which are on the upper side of the head, can be elevated and depressed at the will of the fish. In the range of their vision and acuteness of sight, Fishes are very inferior to the higher classes of Vertebrates, yet at the same time it is evident that they perceive their prey or approaching danger from a considerable distance; and it would appear that the visual powers of a *Periophthalmus*, when hunting insects on mud-flats of the tropical coasts, are quite equal to that of a frog. Again, the discrimination with which fishes sometimes prefer one colour or kind of artificial fly to another affords sufficient evidence that the vision, at least of certain species is by no means devoid of clearness and precision

The eye of *Branchiostoma* is of the most rudimentary condition. It is simply a minute speck coated by dark pigment, and receiving the end of a short nerve. In *Myxinoids* the minute rudiment of the eye is covered by the skin and muscles. This is also the case in many of the blind Teleosteous fishes; however, whilst in the former fishes the organ of sight has not attained to any degree of development, the rudimentary eye of blind Teleostei is a retrogressive formation, in which often a lense and other portions of the eye can be recognised. In fishes with a well-developed eye it is imbedded in a layer of gelatinous and adipose substance, which covers the cavity of the orbit. A lacrymal gland is absent. In the orbit of one fish only, *Chorismodentex*, an organ has been found which can be compared to a *saccus lacrymalis.* It is a round, blind, wide sac, of the size of a pea, situated below the anterior corner of the orbit, between the maxillary bone and the muscles of the cheek, communicating by a rather wide foramen with the orbital cavity. The membrane by which it is formed is continuous with that coating the orbita. In the Chondropterygians the eyeball is supported by and moves on a cartilaginous peduncle of the orbital wall. In the majority of Teleosteans, and in Acipenser, a fibrous ligament attaches the sclerotic to the wall of the orbit. The proper muscles of the eyeball exist in all fishes, and consist of the four *Musculi recti* and the two *M. obliqui.* In many Teleostei the former rise from a subcranial canal, the origin of the *M. rectus externus* being prolonged farthest backwards. The *Recti* muscles are extraordinarily long in the Hammerheaded Sharks, in which they extend from the basis cranii along the lateral prolongations of the head to the eyes, which are situated at the extremities of the hammer.

In all fishes the general integument of the head passes

over the eye, and becomes transparent where it enters the orbit; sometimes it simply passes over the orbit, sometimes it forms a circular fold. The anterior and posterior portions may be especially broad and the seat of an adipose deposit (*adipose eyelids*), as in *Scomber, Caranx, Mugil*, etc. In many of these fishes the extent of these eyelids varies with the seasons; during the spawning season they are so much loaded with fat as nearly to hide the whole eye. Many Sharks possess a *nictitating* membrane, developed from the lower part of the palpebral fold, and moved by a proper set of muscles.

The form of the *bulbus* (Fig. 48) is subhemispherical, the cornea (*co*) being flat. If it were convex, as in higher Vertebrates, it would be more liable to injury; but being level with the side of the head the chances of injury by friction are diminished. The *sclerotica* (*sc*) is cartilaginous in Chondropterygians and Acipensers, fibrous and of varying thickness in Teleosteans, in the majority of which it is supported by a pair of cartilaginous or ossified hemispheroid cups (*c*). In a few fishes, as in *Ceratodus, Xiphias*, the cups are confluent into one cup, which possesses a foramen behind to allow the passage of the optic nerve (*o*). The *cornea* of *Anableps* shows an unique peculiarity. It is crossed by a dark horizontal stripe of the conjunctiva, dividing it into an upper and lower portion; also the iris is perforated by two pupils. This fish is observed to swim frequently with half of its head out of the water, and it is a fact that it can see out of the water as well as in it.

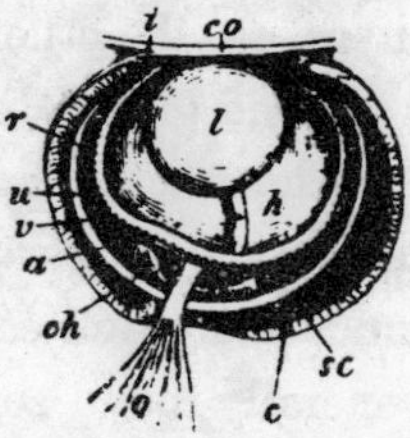

Fig. 48.
Vertical section through eye of Xiphias. (After Owen.)
co, Cornea; *sc*, sclerotica; *o*, nervus opticus; *c*, sclerotic capsule; *a*, membrana argentea; *v*, membrana vasculosa; *u*, membrana uvea; *ch*, choroid gland; *r*, retina; *f*, processus falciformis; *h*, humor vitreus; *l*, lens; *i*, iris.

The membranes situated between the sclerotica and retina are collectively called *choroidea*, and three in number. The one in immediate contact with the sclerotic, and continued upon the iris, is by no means constantly present; it is the *membrana argentea* (*a*), and composed of microscopical crystals reflecting a silvery or sometimes golden lustre. The middle layer is the *membrana vasculosa* s. *halleri* (*v*), the chief seat of the ramifications of the choroid vessels; the innermost layer is the *membrana ruyscheana* or *uvea* (*u*), which is composed of hexagonal pigment-cells, usually of a deep brown or black colour.

In many *Teleostei* a *rete mirabile* surrounds the entry of the optic nerve; it is situated between the membrana argentea and vasculosa, and called the *choroid gland* (*ch*). It receives its arterial blood from the artery issuing from the pseudobranchia; the presence of a choroid gland always being combined with that of a pseudobranchia. Teleosteans without pseudobranchia lack a choroid gland. In the Palæichthyes, on the other hand, the pseudobranchia is present and a choroid gland absent.

The *iris* (*i*) is merely the continuation of the choroid membrane; its capability of contracting and expanding is much more limited than in higher Vertebrates. The *pupil* is generally round, sometimes horizontally or vertically elliptical, sometimes fringed In the Rays and Pleuronectidæ a lobe descends from the upper margin of the pupil, and the outer integument overlying this lobe is coloured and non-transparent; a structure evidently preventing light from entering the eye from above.

In most *Teleostei* a fold of the *Choroidea*, called the *Processus falciformis* (*f*), extends from the vicinity of the entrance of the optic nerve to the lens. It seems to be constantly absent in Ganoids.

The *retina* (*r*) is the membrane into which the optic nerve penetrates, and in which its terminal filaments are distributed. It consists of several layers (Fig. 49). The outermost is an extremely delicate membrane (*a*), followed by a layer of nerve-cells (*b*), from which the terminal filaments issue, passing through several granular strata (*c*, *d*, *e*), on which the innermost stratum rests. This stratum is composed of cylindrical rods (*f*) vertically arranged, between which twin fusiform corpuscles (*g*) are intercalated. This last layer is thickly covered with a dark pigment. The retina extends over a portion of the iris, and a well-defined raised rim runs along its anterior margin.

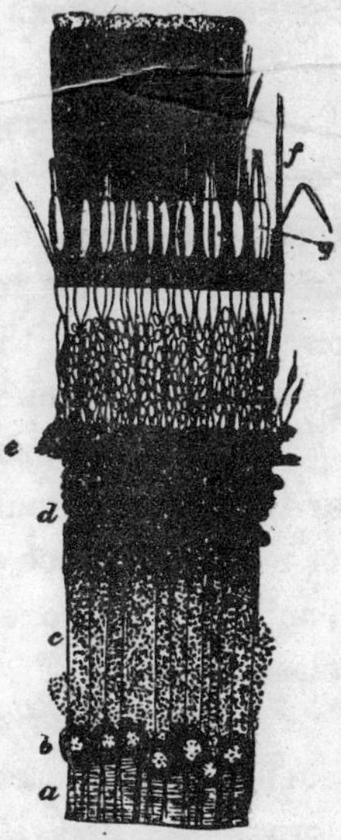

Fig. 49.—Vertical section of the Retina of the Perch, magn. X 350.

The *vitreous humour* (Fig. 48, *h*) which fills the posterior cavity of the eye-ball, is of a firmer consistency than in the higher Vertebrates. The *lens* is spherical, or nearly so; firm, denser towards the centre, and lies in a hollow of the vitreous humour. When a falciform process is present, it is with one end attached to the lens, which is thus steadied in its position. It consists of concentric layers consisting of fibres, which in the nucleus of the body have marginal teeth, by which they are interlocked together. In *Petromyzon* this serrature is absent, or but faintly indicated.

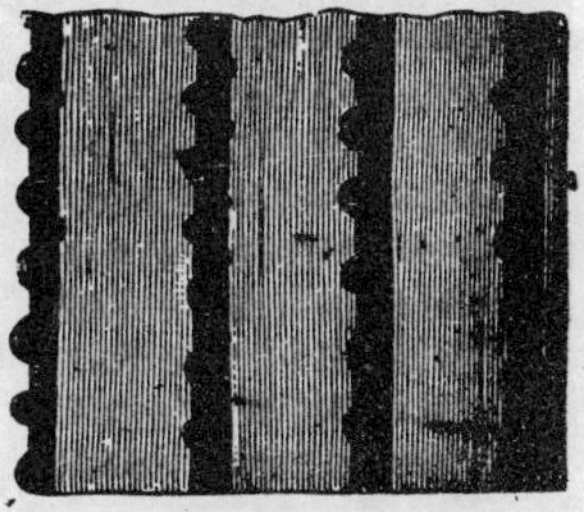

Fig. 50.—Interlocking fibres of lens, highly magnified.

The anterior cavity of the eye is very small in Fishes, in consequence of the small degree of convexity of the cornea; the quantity of the aqueous humour, therefore, is very small, just sufficient to float the free border of the iris, and the lessened refractive power of the aqueous humour is compensated by the greater convexity of the lens.

Organ of Hearing.—No trace of an organ of hearing has been found in *Branchiostoma.* In the *Cyclostomes* the labyrinth is enclosed in externally visible cartilaginous capsules laterally attached to the skull; it consists of a single *semicircular canal* in the Myxinoids, whilst the Petromyzontes possess two semicircular canals with a *vestibulum.*

In all other fishes the labyrinth consists of a vestibule and three semicircular canals, the vestibule dilating into one or more sacs which contain the otoliths. A tympanum, tympanic cavity, and external parts, are entirely absent in the class of fishes.

In the *Chondropterygians* and *Dipnoi*, the labyrinth is enclosed in the cartilaginous substance of the skull. In the former the excavation in the cartilage is larger than the membranous labyrinth, but nearly corresponds to it in form; the part which receives the membranous vestibulum is called *Vestibulum cartilagineum*, from which a canal issues and penetrates to the surface of the skull, where it is closed by the skin in Sharks, but opens by a minute foramen in Rays. The otolithic contents are soft and chalklike.

In the *Holocephali* part of the labyrinth is enclosed in the cartilage of the skull, another part being in the cranial cavity, as in Ganoids and Teleosteans. The membranous vestibulum is continued by a canal to a single opening in the roof of the skull, from which two smaller canals are continued to two small foramina in the skin covering the occipital region.

In the *Teleosteans* the sac which contains the otoliths lies on each side of the base of the cranial cavity and is often divided by a septum into two compartments of unequal size, each containing a firm and solid *otolith;* these bodies (Fig. 51), possess indented margins, frequently other impressions and grooves, in which nerves from the N. acusticus are lodged; they vary much in size and form, but in both respects show a remarkable constancy in the same kind of fishes. The vestibule is outwards in contact with the osseous side wall of the skull, inwards with the metencephalon and medulla oblongata; it contains another firm concretion, and opens by five foramina into the three semicircular canals. The terminations of the acustic nerve are distributed over the vestibular concretion and the ampulliform ends (Fig. 52 *p*) of the semicircular canals, without being continued into the latter, which are filled with fluid. The semicircular canals (Fig. 52 *g*), are sometimes lodged in the cranial bones, sometimes partly free in the cranial cavity. Many Teleostei have fontanelles in the roof of the skull, closed by skin or very thin bone only at the place where the auditory organ approaches the surface, by which means sonorous undulations must be conducted with greater ease to the ear.

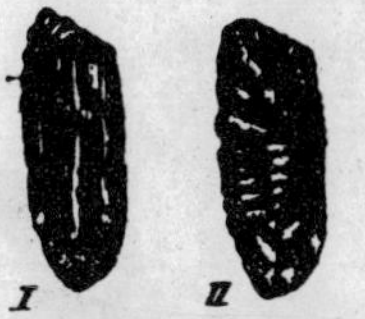

Fig. 51.—Otolith of Haddock (Gadus æglefinus). I. Outer, II. Inner aspect.

In many Teleostei a most remarkable relation obtains between the organ of hearing and the air-bladder. In the most simple form this connection is established in Percoids and the allied families, in which the two anterior horns of the air-bladder are attached to fontanelles of the occipital region of the skull, the vestibulum occupying the opposite side of the membrane by which the fontanelle is closed. The condition is similar, but more complicated in many Clupeoids. The anterior narrow end of the air-bladder is produced into a canal at the base of the skull, and divided into two very narrow branches, which again bifurcate and terminate in a globular swelling. An appendage of the vestibulum meets the anterior of these swellings, and comes into close contact with it. Besides, the two vestibules communicate with each other by a transverse canal, crossing the cranial cavity below the brain.

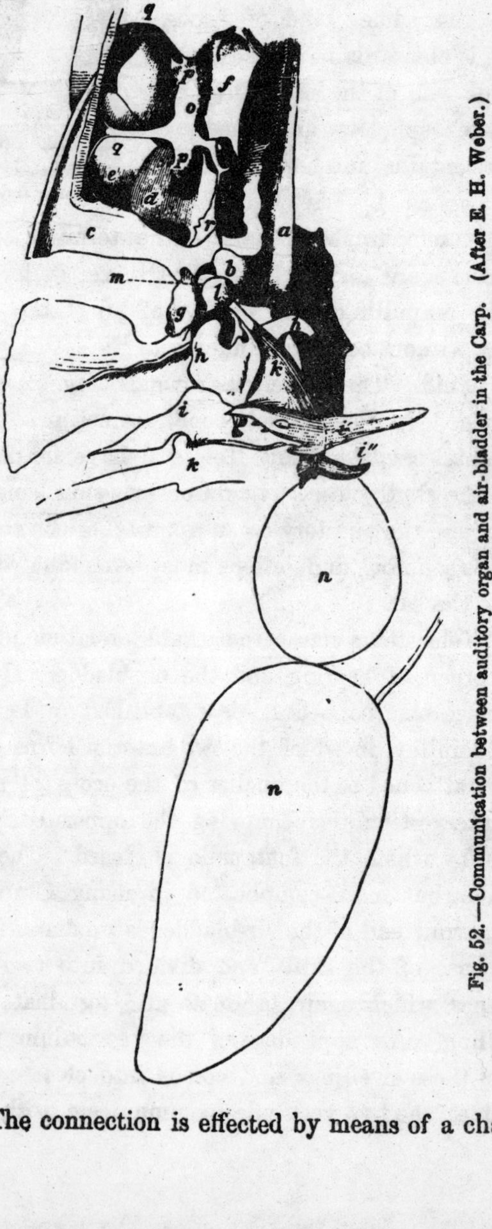

Fig. 52.—Communication between auditory organ and air-bladder in the Carp. (After E. H. Weber.) *a*, Basisphenoid; *b*, Occipital; *c*, Supraoccipital; *d*, Exoccipital; *e*, Paroccipital; *f*, Alisphenoid; *g*, Neural arch of first vertebra; *h*, *i*, *k*, second, third, and fourth vertebræ; *h'*, *i'*, Parapophyses of second and third vertebræ; *i''*, process of the third vertebra for the attachment of the air-bladder; *k*, *l*, *m*, Chain of ossicles; *n*, Air-bladder; *o*, vestibulum; *p*, *p*, Ampullæ; *q*, *q*, Canales semicirculares; *r*, Sinus impar.

The connection is effected by means of a chain of ossicles

in *Siluridæ, Characinidæ, Cyprinidæ* and *Gymnotidæ.* A canal issues from the communication between vestibule and its sac, and meeting that from the other side forms with it a common *sinus impar* (Fig. 52, *r*), lodged in the substance of the basi-occipital; this communicates on each side by a small orifice with two subspherical atria, on the body of the atlas, close to the foramen magnum. Each atrium is supported externally by a small bone (*m*); a third larger bone (*k*) completes the communication with the anterior part of the air-bladder. From the sinus impar a bifid canal penetrates into the alisphenoids, in which it terminates. In *Cobitis* and several Loach-like Siluroids the small air-bladder consists of two globular portions placed side by side, and wholly included within two bullæ, formed by the modified parapophyses of the second and third vertebræ. The three ossicles on each side are present, but concealed by the fore part of the osseous bulla.

Organ of Taste.—Some fishes, especially vegetable feeders, or those provided with broad molar-like teeth, masticate their food; and it may be observed in Carps and other Cyprinoid fish, that this process of mastication frequently takes some time. But the majority of fish swallow their food rapidly, and without mastication, and therefore we may conclude that the sense of taste cannot be acute. The tongue is often entirely absent, and even when it exists in its most distinct state, it consists merely of ligamentous or cellular substance, and is never furnished with muscles capable of producing the movements of extension or retraction as in most higher Vertebrates. A peculiar organ on the roof of the palate of Cyprinoids, is perhaps an organ adapted for perception of this sense; in these fishes the palate between and below the upper pharyngeal bones is cushioned with a thick, soft contractile substance, richly supplied with nerves from the Nervi vagus and glossopharyngeus.

Organs of Touch.—The faculty of touch is more developed than that of taste, and there are numerous fishes which possess special organs of touch. Most fishes are very sensitive to external touch, although their body may be protected by hard horny scales. They perceive impressions even on those parts which are covered by osseous scutes, in the same manner as a tortoise perceives the slightest touch of its carapace. The seat of the greatest sensitiveness, however, appears to be the snout and the labial folds surrounding the mouth. Many species possess soft and delicate appendages, called barbels, which are almost constantly in action, and clearly used as organs of touch. Among the *Triglidæ* and allied families, there are many species which have one or more rays of the pectoral fin detached from the membrane, and supplied with strong nerves. Such detached rays (also found in the *Polynemidæ*, *Bathypterois*) are used partly for locomotion, partly for the purpose of exploring the ground over which the fish moves.

Some fish appear to be much less sensitive than others, or at least lose their sensitiveness under peculiar circumstances. It is well known that a Pike, whose mouth has been lacerated and torn by the hook, continues to yield to the temptation of a bait immediately afterwards. The Greenland Shark when feeding on the carcase of a whale allows itself to be repeatedly stabbed in the head without abandoning its prey. A pair of Congers are so dead to external impression at the time of copulation, and so automatically, as it were, engaged, that they have been taken by the hand together out of the water.

CHAPTER VIII.

THE ORGANS OF NUTRITION AND DIGESTION.

FISHES are either exclusively carnivorous or herbivorous, but not a few feed on vegetable substances as well as animal, or on mud containing alimentary substance in a living or decomposing state. Generally they are very voracious, especially the carnivorous kinds, and the rule of "eat or be eaten" applies to them with unusual force. They are almost constantly engaged in the pursuit and capture of their prey, the degree of their power in these respects depending on the dimensions of the mouth and gullet and the strength of the teeth and jaws. If the teeth are sharp and hooked, they are capable of securing the most slender and agile animals; if this kind of teeth is combined with a wide gullet and distensible stomach, they are able to overpower and swallow other fish larger than themselves; if the teeth are broad, strong molars, they are able to crush the hardest aliments; if they are feeble, they are only serviceable in procuring some small or inert and unresisting prey. Teeth may be wanting altogether. Whatever the prey, in the majority of cases it is swallowed whole; but some of the most voracious fishes, like some Sharks and *Characinidæ,* are provided with cutting teeth, which enable them to tear their prey to pieces if too large to be swallowed whole. Auxiliary organs for the purpose of overpowering their prey, which afterwards is seized or torn by the teeth, like the claws of some carnivorous mammals and birds, are not found in this class; but in a few fishes the jaws themselves are modified for that purpose. In the Sword-fishes the bones of the upper jaw form a long dagger-shaped weapon, with which they not only attack large animals, but also frequently kill fishes on which they feed. The Saw-fishes are armed with a similar but still more complicated weapon, the saw, which is armed on each side with large teeth implanted in deep sockets, specially adapted for killing and tearing the prey before it is seized and masticated by the small teeth within the mouth. Fishes show but little choice in the selection of their food, and some devour their own offspring indiscriminately with other fishes. Their digestive powers are strong and rapid, but subject in some degree to the temperature, which, when sinking below a certain point, lowers the vital powers of these cold-blooded animals. On the whole, marine fishes are more voracious than those inhabiting fresh waters; and whilst the latter may survive total abstinence from food for weeks or months, the marine species succumb to hunger within a few days. The growth of fishes depends greatly on the nature and supply of food, and different individuals of the same species may exhibit a great disparity in their respective dimensions. They grow less rapidly and to smaller dimensions in small ponds or shallow streams than in large lakes and deep rivers. The young of coast fishes, when driven out to sea, where they find a much smaller supply of food, remain in an undeveloped condition, assuming an hydropic appearance. The growth itself seems to continue in most fishes for a great length of time, and we can scarcely set bounds to—certainly we know not with precision—the utmost range of the specific size of fishes. Even among species in no way remarkable for their dimensions we sometimes meet with old individuals, favourably situated, which more or less exceed the ordinary weight and measurement of their kind. However, there are certain evidently short-lived species of fishes which attain a remarkably uniform size within a very short time; for instance, the Stickleback, many species of *Gobius* and *Clupea.*

The organs of nutrition, manducation, and deglutition, are lodged in two large cavities—an anterior (the mouth or *buccal cavity*), and a posterior (the *abdominal cavity*). In the former the alimentary organs are associated with those fulfilling the respiratory functions, the transmission of food to the stomach and of water to the gills being performed by similar acts of deglutition. The abdominal cavity commences immediately behind the head, so, however, that an extremely short thoracic cavity for the heart is partitioned off in front. Beside the alimentary organs it contains also those of the urogenital system and the air-bladder. The abdominal cavity is generally situated in the trunk only, but in numerous fishes it extends into the tail, being continued for some distance along each side of the hæmal apophyses

In numerous fishes the abdominal cavity opens outwards by one or two openings. A single *porus abdominalis* in front of the vent is found in *Lepidosiren* and some Sturgeons; a paired one, one on each side of the vent, in *Ceratodus*, some species of Sturgeon, *Lepidosteus, Polypterus, Amia*, and all Chondropterygians. As in these fishes semen and ova are discharged by proper ducts, the abdominal openings may serve for the expulsion of semen, and those ova only which, having lost their way to the abdominal aperture of the oviduct, would be retained in the abdominal cavity. In those *Teleosteans* which lack an oviduct a single *porus genitalis* opens *behind* the vent.

The *mouth* of fishes shows extreme variation with regard to form, extent, and position. Generally opening in front, it may be turned upwards, or may lie at the lower side of the snout, as in most Chondropterygians, Sturgeons, and some Teleosteans. Vogt regards this position as a persistent fœtal condition. In most fishes the jaws are covered by the skin, which, before passing over the jaws, is often folded, forming more or less fleshy lips. In the Sharks the skin retains its external character even within the teeth, but in other fishes it changes into a mucous membrane. A *tongue* may exist as a more or less free and short projection, formed by the glossohyal and a soft covering, or may be entirely absent. *Salivary* glands and a *velum palati* are absent in fishes.

With regard to the *dentition*, the class of Fishes offers an amount of variation such as is not found in any of the other classes of Vertebrates. As the teeth form one of the most important elements in the classification of fishes, their special arrangement and form will be referred to in the account of the various families and genera. Whilst not a few fishes are entirely edentulous, in others most of the bones of the buccal cavity, or some of them, may be toothed, as the bones of the jaws, the palatines, pterygoids, vomers, basi-sphenoid, glossohyal, branchial arches, upper and lower pharyngeals. In others teeth may be found fixed in some portion of the buccal membrane without being supported by underlying bone or cartilage; or the teeth have been developed in membrane overlying one of the dentigerous bones mentioned, without having become anchylosed to the bone. When the tooth is fixed to the bone the attachment has generally been effected by the ossification of the bone of the tooth, but in some fishes a process of the bone projects into the cavity of the tooth; in others the teeth are implanted in alveoli. In these, again, frequently a process of bone rises from the bottom, on which the tooth rests.

Many fishes, especially predatory fishes with long, lancet-shaped teeth, have all or some of the teeth capable of being bent inwards towards the mouth. Such "hinged" teeth resume at once the upright position when pressure is removed from them. They are, however, depressible in one direction only, thus offering no obstacle to the ingress, but opposing the egress of prey. Mr. C. S. Tomes has shown that the means by which this mechanism is worked are different in different fishes; for whilst, in the *Pediculati* and *Gadoids* (Hake) the elasticity resides solely in the tissue of the hinge (the tooth being as resilient as ever after everything else is severed), in the Pike the hinge is not in the least endowed with elasticity, but the bundles of fibres proceeding from the interior of the dentine cap are exceedingly elastic.

As regards texture the teeth of fishes show considerable variation. The conical teeth of the Cyclostomes and the setiform teeth of many Teleosteans consist of a horny albuminous substance. The principal substance of the teeth of other fishes consists of dentine, with numerous dividing and anastomosing tubercles, sometimes covered by a stratum of unvascular dentine. An enamel-like substance has been observed on the crown of the teeth of *Sargus* and *Balistes*, and an ossification of the capsule of their matrix covers the enamel with a thin coating of cement. The teeth either possess a cavity in which the matrix is received, or, more frequently, they are solid, in which case vascular canals of the underlying bone are continued into the substance of the tooth. In the teeth of some fishes numerous sets of canals and tubes are so arranged that they do not anastomose with one another, each set being surrounded by a layer of dentine and cement. These apparently simple teeth are evidently composed of numerous small teeth, and called *compound* teeth.

The teeth may be, and generally are, very different as regards size or form in the different parts of the mouth; they may be also different according to the age or sex of the fish (*Raja*). The teeth may be few in number and *isolated*, or placed in a single, double, or triple *series*, *distant* from one another or *closely set*; they may form narrow or broad *bands*, or *patches* of various forms. As regards form, they may be cylindrical or conical, pointed, straight, or curved, with or without an angular bent near their base; some are compressed laterally or from the front backwards; the latter may be triangular in shape, or truncated at the top like incisors of mammals; they may have one apex (cusp) only, or be bi- or tri-lobate (bi- or tri-cuspid); or have the margins denticulated or serrated. Compressed teeth may be confluent, and form a cutting edge in both jaws, which assume the shape of a parrot's beak (Fig. 53). In some the apex is hooked or provided with barbs. Again, some teeth are broad, with flat or convex surface, like molar teeth. With regard to size, the finest teeth are like fine flexible bristles, *ciliiform* or *setiform*; or, if very short and anchylosed to the bone, they appear only as inconspicuous asperities of the bone. Very fine conical teeth arranged in a band are termed *villiform* teeth; when they are coarser, or mixed with coarser teeth, they are *card-like* (dents en rape or en cardes) (Fig. 54); molar-like teeth of very small size are termed *granular*.

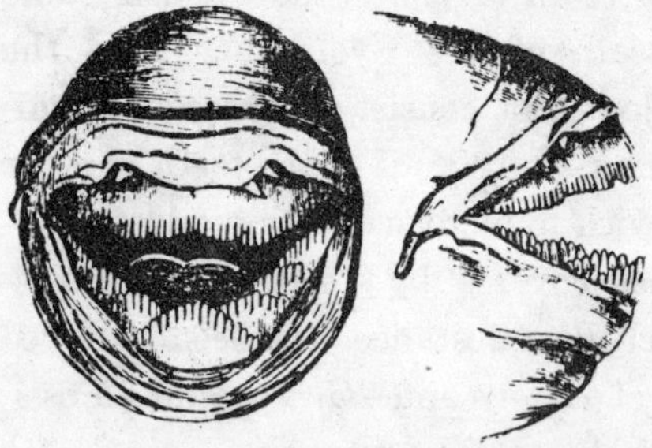

Fig. 53.—Jaws of Calliodon.

In all fishes the teeth are constantly shed or renewed during the whole course of their life. In fishes which have compound teeth, as the Dipnoi, Chimæroids, Scari,[1] Gymnodonts, as well as in those which have apparently permanent teeth, as in the saw of *Pristis*, the detrition of the surface is made up by a constant growth of the tooth from its base. When the teeth are implanted in alveoli, they are generally succeeded by others in the vertical direction, but in others they succeed one another, side by side. In the majority of

[1] On the development and structure of the dentition of *Scarina*, see *Boas*, "Die Zähne der Scaroiden," in Zeitschr. f. Wiss. Zoolog. xxxii. (1878).

fishes the new tooth is not developed (as in reptiles and mammals) in a diverticulum of the sack of its predecessor, but like this from the free surface of the buccal membrane. Generally there are more than one tooth growing, which are in various stages of development, and destined to replace the one in function. This is very conspicuous in Sharks, in which the whole phalanx of their numerous teeth is ever marching slowly forwards (or in some backwards), in rotatory progress, over the alveolar border of the jaw, the teeth being successively cast off after having reached the outer margin, and fulfilled for a longer and shorter period their special function.

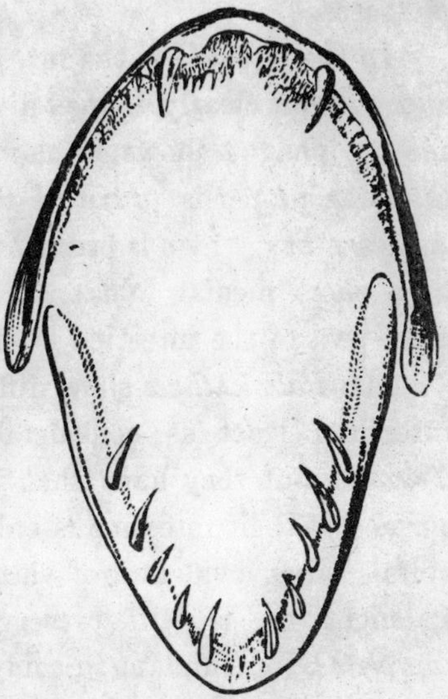

Fig. 54.—Cardlike teeth of Plectropoma dentex, with canines.

[The richest materials for our knowledge of the teeth of fishes are contained in *Owen's* "Odontography." Lond. 1840. 8vo.]

The *intestinal tract* is divided into four portions: œsophagus, stomach, small and large intestine; two or more of these divisions may coalesce in fishes and become indistinguishable. But it is characteristic of the class that the urinary apertures are constantly situated behind the termination of the intestinal tract.

In *Branchiostoma* the whole intestinal tract is straight, and coated with a ciliated mucous membrane. The wide pharynx passes into a narrow œsophagus, this into a gastric cavity, the remainder being again narrower and terminating in the anal aperture, which lies somewhat to the left of the median line. The liver is represented by a green coloured cœcal diverticulum of the stomachic dilatation. A mesenterium is absent.

In the *Cyclostomi* the intestinal tract is likewise straight, and without clearly defined divisions; however, in *Petromyzon* the œsophagus shows numerous longitudinal folds, and the intestine proper is provided with a single longitudinal fold A mesentery, which is present in the Myxinoids, is represented by a short median fold only, by means of which the hindmost part of the intestine is fixed.

The *Palæichthyes* show differences in the structure of their intestinal tract as considerable as are found among the *Teleostei,* but they have that in common that the absorbent surface of their intestine is enlarged by the development of a spiral valve, evidence of the presence of which in extinct Palæichthyes is still preserved in the fossilised fæces or *coproliths,* so abundant in some of the older strata.

In *Chondroptèrygians* (Fig. 55) the stomach is divided into a cardiac and pyloric portion, the former frequently terminating in a blind sac, and the latter varying in length. The pyloric portion is bent at its origin and end, and separated from the short duodenum (called *Bursa entiana* in these fishes) by a valve; the ductus hepaticus and pancreaticus enter the duodenum. This is succeeded by the straight intestine provided with the spiral valve, the coils of which may be either longitudinal and wound vertically about the axis of the intestine, as in *Carcharias, Galeocerdo, Thalassorhinus,* and *Zygœna,* or they may be transverse to that axis, as in the other genera. The number of gyrations in the latter case varies: there may be as many as forty. The short rectum passes into a cloaca, which contains also the orifices of the urogenital ducts. Only the commencement and end of the intestinal tract are fixed by mesenterial folds.

In the *Holocephali* and *Dipnoi,* the intestinal tract is short, straight, and wide, without stomachic dilatation, a pyloric valve, close to which the ductus choledochus enters, indicating

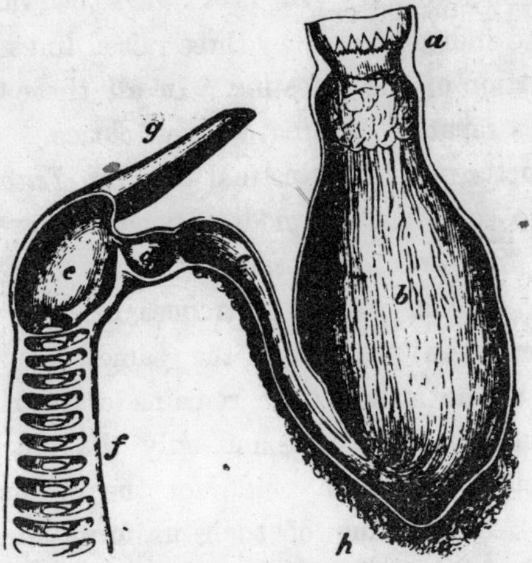

Fig. 55.—Siphonal stomach and spiral valve of Basking-Shark (Selache). (After Home and Owen.)

a, Œsophagus; *b*, Cardiac portion of stomach; *c*, pyloric portion; *d*, pouch intermediate between stomach and duodenum, with circular valves at both ends; *e*, Duodenum; *f*, Valve of intestine; *g*, Ductus hepaticus; *h*, Spleen.

the boundary of the intestine proper (Fig. 57, *p*). The spiral valve is perfect, and makes from three (*Chimæra*) to nine (*Ceratodus*) gyrations. A cloaca is present, as in Chondropterygians. A mesentery fixing the dorsal side of the intestine is absent.

The other *Ganoids* resemble again more the Chondropterygians in the structure of their intestinal tract. The stomach has always a distinct pyloric portion, and has a still more complicated structure in *Acipenser*. The duodenal portion receives the contents of *Appendices pyloricæ* which are confluent into a gland-like mass in *Acipenser*, but separate in *Polyodon*, and numerous and short in *Lepidosteus*, whilst *Polypterus* possesses one such appendage only. A spiral valve is developed in the Sturgeons and Polypterus, but in *Amia*, in which the intestine performs several convolutions, the four gyrations of the valve are situated far back towards the end of the intestine In *Lepidosteus* the valve is rudimentary, and indicated only by three raised lines crossing the terminal portion of the intestine. In all these Ganoids the rectum has a separate opening, without cloaca.

The structure of the intestinal tract of *Teleosteous* fishes is subject to so numerous modifications that we should go beyond the limits of the present work if we would attempt to enter into details. Great differences in this respect may be found even in groups of the same natural families. Frequently the intestinal tract remains of nearly the same width throughout its course, and only the entrance of the various ducts serves as a guide for the distinction of its divisions. An intestine of such uniform width may be straight and short, as in *Scombresocidæ*, *Symbranchidæ*, or it may be more or less convoluted and long, as in many *Cyprinidæ*, *Doradina*, etc. On the whole, carnivorous fishes have a much shorter and simpler intestinal tract than herbivorous.

In the majority of Teleosteans, however, œsophagus, stomach, duodenum, small intestine and rectum, can be more or less distinctly, even externally distinguished.

There are two predominant forms of the stomach, intermediate forms being, however, numerous. In the first, the *siphonal*, it presents the form of a bent tube or canal, one-half of the horse-shoe being the cardiac, the other the pyloric portion. In the second, the *cæcal*, the cardiac division is prolonged into a long descending blind sac, the cardiac and pyloric openings of the stomach lying close together (*Clupea Scomber*, *Thynnus*, etc.)

The duodenum receives always the hepatic and pancreatic secretions, and, besides, those of the appendices pyloricæ, which, in varying numbers (from 1 to 200), are of very common occurrence in Teleosteans (Fig. 56). They vary also in length

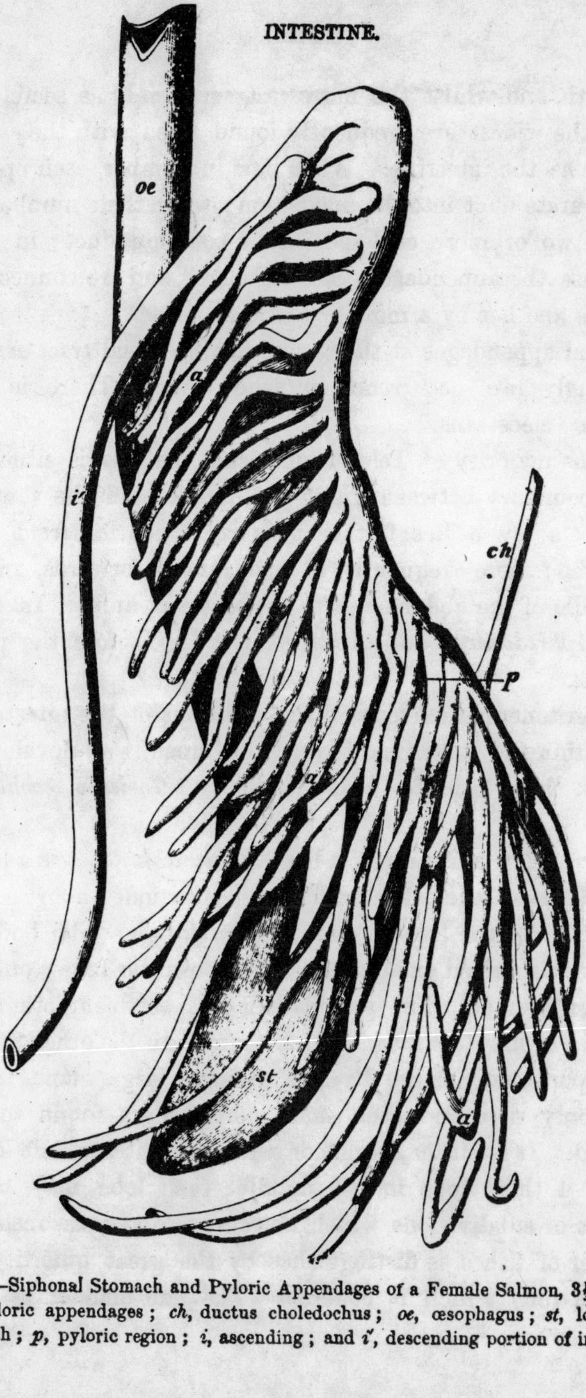

Fig. 56.—Siphonal Stomach and Pyloric Appendages of a Female Salmon, 3⅓ feet long. *a a a*, Pyloric appendages; *ch*, ductus choledochus; *oe*, œsophagus; *st*, lower end of stomach; *p*, pyloric region; *i*, ascending; and *i″*, descending portion of intestine.

and width, and whilst the narrowest serve only as secretory organs, the widest are frequently found filled with the same contents as the intestine. When few in number, each opens by a separate duct into the duodenum; when their number is greater two or more coalesce into a common duct; in the latter case the appendages cease to be free, and are connected with one another by a more or less firm tissue.

Cœcal appendages at the end of the intestinal tract are of exceedingly rare occurrence in fishes (*Box*). There is no *cloaca* in Teleosteans.

In the majority of Teleosteous fishes the *vent* is situated on the boundary between trunk and tail, behind the ventral fins. In a few it lies farther backwards, not far from the caudal fin; more frequently it is advanced forwards, under the middle of the abdomen or to the scapular arch. In two fishes, *Aphredoderus* and *Amblyopsis*, it lies before the pectoral fins.

A peritoneum envelops all the divisions of the intestinal tract within the abdominal cavity. A broad, well-developed *omentum* has hitherto been found in *Gobiesox cephalus* only.

Liver.—The existence of a liver in *Branchiostoma* as a long diverticulum of the intestine has been mentioned above. In the Myxinoids the liver is divided into two glandular bodies, an anterior rounded smaller one, and a posterior larger one of an elongate shape. The gall-bladder lies between both, and receives a cystic duct from each of them. In the other fishes the proportionally large liver is a single large gland, from which only now and then small portions are found to be detached. It is either simple, or with a right and left lobe, or with a third lobe in the middle; each lobe may have incisions or subdivisions, which, however, are very inconstant. The liver of fishes is distinguished by the great quantity of fluid fat (oil) which it contains. The gall-bladder is but rarely absent, and attached to the right lobe, or towards the centre; however, in some fishes it is detached from the liver and connected with it by the cystic duct only. The bile may be conveyed by one or more hepatic ducts into a common duct which is continued towards the gall-bladder as *ductus cysticus*, and towards the duodenum as *ductus choledochus;* or some of the hepatic ducts enter directly the gall-bladder, or directly the duodenum, without communicating with the common duct. Individual variations in this respect are of common occurrence.

A *pancreas* has been found hitherto in all Chondropterygians, Acipenser, and many Teleosteans. In the first it is a glandular mass of considerable size behind the stomach, close to the spleen; its duct leads into the duodenum. In the Sturgeons the pancreas is attached to the duodenum, and opens close to the ductus choledochus. In *Silurus glanis* it is very large, and the ductus choledochus passes through its substance; it is smaller in *Belone* and *Pleuronectes*, and situated in the mesentery; its duct accompanies the terminal portion of the ductus choledochus. In the Salmon, which possesses a large lobed pancreas, the duct is so intimately connected with the ductus choledochus that both appear externally as a single duct only.

The *spleen*, which is substantially a lymphatic gland, may be mentioned here, as it is constantly situated in the immediate vicinity of the stomach, generally near its cardiac portion. With the exception of *Branchiostoma*, it is found in all fishes and appears as a rounded or oblong organ of dark-red colour. In the Sharks frequently one or more smaller pieces are detached from the principal body. In the Dipnoi a thin layer of a very soft substance of brownish-black colour below the mucous membrane of the stomach and upper part of the intestine has been regarded as the homologue of the spleen (Fig. 57. *m*). In most *Tcleostci* the spleen is undivided, and appended by its vessels and a fold of the peritoneum to the pyloric bend of the stomach or the beginning of the intestine.

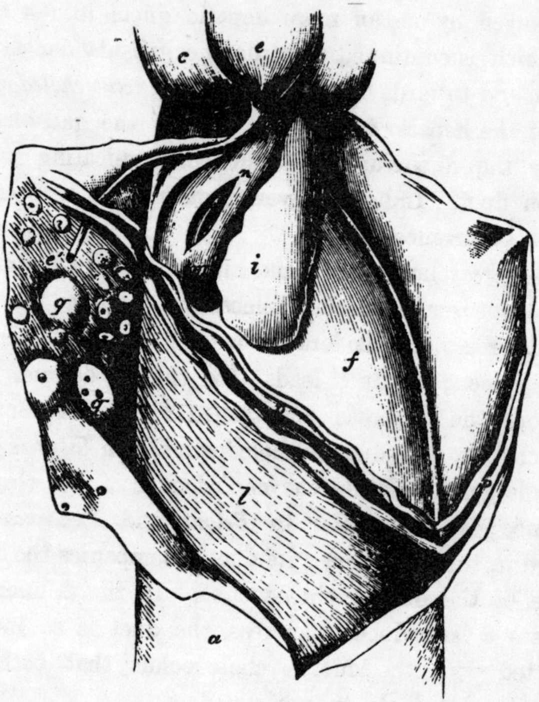

Fig. 57.—Upper part of Intestine of Ceratodus. The anterior wall of the intestine is opened, the liver (*c*) and gall-bladder (*e*) being drawn forward. A slit is made at *n*, through which part of the next compartment of the spirally wound intestine may be seen.

e', Mouth of ductus choledochus; *f*, stomach; *i*, adipose agglomeration; *l*, first compartment of intestinal spire; *m*, spleen; *oe*, lower part of œsophagus, opened; *p*, double pyloric fold; *q q*, glandular patches.

CHAPTER IX.

ORGANS OF RESPIRATION.

Fishes breathe the air dissolved in water by means of gills or branchiæ. The oxygen consumed by them is not that which forms the chemical constituent of the water, but that contained in the air which is dissolved in water. Hence fishes transferred into water from which the air has been driven out by a high temperature, or in which the air absorbed by them is not replaced, are speedily suffocated. The absorption of oxygen by fishes is comparatively small. and it has been calculated that a man consumes 50,000 times more than is required by a Tench. However, some fishes evidently require a much larger supply of oxygen than others: Eels and Carps, and other fishes of similar low vitality, can survive the removal out of their elements for days, the small quantity of moisture retained in their gill-cavity being sufficient to sustain life, whilst other fishes, especially such as have very wide gill-openings, are immediately suffocated after being taken out of the water. In some fishes noted for their muscular activity, like the *Scombridæ*, the respiratory process is so energetic as to raise the temperature of their blood far beyond that of the medium in which they live. A few fishes, especially such as are periodically compelled to live in water thickened into mud by desiccation and vitiated by decomposing substances, breathe atmospheric air, and have generally special contrivances for this purpose. These are so much habituated to breathing air that many of them, even when brought into pure water of normal condition, are obliged to rise to the surface at frequent intervals to take in a quantity of air, and if they be kept beneath the surface by means of a gauze net, they perish from suffocation. The special contrivances consist of additional respiratory organs, lodged in cavities either adjoining the gill-cavity or communicating with the ventral side of the œsophagus, or of the air-bladder which enters upon respiratory functions (Dipnoi, Lepidosteus, Amia).

The water used by fishes for respiration is received by the mouth, and by an action similar to that of swallowing driven to the gills, and expelled by the gill-openings, of which there may be one or several on each side behind the head; rarely one only in the median line of the ventral surface.

The *gills* or *branchiæ* consist essentially of folds of the

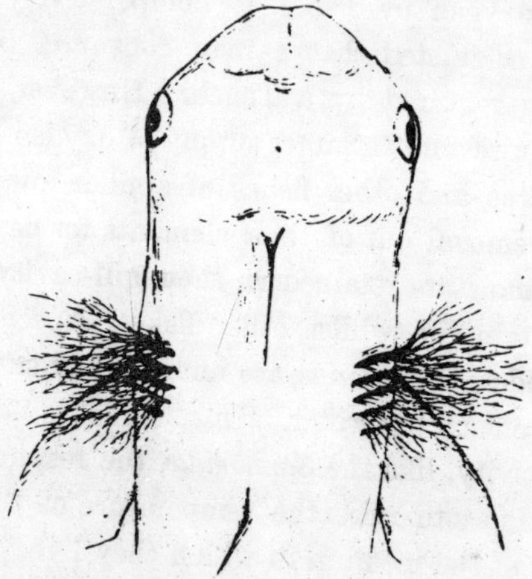

Fig. 58.—Fore-part of the body of an embryon of Carcharias, showing the branchial filaments (natural size).

mucous membrane of the gill-cavity (*laminæ branchiales*), in which the capillary vessels are distributed. In all fishes the gills are lodged in a cavity, but during the embryonic stage the Chondropterygians have the gill-laminæ prolonged into long filaments projecting beyond the gill-cavity (Fig. 58), and in a few young Ganoids external gills are superadded to the internal.

In *Branchiostoma* the dilated pharynx is perforated by numerous clefts, supported by cartilaginous rods (Fig. 29, *h*). The water passes between these clefts into the peritoneal cavity, and makes its exit by the porus abdominalis situated considerably in advance of the vent. The water is propelled by cilia.

In the *Cyclostomes* the gills of each side are lodged in a series of six or more antero-posteriorly compressed sacs, separated from each other by intervening septa. Each sac communicates by an inner duct with the œsophagus, the water being expelled by an outer duct. In *Bdellostoma* each outer duct has a separate opening, but in *Myxine* all the outer ducts pass outwards by one common gill-opening on each side. In the Lampreys the ducts are short, the outer ones having separate openings (Fig. 2, p. 39). The inner ducts lead into a single diverticulum or bronchus, blind behind, situated below the œsophagus, and communicating in front with the pharynx, where it is provided with two valves by which the regurgitation of the water into the buccal cavity is prevented.

The same type of branchial organs persists in *Chondropterygians*, which possess five, rarely six or seven, flattened pouches with transversely plaited walls. The septa between them are supported by cartilaginous filaments rising from the hyoidean and branchial arches. Each pouch opens by a cleft outwards, and by an aperture into the pharynx, without intervening ducts. The anterior wall of the first pouch is supported by the hyoidean arch. Between the posterior wall of the first and the anterior of the second sac, and between the adjacent walls of the succeeding, a branchial arch with its two series of radiating cartilaginous filaments is interposed. Consequently the first and last pouch have one set of gill-laminæ only, viz. the first on its posterior and the last on its anterior wall. The so-called *spiracles* on the upper surface of the head of Chondropterygians are to be referred to in connection with the respiratory organs. They are the external openings of a canal leading on each side into the pharynx, and situated generally close to and behind the orbit. They frequently possess valves or an irregularly indented margin, and are found in all species during the embryonic stage, but remaining persistent in a part only. The spiracles are the remains of the first visceral cleft of the embryo, and in the fœtal state long branchial filaments have been observed to protrude, as from the other branchial clefts.

The *Holocephali* and *Ganoidei* show numerous deviations from the Chondropterygian type, all leading in the direction towards the Teleosteans. As a whole they take an intermediate position between the preceding types and the Teleosteans, but they show a great variation among themselves, and have in common only the imperfect separation of the branchial sacs and the presence of a single outer branchial aperture.

In *Chimæra* the septum separating the branchial sacs is confluent with the wall of the gill-cavity in a part of its extent only, and still more imperfect is the separation of those branchial divisions in *Ceratodus* (Fig. 60). The other Ganoids show no such division whatever. In *Chimæra* the first gill is incomplete (uniserial), and belongs to the hyoid; then follow three complete gills; the last, belonging to the fourth branchial arch, being again incomplete. *Acipenser*, *Scaphirhynchus*, *Lepidosiren*, *Protopterus*, and *Lepidosteus*, possess likewise an anterior incomplete gill (*opercular gill*), followed by four complete gills in the Sturgeons and *Lepidosteus*, whilst in

Lepidosiren and *Protopterus* a part of the branchial arches is gill-less. In *Polyodon, Ceratodus,* and *Polypterus,* an opercular gill is absent, the two former having four complete gills, the latter three and a half only. *Spiracles* are still in some Ganoids present, viz. in the Sturgeons and *Polypterus.* In all the Ganoids an osseous gill-cover is now developed.

In the *Teleostei* the gills with their supporting branchial arches lie in one undivided cavity; more or less wide clefts between the arches lead from the pharynx to the gills, and a more or less wide opening gives exit to the water after it has washed the gills. The interbranchial clefts have sometimes nearly the same extent as the branchial arches; sometimes they are reduced to small openings, the integuments stretching from one arch to the other. Sometimes there is no cleft behind the fourth arch, in which case this arch has only an uniserial gill developed. The gill-opening likewise varies much in its extent, and when reduced to a foramen may be situated at any place of the posterior boundary of the head. In the *Symbranchidæ* the gill-openings coalesce into a single narrow slit in the median line of the isthmus. In the majority of Teleosteans the integument of the concave side of the branchial arches develops a series of horny protuberances of various form, the so-called *gill-rakers.* They are destined to catch any solid corpuscles or substances which would be carried into the gill-cavity with the water. In some fishes they are setiform, and form a complete sieve, whilst in others they are merely rough tubercles, the action of which must be very incomplete if they have any function at all.

Most Teleosteans possess four complete gills, but frequently the fourth arch is provided with an uniserial gill only, as mentioned above, or even entirely gill-less. The most imperfect gills are found in *Malthe,* which has two and a half gills only, and in *Amphipnous cuchia,* in which one small gill is fixed to the second arch.

The gills of the Teleosteans as well as of the Ganoids are supported by a series of solid cartilaginous or horny pointed rods, arranged along the convex edges of the branchial arches. Arches bearing a complete gill have two series of those rods, one along each edge; those with uniserial gills bear one row of rods only. The rods are not part of the arch, but fixed in its integument, the several rods of one row corresponding to those of the other, forming pairs (*feuillet*, Cuvier) (Fig. 59). Each rod is covered by a loose mucous membrane passing from one rod to its fellow opposite, which again is finely transversely plaited, the general surface being greatly increased by these plaits. In most Teleostei the branchial lamellæ are compressed, and taper towards their free end, but in the Lophobranchs their base is attenuated and the end enlarged. The mucous membrane contains the finest terminations of the vessels, which, being very superficial, impart the blood-red colour to living gills. The *Arteria branchialis*, the course of which lies in the open canal in the convexity of the branchial arch, emits a branch (*a*) for every pair of lamellæ which ascends (*b*) along the inner edge of the lamella, and supplies every one of the transverse plaits with a branchlet. The latter break up into a fine net of capillaries, from which the oxygenised blood is collected into venous branchlets, returning by the venous branch (*d*), which occupies the outer edge of the lamella.

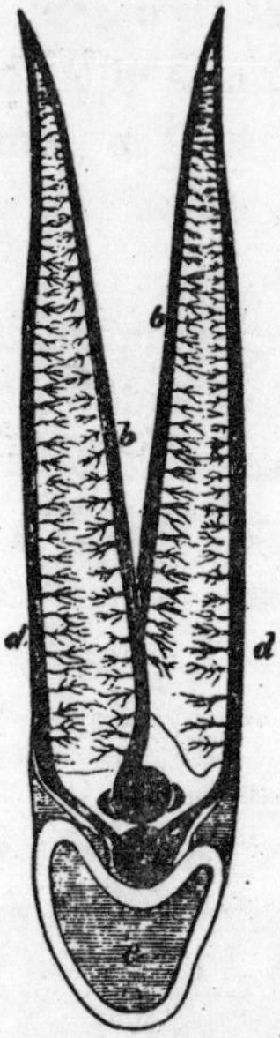

Fig. 59.—A pair of branchial lamellæ (magnified) of the Perch.
a, Branch of Arteria branchialis; *b*, Ascending branch of the same; *c*. Branch of Vena branchialis; *d*, Descending branch of the same; *e*, Transverse section through the branchial arch.

The so-called *Pseudobranchiæ* (Fig. 60) are the remains of an anterior gill which had respiratory functions during the embryonic life of the individuals. By a change in the circulatory system these organs have lost those functions, and appear in the adult fish as retia mirabilia, as they receive oxygenised blood, which, after having passed through their capillary system, is carried to other parts of the head. In Palæichthyes the pseudobranchia is a rete mirabile caroticum for the brain and eye; in Teleosteans a rete mirabile ophthalmicum only. Pseudobranchiæ are as frequently absent as present in Chondropterygians as well as Teleosteans. As to the Ganoids, they occur in *Ceratodus*, *Acipenser*, *Polyodon*, and *Lepidosteus*, and are absent in *Lepidosiren*, *Protopterus*, *Scaphirhynchus*, *Polypterus*, and *Amia*.

Fig. 60.—Gills of Ceratodus. *x*, Arcus aortæ; *gl*, Glossohyal; *ch*, Ceratohyal; *u*, Attachment of the first gill to the walls of the gill-cavity; *h*, Pseudobranchia; *x'*, *x''*, two series of gill-rakers belonging to the Pseudobranchia.

In Chondropterygians and Sturgeons the pseudobranchiæ are situated within the spiracles; in those, in which spiracles have become obliterated, the pseudobranchiæ lie on the suspensorium, hidden below cellular tissue; but pseudobranchiæ are not necessarily co-existent with spiracles. In the other Ganoids and Teleosteans the pseudobranchiæ (Fig. 60, *h*) are within the gill-cavity, near the base of the gill-cover; in *Ceratodus* even rudiments of the gill-rakers (*x'*, *x''*) belonging to this embryonic gill are preserved, part of them (*x''*) being attached to the hyoid arch. Pseudobranchiæ are frequently hidden below the integuments of the gill-cavity, and have the appearance of a glandular body rather than of a gill.

[See Müller, "Vergleichende Anatomie des Gefäss-systems der Myxinoiden:" and "Ueber den Bau und die Grenzen der Ganoiden."]

Accessory respiratory organs for retaining water or breathing air, such as are found in the *Labyrinthici, Ophiocephalidæ,* certain *Siluridæ,* and *Lutodira,* are structures so specialised that they are better described in the accounts of the Fishes in which they have been observed.

Air-Bladder.—The air-bladder, one of the most characteristic organs of fishes, is a hollow sac, formed of several tunics, containing gas, situated in the abdominal cavity, but without the peritoneal sac, entirely closed or communicating by a duct with the intestinal tract. Being compressible, its special functions consist in altering the specific gravity of the fish or in changing the centre of gravity. In a few fishes it assumes the function of the organ of higher Vertebrates, of which it is the homologue—viz. of a *lung.*

The gas contained in the air-bladder is secreted from its inner surface. In most fresh-water fishes it consists of nitrogen, with a very small quantity of oxygen and a trace of carbonic acid; in sea-fishes, especially those living at some depth, oxygen predominates, as much as 87 per cent having been found. Davy found in the air-bladder of a fresh-run Salmon a trace of carbonic acid and 10 per cent of oxygen, the remainder of the gas being nitrogen.

An air-bladder is absent in *Leptocardii, Cyclostomi, Chondropterygii,* and *Holocephali;* but occurs in all Ganoids, in which, besides, its respiratory functions more or less clearly manifest themselves. Its occurrence in Teleosteans is most irregular, closely allied species sometimes differing from each other in this respect; it shows in this sub-class the most extraordinary modifications, but has no respiratory function whatever.

Constantly situated within the abdominal cavity, below the vertebral column, but without the sac of the peritoneum which covers only its ventral portion, the air-bladder is frequently prolonged into the tail, the prolongation being either simple and lodged between the non-united parapophyses, or double and penetrating between the muscles and hæmapophyses of each side. In the opposite direction processes of the air-bladder may penetrate into the skull, as has been mentioned above (p. 117). In some fishes the air-bladder is almost loose in the abdominal cavity, whilst in others it adheres most intimately by firm and short tissue to the vertebral column, the walls of the abdomen, and the intestines. In the Cobitina and many Siluroids it is more or less completely enclosed in osseous capsules formed by the vertebræ.

The tunics of the majority of air-bladders are an extremely fine internal one, frequently shining silvery, containing crystalline corpuscles, sometimes covered with a pavement-epithelium; and a thicker outer one of a fibrous texture, which sometimes attains to considerable thickness and yields isinglass. This wall is strengthened in many fishes by muscular layers for the compression of the whole organ or of some portion of it.

A distinction has been made between air-bladders which communicate by a duct with the intestinal tract and those which are entirely closed. However, it is to be remembered that at an early stage of development all air-bladders are provided with such a duct, which in a part of the fishes more or less completely obliterates, being then represented by a fine ligament only. In young *Lucioperca* of six to eight inches in length the duct may be found still open for a considerable distance; and, on the other hand, in adult *Physostomi*, that is Teleosteous fishes with a ductus pneumaticus, not rarely the whole duct is found very narrow, or, for some part of its length, even entirely closed.

Air-bladders without duct are found in Acanthopterygians, Pharyngognaths, Anacanths, and Lophobranchs. They may consist of a single cavity or divided by constrictions into two or three partitions situated behind one another; they may consist of two lateral partitions, assuming a horseshoe-like form, or they may be a single sac with a pair of simple or bifid

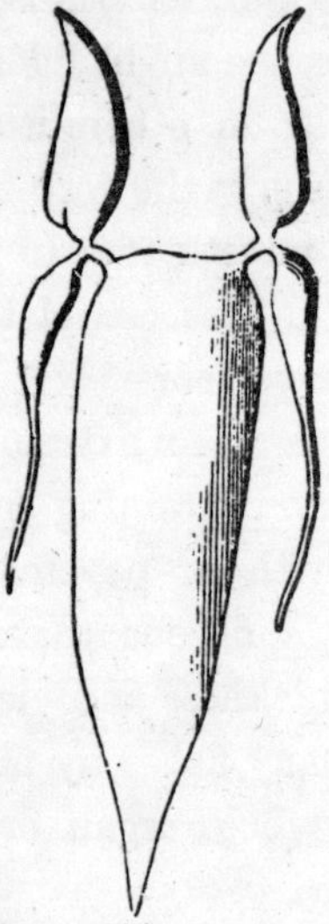

Fig. 61.—Air-bladder of Otolithus sp.

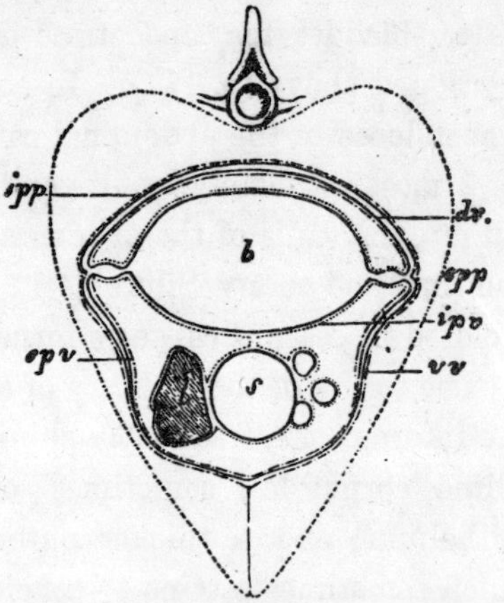

Fig. 62.—Vertical section through abdominal cavity of Collichthys lucida. *b*, air-bladder; *l*, liver; *s*, stomach; *epp* and *ipp*, external and internal laminæ of peritoneum parietale; *epv* and *ipv*, external and internal laminæ of peritoneum viscerale; *dv*, dorsal air-vessels; *vv*, ventral air-vessels.

processes in front or behind (Fig. 61). The families of *Sciænidæ* and *Polynemidæ* possess air-bladders with a most extraordinary development of appendages rising from each side of the air-bladder. In the Sciænoid (Fig. 63) fifty-two branches issue from each side, each branch being bifurcate and bearing smaller appendages. In *Pogonias chromis* (Fig. 64) the sides of the anterior half is provided with irregular broad-fringed appendages, the hindmost of which communicates by a narrow duct with the posterior extremity of the air-bladder. In *Collichthys lucida* (Fig. 62) twenty-five appendages issue from each side; the anterior ones are directed towards the front, but the lateral assume a more posterior direction, the nearer they are to the posterior extremity of the air-bladder, where they form an assemblage giving the appearance of a cauda equina. All these appendages soon bifurcate in a dorsal and ventral stem; these stems bifurcate again and again, and either terminate after the first or second bifurcation or are so far prolonged as to reach the median line of the ventral and dorsal sides, anastomosing with the branches of the other side. The branches being enveloped in laminæ of the peritonæum, form a dorsal and ventral sac of beautiful appearance, caused by the regular arrangement of the air-vessels. The dorsal sac is situated between the air-bladder and the roof of the abdominal cavity without being attached to the latter. The ventral sac receives within its cavity the intestine, liver, and ovaries.—A peculiar mechanism has been observed in the air-bladder of the *Ophidiidæ*, the anterior portion of which can be prolonged by the contraction of two muscles attached to its anterior extremity, with or without the addition of a small bone.

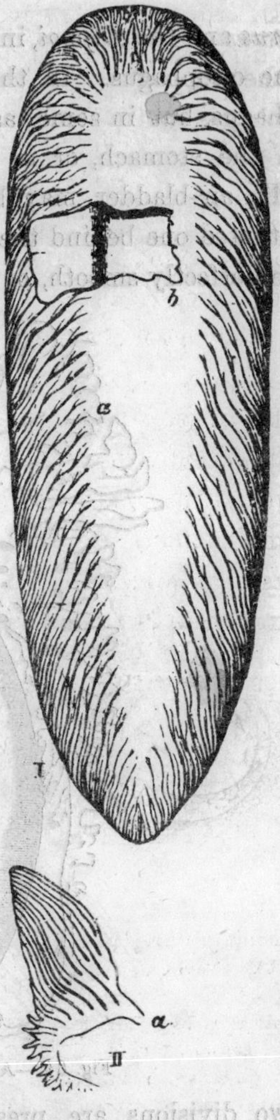

Fig. 63.—Air-bladder of a Sciænoid.
I. Visceral surface opened at *b*, to show openings of the lateral branches.
II. Isolated lateral branch; *a*, its opening into the cavity of the air-bladder.

Air-bladders with a pneumatic duct are found in Ganoids and Physostomes, the duct entering the dorsal side of the intestinal tract, with the exception of *Polyp terus* and the *Dipnoi*, in which it enters on the ventral side of the œsophagus. In the majority the orifice is in the œsophagus, but in some, as in *Acipenser*, in the cardiac portion of the stomach, or in its blind sac, as in many Clupeoids. The air-bladder may be single, or consist of two divisions situated one behind the other (Fig. 52); its inner surface may be perfectly smooth, or form manifold pouches and cells. If

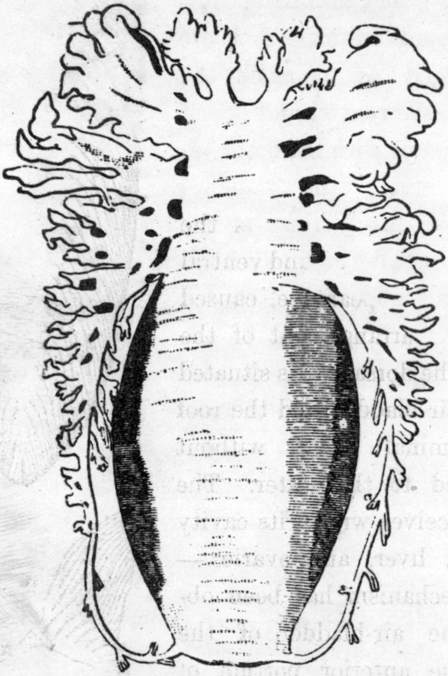

Fig. 64.—Air-bladder of Pogonias chromis.

two divisions are present the anterior possesses a middle elastic membrane which is absent in the posterior; each division has a muscular layer, by which it can be separately compressed, so that part of the contents of the posterior may be driven into the elastic anterior division, and *vice versa.* The posterior division being provided with the ductus pneumaticus does not require the elasticity of the anterior.

Some Siluroids possess a peculiar apparatus for voluntarily exercising a pressure upon the air-bladder. From the first vertebra a process takes its origin on each side, expanding at its end into a large round plate; this is applied to the side of the air-bladder, and by pressing upon it expels the air through the duct; the small muscle moving the plate rises from the skull.

The connection of the air-bladder with the organ of hearing in some Physostomes has been described above, p. 117.

In the modifications of the air-bladder, hitherto mentioned, the chief and most general function is a mechanical one; this organ serves to regulate the specific gravity of the fish, to aid it in maintaining a particular level in the water, in rising or sinking, in raising or depressing the front part of its body as occasion may serve. Yet a secretion of gas from the blood into its cavity must take place; and if this be so, it is not at all impossible that also an exchange of gases between the two kinds of blood is effected by means of the extraordinary development of *retia mirabilia* in many air-bladders.

In all fishes the arteries of the air-bladder take their origin from the aorta or the system of the aorta, and its veins return either to the portal, or vertebral, or hepatic veins; like the other organs of the abdominal cavity it receives arterial blood and returns venous blood. However, in many fishes the arteries as well as veins break up below the inner membrane into *retia mirabilia* in various ways. The terminal ramifications of the arteries may dissolve into fan-like tufts of capillaries over almost every part of the inner surface, as in Cyprinoids. Or these tufts of radiating capillaries are more localised at various places, as in *Esocidæ;* or the tufts are so aggregated as to form gland-like, *red bodies,* the capillaries reuniting into larger vessels, which again ramify freely round the border of the red body; the red bodies are formed not only by minute arteries but also by minute veins, both freely anastomosing with its kind, and being inextricably inter-

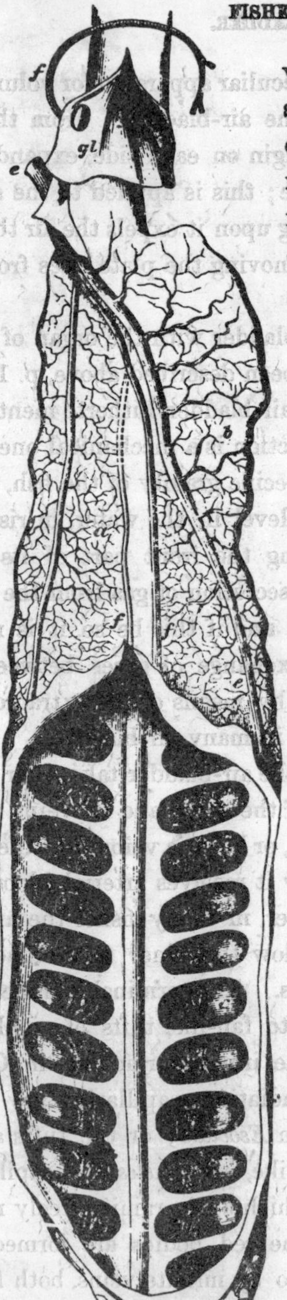

Fig. 65.—Lung of Ceratodus opened in its lower half to show its cellular pouches. *a*, Right half; *b*, Left half; *c*, Cellular pouches; *e*, Vena pulmonalis; *f*, Arterial blood-vessel; *oe*, Œsophagus opened, to show glottis (*gl.*)

woven. The rest of the inner surface of the air-bladder receives its blood, not from the red bodies, but from normally ramifying vessels. This kind of rete mirabile or "vaso-ganglion" is found in the Perch and Gadoids; it is generally distributed in closed air-bladders, but also sometimes observed in air-bladders with pneumatic duct. In *Anguilla* and *Conger* two similar vaso-ganglia are situated at the sides of the opening of the pneumatic duct.

Whilst the air-bladders of some *Ganoids*, anatomically as well as functionally, closely adhere to the Teleosteous type, that of *Amia* is more cellular and lung-like in its interior than the Teleosteous air-bladder, and *Polypterus* approaches the Dipnoi not only in having a laterally divided air-bladder but also in its pneumatic duct entering the *ventral* side of the œsophagus. The air-bladder of the *Dipnoi* possesses still more the anatomical characteristics of a lung and assumes its functions, though, as it co-exists with gills, only periodically or in an auxiliary manner. The ductus pneumaticus is a membranous bronchus, entering the ventral side of the œsophagus, and provided at its entrance with a *glottis.* In *Ceratodus* (Fig. 65) the lung is still a single cavity, but with a symmetrical arrangement of its internal pouches; it has no pulmonal artery, but receives branches from the *arteria cœliaca.* Finally, in *Lepidosiren* and *Protopterus* the lung is completely divided into lateral halves, and by its cellular structure approaches most nearly that of a reptile; it is supplied with venous blood by a true pulmonary artery.

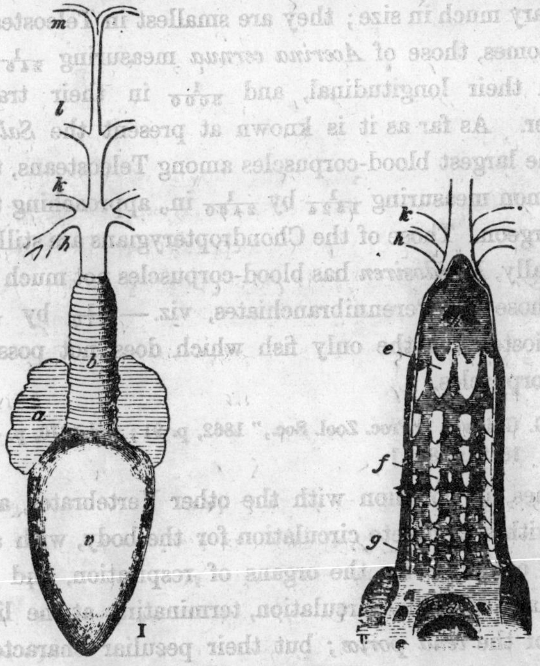

Fig. 66.—Heart of Lepidosteus osseus.

I. External aspect. II. Conus arteriosus opened.

a, Atrium; *b*, Conus arteriosus; *v*, Ventricle; *h*, Branchial artery for 3d and 4th gill; *k*, for the second; *l*, for the first; *m*, branch for the opercular gill; *d*, Single valve at the base of the conus; *e-g*, Transverse rows of Ganoid valves.

CHAPTER X.

ORGANS OF CIRCULATION.

The *Blood-corpuscles* of fishes are, with one exception, of an elliptic shape; this exception is *Petromyzon*, which possesses circular, flat, or slightly biconvex blood-corpuscles. They vary much in size; they are smallest in Teleosteans and Cyclostomes, those of *Acerina cernua* measuring $\frac{1}{2461}$ of an inch in their longitudinal, and $\frac{1}{3000}$ in their transverse diameter. As far as it is known at present the *Salmonidæ* have the largest blood-corpuscles among Teleosteans, those of the salmon measuring $\frac{1}{1524}$ by $\frac{1}{2460}$ in., approaching those of the Sturgeon. Those of the Chondropterygians are still larger, and finally, *Lepidosiren* has blood-corpuscles not much smaller than those of Perennibranchiates, viz.—$\frac{1}{570}$ by $\frac{1}{941}$ in. Branchiostoma is the only fish which does not possess red blood-corpuscles.

[See G. Gulliver, "Proc. Zool. Soc.," 1862, p. 91; and 1870, p. 844; and 1872, p. 833.]

Fishes, in common with the other Vertebrates, are provided with a complete circulation for the body, with another equally complete for the organs of respiration, and with a particular abdominal circulation, terminating at the liver by means of the *vena portæ;* but their peculiar character consists in this, that the branchial circulation alone is provided at its base with a muscular apparatus or *heart*, corresponding to the right half of the heart of Mammalia and Birds.

The *Heart* is situated between the branchial and abdominal cavities, between the two halves of the scapulary arch, rarely farther behind, as in *Symbranchidæ*. It is enclosed in a *pericardium*, generally entirely separated from the abdominal cavity by a diaphragma, which is, in fact, the anterior portion of the peritoneum, strengthened by aponeurotic fibres. However, in some fishes there is a communication between the pericardial and peritoneal sacs, viz. in the Chondropterygians and Acipenser, whilst in the Myxinoids the pericardial sac is merely a continuation of the peritoneum.

The heart is, relatively to the size of the body, very small, and consists of three divisions: the *atrium*, with a large *sinus venosus* into which the veins enter; the *ventricle;* and a conical hollow swelling at the beginning of the arterial system, the structure of which forms one of the most important characters used in the classification of fishes. In all *Palæichthyes* (Figs. 66 and 67) this swelling is still a division of the pulsating heart, being provided with a thick muscular stratum; it is not separated from the ventricle by two valves opposite to each other, but its interior is fitted with a plurality of valves, arranged in transverse series more or less numerous in the various groups of *Palæichthyes*. *Lepidosiren* and *Protopterus* offer an example of a modification of this valvular arrangement, their valves being longitudinal, each valve in fact being formed by the confluence of several smaller ones situated behind one another. This Palæichthyan type is called *conus arteriosus*.

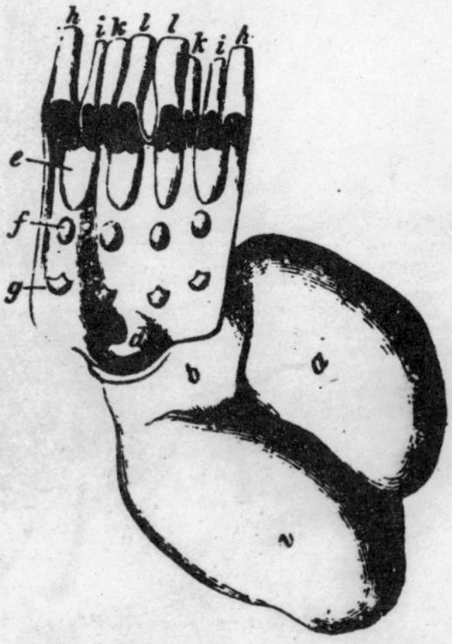

Fig. 67.—Heart of Ceratodus. *a*, Atrium; *b*, Conus arteriosus; *d*, Papillary valve within the conus; *e-g*, Transverse rows of Ganoid valves; *h*, *i*, Anterior arcus aortæ; *k*, *l*, Posterior arcus aortæ; *v*, Ventricle.

In Cyclostomes and Teleosteans (Fig. 68) the enlargement

is a swelling of the artery, without muscular stratum and without contractility; with the exception of the Myxinoids its walls are thick, fibrous, with many trabeculæ and pouches, but it has no valves in its interior, and is separated from the ventricle by two valves opposite to each other. This Teleostean type is called *bulbus aortæ*.

The sinus venosus sends the whole of the venous blood by a single orifice of its anterior convexity into the atrium;

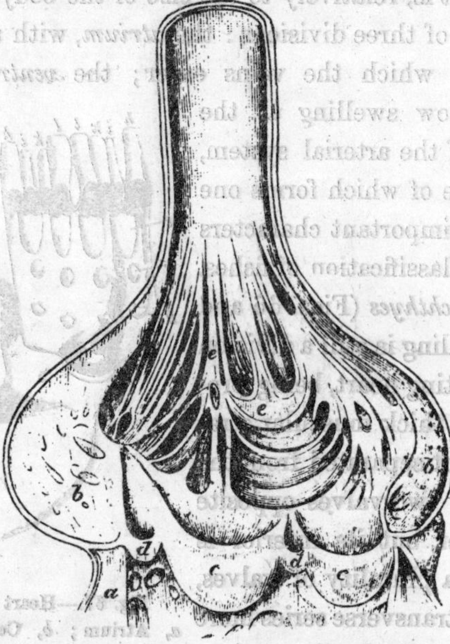

Fig. 68.—Bulbus aortæ of Xiphias gladius, opened.
a, Section through part of the wall of ventricle; *b*, Section through the bulbus; *c*, Teleosteous valves of the ostium arteriosum; *d*, Accessory valves, of rudimentary nature and inconstant; *e*, Trabeculæ carneæ of the bulbus.

two thin membranous valvules turned towards the atrium prevent the blood from re-entering the sinus. A pair of other valves between atrium and ventricle have the same function. The walls of the ventricle are robust, and, internally, it is furnished with powerful fleshy trabeculæ.

The bulbus or conus arteriosus is prolonged into the branchial artery which soon divides, sending off a branch to each branchial arch. On returning from the respiratory organ the branchial veins assume the structure and functions of arteries. Several branches are sent off to different portions of the head and to the heart, but the main trunks unite to form the great artery which carries the blood to the viscera and all the parts of the trunk and tail, and which, therefore, represents the *aorta* of higher animals.

In the majority of Teleosteans the *aorta* has proper walls formed by its own membranes, but in the Sturgeons it is independent at its commencement only, and replaced by a canal formed by hæmal elements of the vertebral column, and clothed inside with a perichondrium. In many Chondropterygians and some Teleosteans (*Esox, Clupea, Silurus*), the aorta possesses its own firm membranes along its ventral side, dorsally being protected by a very thin membrane only, attached to the concavity of the centra of the vertebræ.

The circulatory system of *Branchiostoma* and of the *Dipnoi* shows essential differences from that of other fishes.

Branchiostoma is the only fish which does not possess a muscular heart, several cardinal portions of its vascular system being contractile. A great vein extends forwards along the caudal region below the notochord, and exhibits contractility in a forward direction; it is bent anteriorly, passing into another tube-like pulsatile trunk, the branchial heart, which runs along the middle of the base of the pharynx, sending off branches on each side to the branchiæ; each of these branches has a small contractile dilatation (*bulbillus*) at its base. The two anterior branches pass directly into the aorta, the others are branchial arteries, the blood of which returns by branchial veins emptying into the aorta. The blood of the intestinal veins is collected in a contractile tube, the portal vein, situated below the intestine, and distributed over the rudimentary liver. Of all other fishes, only in *Myxinoids* the portal vein is contractile. All the blood-corpuscles of *Branchiostoma* are colourless and without nucleus.

In *Dipnoi* a rudimentary division of the heart into a right and left partition has been observed; this is limited to the ventricle in *Ceratodus*, but in *Lepidosiren* and *Protopterus* an incomplete septum has been observed in the atrium also. All Dipnoi have a pulmonal vein, which enters the atrium by a separate opening, provided with a valve. The pulmonal artery rises in *Lepidosiren* and *Protopterus* from an arch of the aorta, but in *Ceratodus* it is merely a subordinate branch, rising from the *Arteria cœliaca*.

CHAPTER XI.

URINARY ORGANS.

In *Branchiostoma* no urinary organs have been found.

In Myxinoids these organs are of a very primitive structure: they consist of a pair of ducts, extending from the urogenital porus through the abdominal cavity. Each duct sends off at regular intervals from its outer side a short wide branch (the uriniferous tube), which communicates by a narrow opening with a blind sac. At the bottom of this sac there is a small vaso-ganglion (*Malpighian corpuscle*), by which the urine is secreted.

In the Lampreys the kidneys form a continuous gland-like body, with irregular detached small portions. The ureters coalesce before they terminate in the urogenital papilla.

In Chondropterygians the kidneys occupy the posterior half or two-thirds of the back of the abdominal cavity, without the sac of the peritoneum (as in all fishes) which forms a firm tendinous horizontal septum. The kidneys of the two sides are never confluent, and generally show a convoluted or lobulated surface. The ureters are short; each is dilated into a pouch, and communicating with its fellow terminates by a single urethra (which also receives the vasa deferentia) behind the end of the rectum in the large common cloaca.

In Ganoids the kidneys occupy a similar position as in Chondropterygians, but these fishes differ considerably with regard to the termination and the arrangement of the ends of the urogenital ducts. The Dipnoi possess a cloaca. In *Ceratodus* the ureters open into it by a common opening, separate from the genital opening; and no closed urinary bladder has been developed. *Lepidosiren* has a small urinary bladder; the ureters do not communicate directly with it, but terminate separately on small papillæ in the dorsal compartment of the cloaca. The other Ganoids lack a cloaca, and the urogenital opening is behind the vent as in Teleosteans. In all the genital and urinary ducts coalesce towards their end. The Sturgeons have no urinary bladder, whilst it is present in *Amia*, the ureters opening separately into it.

The *kidneys* of Teleosteans are situated likewise without the peritoneal cavity, immediately below some part of the vertebral column, and vary exceedingly with regard to form and extent. Sometimes they reach from the skull to between the muscles of the tail, sometimes they are limited to the foremost part of the abdominal cavity (in advance of the diaphragm), but generally their extent corresponds to that of the abdominal portion of the vertebral column. Frequently they are irregular on their dorsal surface, filling every available recess, flat, attenuated on the sides, more or less coalescent towards the middle; in other fishes they are more compact bodies. The ureters terminate, either separate or united, in a urinary bladder, varying in shape, which opens by a short urethra behind the vent. The urinary opening may be separate or confluent with that of the genital ducts, and is frequently placed on a more or less prominent papilla (*papilla urogenitalis*). If separate, the urinary opening is behind the genital; and if a papilla is developed, its extremity is perforated by the urethra, the genital opening being situated nearer the base. A few Teleosteans show an arrangement similar to that of Chondropterygians and Dipnoi, the urogenital openings being in the posterior wall of the rectum (*Symbranchidæ*, *Pediculati*, and some *Plectognathi*).

CHAPTER XII.

ORGANS OF REPRODUCTION.

ALL fishes are *dioecious*, or of distinct sex. Instances of so-called *hermaphroditism* are, with the exception of *Serranus*, abnormal individual peculiarities, and have been observed in the Cod-fish, some Pleuronectidæ, and in the Herring. Either the generative organ of one side was found to be male, that of the other female; or the organ of one or both sides was observed to have been developed partly into an ovary partly into a testicle. In the European species of Serranus a testicle-like body is attached to the lower part of the ovary; but many specimens of this genus are undoubtedly males, having normally developed testicles only.

The majority of fishes are oviparous, comparatively few viviparous; the embryos being developed either in the ovarium or in some dilated portion of the oviduct. In viviparous fishes actual copulation takes place, and the males of most of them are provided with copulatory or intromittent organs. In oviparous fishes the generative products are, during sexual excitement, discharged into the water, a very small quantity of semen being sufficient for effectual impregnation of a number of ova dispersed in a considerable quantity of water; circumstances which render *artificial impregnation* more practicable than in any other class of animals.

In *Branchiostoma* the generative organs occupy the ventral side of the abdominal cavity, into which they discharge their contents. No ducts are developed in either sex.

In the *Cyclostomes* the generative organ is single, and fixed to or suspended from the median line of the back of the visceral cavity by a duplicature of the peritoneum (*mesoarium*); the testicle and ovary being distinguishable by their contents only. These escape by dehiscence of the cells or capsules and rupture of the peritoneal covering into the abdominal cavity, and are expelled by reciprocal pressure of the intertwined sexes through the *porus genitalis*, which is sunk between two labia of the skin in *Myxine*, and produced into a long papilla in Petromyzon.

The ova of the Lampreys are small, globular, like those of Teleosteans. Those of Myxine have a very peculiar shape when mature; they are of an oval form, about 15 millimetres long and 8 millimetres broad, enveloped in a horny case, which at each end is provided with a bundle of short threads, each thread ending in a triple hook. Whilst in the mesoarial fold the eggs are attached to one another by means of these hooks, and after being expelled they probably fix themselves by the same means to other objects. As in all fishes producing ova of large size, the number of ova matured in one season is but small.

Fig. 69.—Ovum of Myxine glutinosa, enlarged.

In *Teleosteans* the generative organs are comparatively large. In some families the ovaries are without closed covering and without oviducts, as in *Salmonidæ, Galaxiidæ, Notopteridæ, Murænidæ*, and others. The surface of such an open ovary—as, for instance, that of the Salmon—is transversely plaited, the ova being developed in capsules in the stroma of the laminæ; after rupture of the capsules the mature ova drop into the abdominal cavity, and are expelled by the porus genitalis. The ovaries of the other Teleosteans are closed sacs, continued into oviducts. Frequently such ovaries coalesce into a single body, or one in which the division is effected internally only by a more or less complete septum. Fixed by a mesoarium, the ovaries occupy generally a position outwards of the intestine or air-bladder; their form varies as well as the thickness and firmness of their covering, which frequently is an extremely thin transparent membrane. The inner surface of the ovarian sac is transversely or longitudinally plaited or covered with fringes, on which the ova are developed, as in the open ovaries. In the viviparous Teleosteans the embryons are likewise developed within the ovary, notably in the *Embiotocidæ*, many *Blenniidæ*, and *Cyprinodontidæ*, *Sebastes viviparus*, etc.

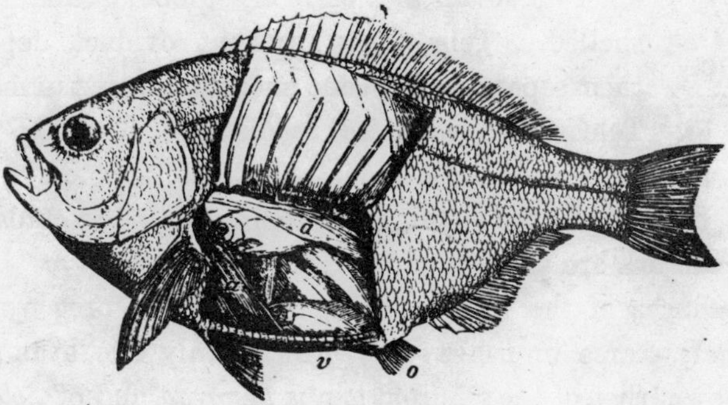

Fig. 70.—Ditrema argenteum, with fully developed young, ready for expulsion by the genital orifice, *o*; *a*, folds of the ovarian sac; *v*, vent.

Among the Cyprinodonts the end of the oviduct is attached to the anterior anal rays, which are modified into supports of its termination. In *Rhodeus* the oviduet is periodically prolonged into a long oviferous tube, by means of which the female deposits her ova into the shells of living Bivalves.

The *ova* of Teleosteous Fishes are extremely variable in size, quite independently of the size of the parent species. The ova of large and small individuals of the same species, of course, do not differ in size; but, on the whole larger individuals produce a greater number of ova than smaller ones of the same species. The larger the size of the ova is in a species, the smaller is the number produced during one season. The ova of the Eel are almost microscopic. The small sized roe in the Herring, Lump-fish, Halibut, and Cod-fish, have been estimated at respectively 25,000, 155,000, 3,500,000, and 9,344,000. Larger in size and fewer in number are those of *Antennarius*, *Salmo*, *Aspredo*, *Lophobranchs*, etc. Comparatively largest are those of *Gastrosteus*; and the Siluroid genus *Arius*, the males of which take care of their progeny, produces ova from 5 to 10 millimeters in diameter. The ova of all Teleosteans are perfectly globular and soft-shelled. Teleosteans without oviduct, deposit them separated from one another; whilst in many Teleosteans with an oviduct the ova are enveloped in a glutinous substance, secreted by its glands, swelling in the water and forming lumps or cords, in which the ova are aggregated.

Fig. 71. Ovum of Arius boakii (Ceylon), showing embryo. Nat. size.

Instances of the female taking care of her progeny are extremely scarce in fishes. At present only two examples are known, that of the Siluroid genus *Aspredo*, and of *Solenostoma*. In the former, during the time of propagation, the integuments of the lower side of the flat trunk of the female assume a soft and spongy texture. After having deposited the eggs, the female attaches them to, and presses them into, the spongy integument, by merely lying over them. She carries them on her belly, as the Surinam Toad (*Pipa*) carries her ova on the back. When the eggs are hatched the excrescence on the skin disappears, and the abdomen becomes as smooth as before. In *Solenostoma* the inner side of the long and broad ventral fins coalesces with the integuments of the body, a large pouch being formed for the reception of the eggs. There is a peculiar provision for the retention of the eggs in the sac, and probably for the attachment of the embryo.

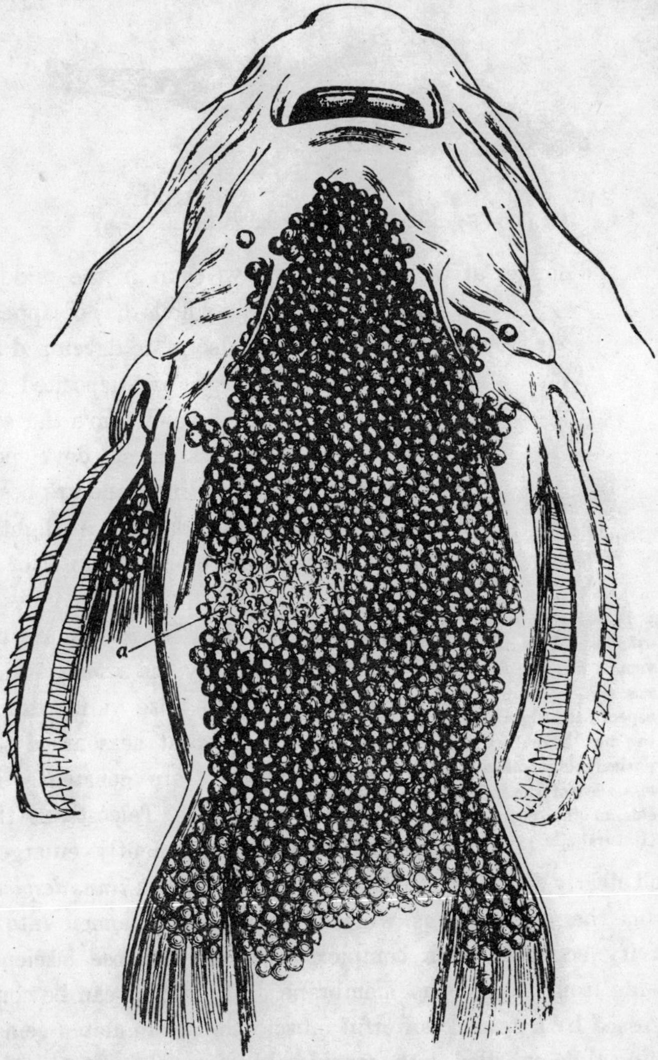

Fig. 72.—Abdomen of *Aspredo batrachus*, with the ova attached; at *a*, the ova are removed, to show the spongy structure of the skin, and the processes filling the interspaces between the ova. (Natural size.)

The inner walls of the sac are lined with long filaments,

arranged in series along the ventral rays, and more nume-

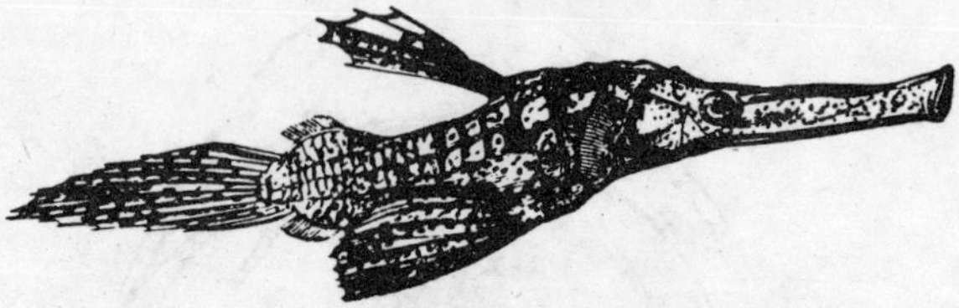

Fig. 73.—Solenostoma cyanopterum ♀ (Indian Ocean).

rous and longer at the base of the rays than in the middle of their length, behind which they disappear entirely. They are also more developed in examples in which eggs are deposited in the sac than in those which have the sac empty. The filaments most developed have a length of half an inch, and are beset with mamilliform appendages. A slightly undulated canal runs along the interior of the filament.

Fig. 74.—Pouch with ova, formed by the ventral fins of *Solenostoma*. Lower aspect; the edges of the fins have been pushed aside to allow of a view of the inside of the pouch. (Natural size.)

The *Testicles* of the *Teleosteans* are always paired, and occupy the same position as the ovaries. Their size varies extraordinarily at the different seasons of the year. Vasa deferentia are constant. In the males of viviparous Teleosteans the urogenital papilla is frequently enlarged, and clearly serves as an intromittent organ. In *Clinus despicillatus* the vas deferens widens within the abdomen into a cavity occupied by a complex network of loose fasciculi, rising from the mucous membrane. The cavity can be compressed by a special powerful muscle, the accumulated semen being thus expelled with considerable force through the narrow aperture of the penis. In many Cyprinodonts the vas deferens runs along the anterior anal rays, which may be thickened, and prolonged into a long slender organ.

Many Teleostei take care of their progeny, but with the

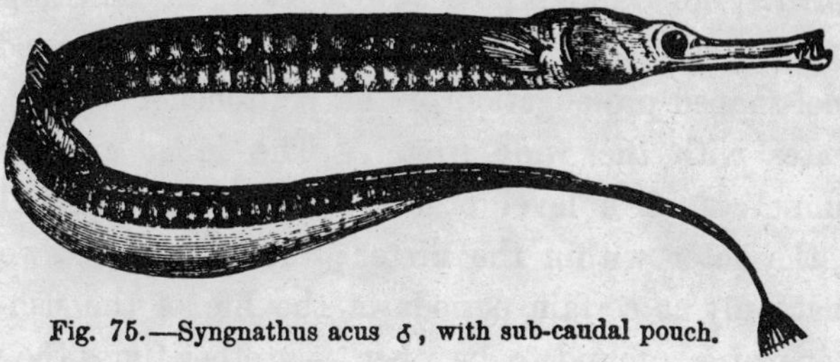

Fig. 75.—Syngnathus acus ♂, with sub-caudal pouch.

exception of *Aspredo* and *Solenostoma*, mentioned above (p 160), it is the male on which this duty devolves. In some. as in *Cottus, Gastrosteus, Cyclopterus, Antennarius, Ophiocephalus Callichthys*, the male constructs with more or less skill a nest, and jealously guards the ova deposited in it by the female. The male of some species of *Arius* carries the ova (Fig. 71) about with him in his capacious pharynx. The species of *Chromis*, inhabiting the sea of Galilee, are said to take care of their ova in the same manner. And, finally, in the Lophobranchs, nature has aided this instinct by the development of a pouch on the abdomen or lower side of the tail. In the Syngnathidæ this pouch is formed by a fold of the skin developed from each side of the trunk and tail, the free margins of the fold being firmly united in the median line, whilst the eggs are being hatched in the inside of the pouch. In *Hippocampus* the pouch is completely closed, with a narrow anterior opening.

Fig. 76.—Sub-caudal pouch of Syngnathus acus, with the young, ready to leave the pouch. One side of the membrane of the pouch is pushed aside to admit of a view of its interior. (Natural size.)

The genital organs of *Ganoids* show similar diversity of structure as those of Teleosteans, but on the whole they approach the Batrachian type. The ovaries are not closed, except in *Lepidosiren;* all Ganoids possess oviducts. In the Sturgeons the oviduct as well as the vas deferens is represented by a funnel-shaped prolongation of the peritoneum, which communicates with the wide ureter. The inner aperture of the funnel is on a level of the middle of the testicle or ovary, the outer within the ureter; and it is a noteworthy fact that only at certain periods of the life of the fish this outer aperture is found to be open,—at other times the peritoneal funnel appears as a closed blind sac within the ureter. The mode of passage of the semen into the funnel is not known.

In *Polypterus* and *Amia,* proper oviducts, with abdominal apertures in about the middle of the abdominal cavity, are developed; they coalesce with the ureters close to the common urogenital aperture.

In *Ceratodus* (Fig. 77), a long convoluted oviduct extends to the foremost limit of the abdominal cavity, where it opens by a slit at a considerable distance from the front end of the long ovary; this aperture is closed in sexually immature specimens. The oviducts unite close to their common opening in the cloaca. During their passage through the oviduct the ova receive a gelatinous covering secreted by its mucous membrane. This is probably also the case in *Lepidosiren,* which possesses a convoluted oviduct with secretory glands in the middle of its length. The oviduct begins with a funnel-shaped dilatation, and terminates in a wide pouch, which posteriorly communicates with that of the other side, both opening by a common aperture behind the urinary bladder.

The ova of Ganoids, as far as they are known at present, are small, but enveloped in a gelatinous substance. In the Sturgeon have been counted as many as 7,635,200. Those of *Lepidosteus* seem to be the largest, measuring 5 millimetres in diameter with their envelope, and 3 millimetres without it. They are deposited singly, like those of Newts.

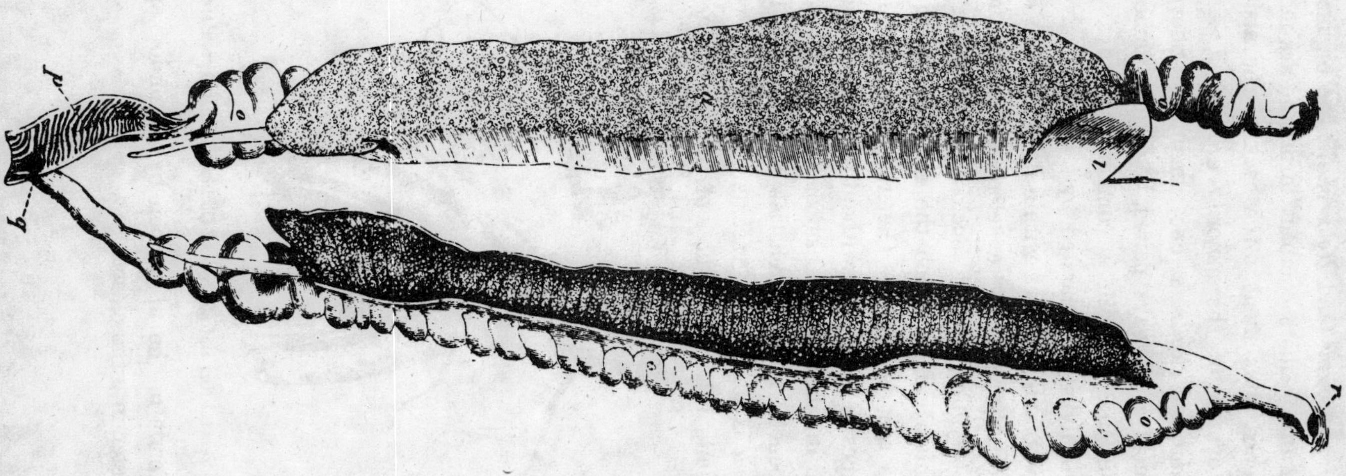

Fig. 77.—Ovaries of Ceratodus.

a, Right ovary shown from the inner surface, which is covered by the peritoneum; *a′*, Left ovary, showing its outer surface; *l*, Portion of liver; *o*, Oviduct; *p*, the lower part of the oviduct is opened to show the folds of its inner membrane; *q*, Opening of the left oviduct into the right; *r*, Abdominal orifice of the oviduct.

In *Chondropterygians* (and *Holocephali*) the organs of reproduction assume a more compact form, and are more free from a lengthened attachment to the back of the abdominal cavity. The ovaries of the majority are paired, single in the *Carchariidæ* and *Scylliidæ*, one remaining undeveloped. But the oviducts are always paired, beginning immediately behind the diaphragma with a common aperture. They consist of two divisions, separated by a circular valve; the upper is narrow, and provided within its coats with a gland which secretes the leathery envelope in which most of the Chondropterygian ova are enclosed; the lower forms the uterine dilatation, in which the embryoes of the viviparous species are developed. Generally the vitelline sac of the embryoes is free, and without connection with the uterus, which in these cases has merely the function of a protecting pouch; but in Carcharias and Mustelus lævis a *placenta uterina* is formed, the vascular walls of the vitelline sac forming plaits fitting into those of the membrane of the

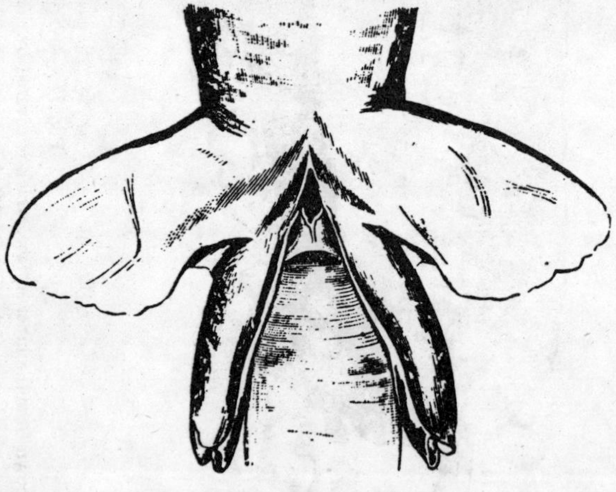

Fig. 78.—Ventral fins and claspers of Chiloscyllium trispeculare.

uterus. The ends of the uteri open by a common aperture behind the ureter into the cloaca.

The testicles are always paired, rounded, and situated in the anterior part of the abdominal cavity, covered by the liver. *Vasa efferentia* pass the semen into a much-convoluted *epididymis*, which is continued into the *vas deferens;* this, at the commencement of its course, is spirally wound, but becomes straight behind, and has its end dilated into a seminal reservoir. It opens with the urethra in a papilla within the cloaca.

The so-called *claspers* of Chondropterygians (Fig. 78) are characteristic of all male individuals. They are semi-ossified appendages of the pubie, with which they are movably joined, and special muscles serve to regulate their movements. Sometimes they are armed with hook-like osseous excrescences (*Selache*). They are irregularly longitudinally convoluted, and, when closely adpressed to each other, form a canal open at their extremity. A gland, abundantly discharging a secretion during the season of propagation, is situated at, and opens into, the base of the canal. It is still doubtful whether the generally-adopted opinion that their function consists in holding the female during copulation is correct, or whether they are not rather an intromittent organ, the canal of which not only conducts the secretion of their proper gland but also the impregnating fluid.

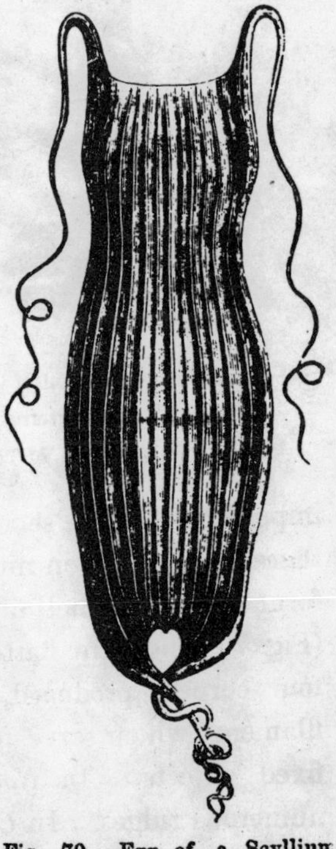

Fig. 79.—Egg of a Scyllium from Magelhan's Straits (? Sc. chilense). Natural size.

The ova of the oviparous Chondropterygians are large and few in number; they are successively impregnated, and the impregnation must take place before they are invested with a tough leathery envelope which would be

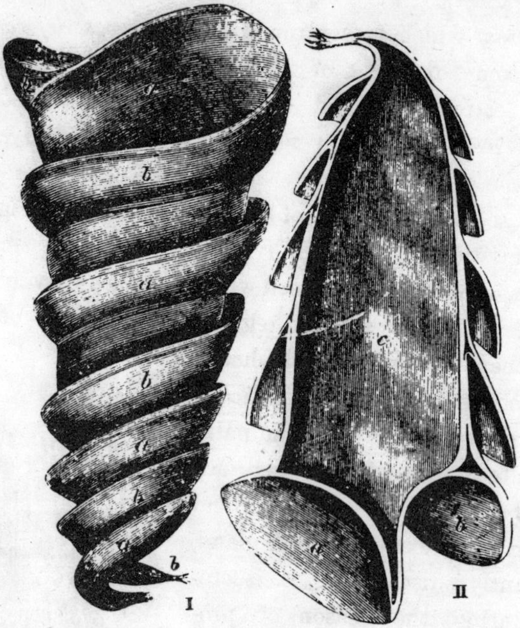

Fig. 80.—Egg-shell of Cestracion philippi, half natural size, linear.
I. External view. II. Vertical section.
a, One spiral ridge ; *b*, The other spiral ridge ; *c*, Cavity for the ovum.

impenetrable to the semen, that is, before they enter the uterus; therefore, copulation must take place in all these fishes. The form of the egg-shell differs in the various genera ; generally (Fig. 79) they are flattened, quadrangular, with each of the four corners produced, and frequently prolonged into long filaments which serve for the attachment of the ova to other fixed objects. In *Notidanus* the surfaces are crossed by numerous ridges. In *Cestracion* (Fig. 80) the egg is pyriform, with two broad ridges or plates, wound edgewise round it, the two ridges forming five spires. The eggs of *Callorhynchus*

(Fig. 81) have received a protective resemblance to a broad-leaved fucus, forming a long depressed ellipse, with a plicated and fringed margin.

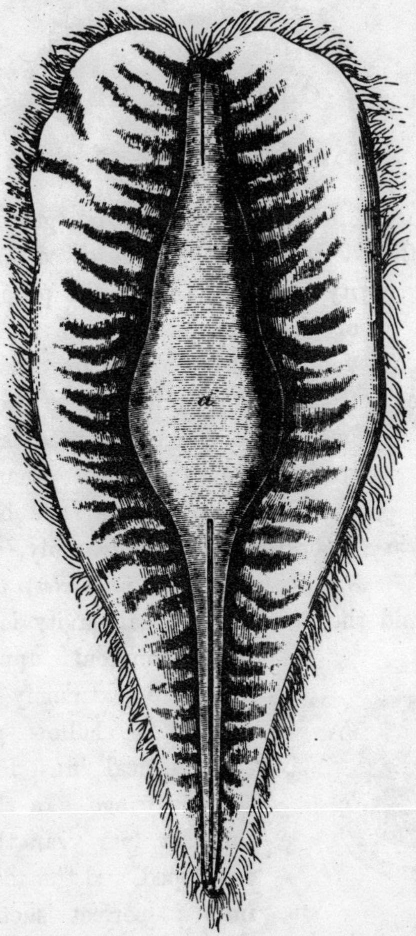

Fig. 81.—Egg of Callorhynchus antarcticus.
a, Cavity for the embryo.

CHAPTER XIII.

GROWTH AND VARIATION OF FISHES.

CHANGES of form normally accompanying growth (after absorption of the vitelline sac) are observed in all fishes; but in the majority they affect only the proportional size of the various parts of the body. In young fishes the eyes are constantly larger than in adult relatively to the size of the head; and again, the head is larger relatively to that of the body. Changes amounting to metamorphosis have been hitherto observed in *Petromyzon* only. In the larval condition (*Ammocœtes*) the head is very small, and the toothless buccal cavity is surrounded by a semicircular upper lip. The eyes are extremely small, hidden in a shallow groove; and the vertical fins form a continuous fringe. In the course of three or four years the teeth are developed, and the mouth changes into a perfect suctorial organ; the eyes grow; and the dorsal fin is divided into two divisions. In Malacopterygians and Anacanths the embryonal fringe from which the vertical fins are developed, is much longer per-

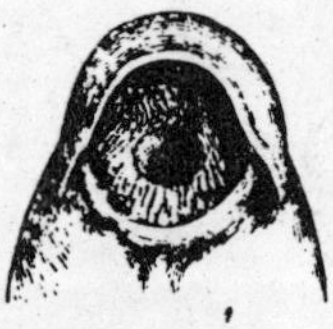

Fig. 82.—Mouth of Larva of Petromyzon branchialis.

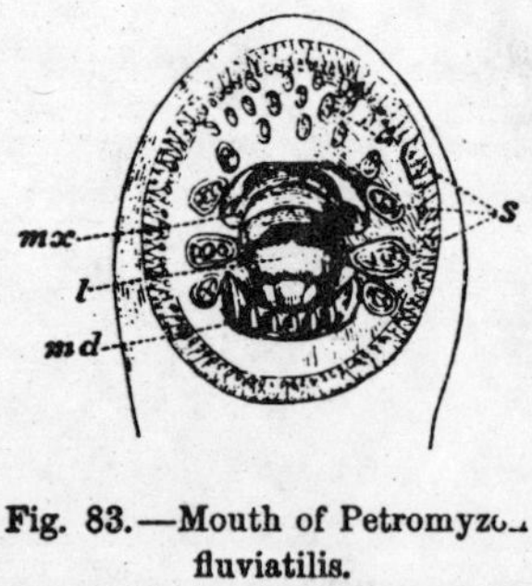

Fig. 83.—Mouth of Petromyzon fluviatilis.
mx, Maxillary tooth; *md*, Mandibulary tooth; *l*, Lingual tooth; *s*, Suctorial teeth.

sistent than in Acanthopterygians. A metamorphosis relating to the respiratory organs, as in Batrachians, is indicated in the class of Fishes by the external gills with which fœtal Plagiostomes (Fig. 58, p. 136) and the young of some Ganoids, viz. the *Protopterus* and *Polypterus*, are provided.

One of the most extraordinary changes by which, during growth, the form and position of several important organs are affected, occurs in Flat-fishes (*Pleuronectidæ*); their young are symmetrically formed, with a symmetrical mouth, and with one eye on each side, and, therefore, keep their body in a vertical position when swimming. As they grow they live more on the bottom, and their body, during rest, assumes a horizontal position; in consequence, the eye of the lower side moves towards the upper, which alone is coloured; and in many genera the mouth is twisted in the opposite direction, so that the bones, muscles, and teeth are much more developed on the blind side than on the coloured. In a great number of other *Teleostei* certain bones of the head show a very different form in the young state. Ossification proceeds in those bones in the direction of lines or radii which project in the form of spines or processes; as the interspaces between

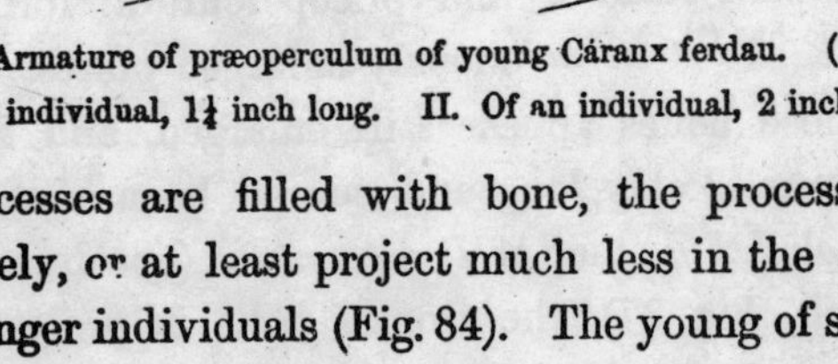

Fig. 84.—Armature of præoperculum of young Caranx ferdau. (Magnified.)
I. Of an individual, 1¼ inch long. II. Of an individual, 2 inches long.

these processes are filled with bone, the processes disappear entirely, or at least project much less in the older than in the younger individuals (Fig. 84). The young of some fishes may be armed with a long powerful præopercular or scapular spine, or show a serrature of which nothing remains in the adult fish except some ridges or radiating lines. These processes seem to serve as weapons of defence during a period in the life of the fish in which it needs them most. In not a few instances a portion of this armature is so much

Fig. 85.—Tholichthys osseus. Six times the natural size.

developed that the disappearance of its most projecting parts with the growth of the fish is not only due to its being surrounded by other bone, but, partially at least, caused by absorption. The *Carangidæ*, *Cyttidæ*, *Squamipinnes*, *Xiphiidæ*, offer instances of such remarkable changes. A fish, described as *Tholichthys osseus* (Fig. 85), is probably the young of a Cyttoid, the supra-scapula, humerus, and præoperculum forming enormously enlarged plates. In the fish Fig. 86 those bones appear still enlarged, and the frontals develop a remarkably long and curved horn above the orbit. In the *Tholichthys*-stage of *Pomacanthus* (specimens 10 millimetres long, Fig. 87), the frontal bone is prolonged into a straight lancet-shaped process, nearly half as long as the body; the suprascapular and præopercular processes cover

Fig. 86.—Tholichthys-stage of Heniochus (?).

and hide the dorsal and ventral fins. The plates attached to the shoulder-girdle remain persistent until the young fish

Fig. 87.—Tholichthys-stage of Pomacanthus (magn.) Atlantic.

has assumed the form of the adult; thus they are still visible in young *Chætodon citrinellus*, 30 millimetres long, in which the specific characters are already fully developed.—The Sword-fishes with ventral fins (*Histiophorus*) belong to the Teleosteans of the largest size; in young individuals, 9 millimetres long (Fig. 89), both jaws are produced, and armed with pointed teeth; the supra-orbital margin is ciliated; the parietal and præoperculum are prolonged into long spines; the dorsal and anal fins are a low fringe, and the ventrals make their appearance as a pair of short buds. When 14 millimetres long (Fig. 90) the young fish has still the same armature of the head, but the dorsal fin has become much higher, and the ventral

Fig. 88.—Young Chætodon citrinellus (30 mill. long).

filaments have grown to a great length. At a third stage,

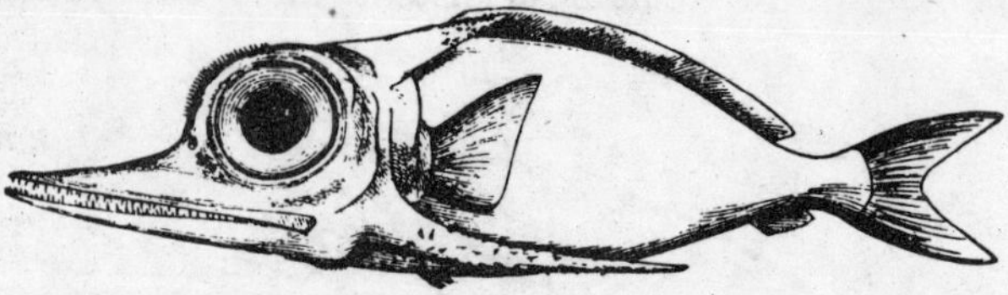

Fig. 89.—Young Sword-fish (Histiophorus), 9 mill. long. Atlantic. (Magn.)

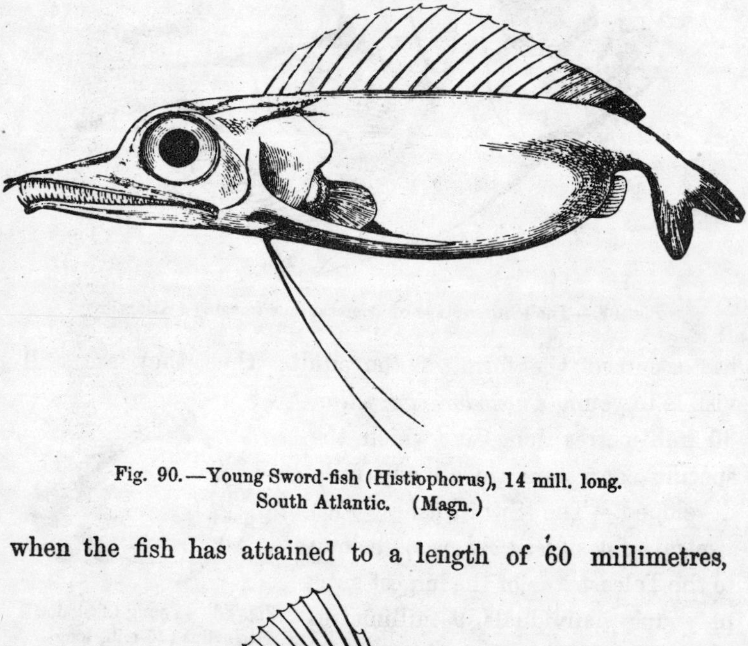

Fig. 90.—Young Sword-fish (Histiophorus), 14 mill. long. South Atlantic. (Magn.)

when the fish has attained to a length of 60 millimetres,

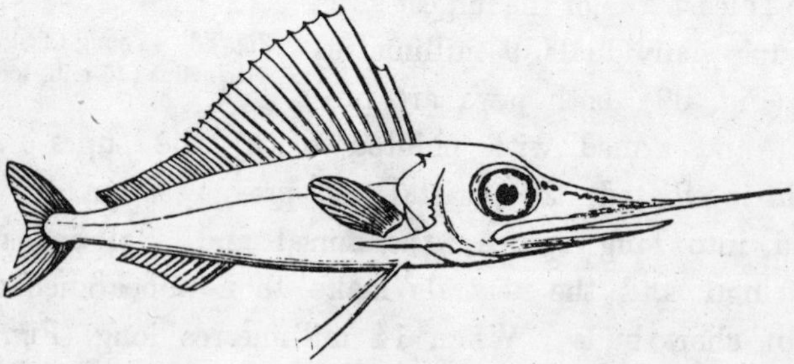

Fig. 91.—Young Sword-fish (Histiophorus), 60 mill. long. Mid-Atlantic.

the upper jaw is considerably prolonged beyond the lower,

losing its teeth; the spines of the head are shortened, and the fins assume nearly the shape which they retain in mature individuals. Young Sword-fishes without ventral fins (*Xiphias*) undergo similar changes; and, besides, their skin is covered with small rough excrescences longitudinally arranged, which continue to be visible after the young fish has assumed the form of the mature in other respects (Fig. 92).

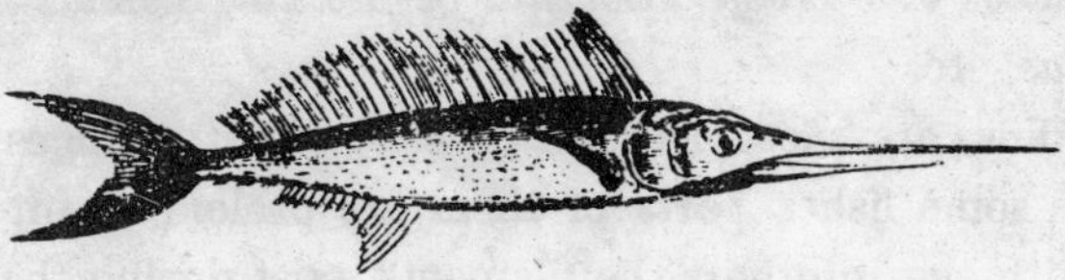

Fig. 92.—Xiphias gladius, young, about 8 inches long.

The Plectognaths show no less extraordinary changes: an extraordinary form taken in the South Atlantic, and named *Ostracion boops*, is considered by Lütken to be the young of a Sunfish (*Orthagoriscus*). In very young more advanced Sun-fishes (18 to 32 millimetres) the vertical diameter of the body exceeds, or is not much less than, the longitudinal; and small conical spines are scattered over its various parts. The caudal

Fig. 93.—"Ostracion boops" (much magnified).

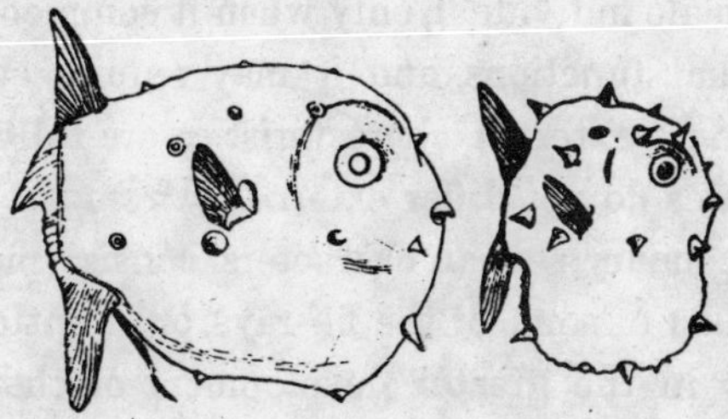

Fig. 94.—Young of Orthagoriscus, 18 and 32 mill. long. (Natural size.)

fin is developed long after the other vertical fins.

Similar changes take place in a number of other fishes, and in many cases the young are so different that they were described as distinct genera: thus *Priacantichthys* has proved to be the young of *Serranus*, *Rhynchichthys* that of *Holocentrum*, *Cephalacanthus* of *Dactylopterus*, *Dicrotus* of *Thyrsites*, *Nauclerus* of *Naucrates*, *Porthmeus* of *Chorinemus*, *Lampugus* of *Coryphœna*, *Acronurus* of *Acanthurus*, *Keris* of *Naseus*, *Porobronchus* of *Fierasfer*, *Couchia* of *Motella*, *Stomiasunculus* of *Stomias*, etc.

The fins are most frequently subject to changes; but, whilst in some fishes parts of them are prolonged into filaments with age, in others the filaments exist during the early life-periods only; whilst in some a part of the dorsal or the ventral fins is normally developed in the young only, in others those very parts are peculiar to the mature age. The integuments are similarly altered: in some species the young only has asperities on the skin, in others the young are smooth and the old have a tubercular skin; in some the young only have a hard bony head; in others (some Siluroids) the osseous carapace of the head and neck, as it appears in the adult, is more or less covered with soft skin whilst the fish is young.

In not a few fishes the external changes are in relation to the sexual development (*Callionymus*, many *Labyrinthici*, Cyprinodonts). These *secondary sexual differences* show themselves in the male individual, only when it commences to enter upon his sexual functions, and it may require two or more seasons before its external characteristics are fully developed. Immature males do not differ externally from the old female The male secondary sexual characters consist principally in the prolongation of some of the fin-rays, or of entire fins; and in *Salmonidœ* in the greater development of the jaw-bones. The coloration of the male is in many fishes much brighter and more variegated than that of the female, but in comparatively few permanent (as in some *Callionymus*, *Labrus mixtus*); generally it is acquired immediately before and during the season of propagation only, and lost afterwards. Another periodical change in the integuments, also due to sexual influence and peculiar to the male, is the excrescence of wart-like tubercles on the skin of many *Cyprinoids*; they are developed chiefly on the head, but sometimes extend over the whole body and all the fins.

With regard to size, it appears that in all Teleosteous fishes the female is larger than the male; in many Cyprinodonts the male may be only one-sixth or even less of the bulk of the female. The observations on the relative size of the sexes are few in Palæichthyes, but such as have been made tend to show that, if a difference exists at all, the male is generally the larger (*Lepidosteus*). In the Rays (*Raja*) the sexes, after they have attained maturity, differ in the development of dermal spines and the form of the teeth, the female being frequently much rougher than the male. There is much variation in this respect in the different species; but the males are constantly distinguished by an oblong patch of erectile clawlike spines on each pectoral fin, and by having the teeth (all, or only a portion) pointed, and not obtuse, like those of the females. In Sharks no secondary sexual differences have been observed; the male *Chimæridæ* (see Fig. 96, p. 184), possess a singular comblike cartilaginous appendage on the top of the head, which can be erected or depressed into a groove, both the appendage and the anterior part of the groove being armed with hooklets. The use of this singular organ is not known.

The majority of Teleostei are *mixogamous*—that is, the males and females congregate on the spawning-beds, and the number of the former being in excess, several males attend to the same female, frequently changing from one female to another. The same habit has been observed in

Lepidosteus. *Gastrosteus* is truly polygamous, several females depositing their ova into the same nest, guarded by one male only. Some Teleostei (*Ophiocephalus*), and probably all Chondropterygians, are monogamous; and it is asserted that the connection between the pair is not merely temporary, but lasts until they are separated by accident. Monogamous are probably also all those Teleosteans which bring forth living young, and those, the males of which, for the attraction of the female, are provided with appendages, or ornamented with a bright coloration.

Hybridism is another source of changes and variations within the limits of a species, and is by no means so scarce is has been believed hitherto; it is only apparently of exceptional occurrence, because the life of fishes is more withdrawn from our direct observation than that of terrestrial animals. It has been observed among species of *Serranus*, *Pleuronectidæ*, *Cyprinidæ*, *Clupeidæ*, and especially *Salmonidæ*. As in other animals, the more certain kinds of fishes are brought under domestication, the more readily do they interbreed with other allied species. It is characteristic of hybrids that their characters are very variable, the degrees of affinity to one or the other of the parents being inconstant; and as these hybrids are known readily to breed with either of the parent race, the variations of form, structure, and colour are infinite. Of internal organs the dentition, gill-rakers, pyloric appendages, are those particularly affected by such mixture of species.

Some fishes are known to grow rapidly (in the course of from one to three years) and regularly to a certain size, growth being definitely arrested after the standard has been attained. Such fishes may be called "full-grown," in the sense in which the term is applied to warm-blooded Vertebrates—the Sticklebacks, most Cyprinodonts, and many Clupeoids (Herring,

Sprat, Pilchard) are examples of this regular kind of growth.[1] But in the majority of fishes the rate of growth is extremely irregular, and it is hardly possible to know when growth is actually and definitely arrested. All seems to depend on the amount of food and the more or less favourable circumstances under which the individual grows up. Fishes which rapidly grow to a definite size are short-lived, whilst those which steadily and slowly increase in size attain to a great age, Teleosteans as well as Chondropterygians. Carp and Pike have been ascertained to live beyond a hundred years.

It is evident that such diversity and irregularity of growth in the same species is accompanied by considerable differences in the appearance and general development of the fish. No instance is more remarkable than that of the so-called *Leptocephali*, which for a long time have been regarded either as a distinct group of Fishes, or as the larval stages of various genera of fishes.

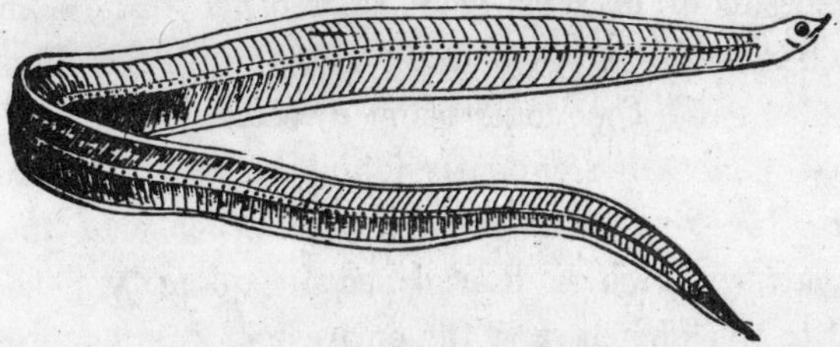

Fig. 95.—Leptocephalus.

The *Leptocephali* proper are small, narrow, elongate, more or less band-shaped fishes, pellucid in a fresh state, but assum-

[1] This applies to individuals only growing up under normal conditions. Dr. H. A. Meyer has made observations on young Herrings. Individuals living in the sea had attained at the end of the third month a length of 45 to 50 millimetres, whilst those reared from artificially-impregnated ova were only from 30 to 35 millimetres long. When the latter had been supplied with more abundant food, they grew proportionally more rapidly in the following months, so that at the end of the fifth month they had reached the same length as their brethren in the sea, viz. a length of 65 to 70 millimetres.

ing a white colour when preserved in spirits, resembling a tapeworm, being quite as soft and flexible. The skeleton is entirely cartilaginous, or slight ossifications are only now and then visible, especially towards the end of the vertebral column. The latter is replaced by a chorda dorsalis which, in many specimens, is found to be divided into numerous segments. Neural arches are sometimes present in their rudimentary condition. The anterior end of the chorda passes into the cartilaginous base of the skull, the connection not being by means of joint and ligaments. Hæmal arches are found on the caudal portion. Ribs none. The skull, like the vertebral column, is nearly entirely cartilaginous. The basi-sphenoid, frontal, and jaw-bones are the first which may be distinguished, and the mandible has generally ossifications.

The muscles are generally not attached to the chorda, which is surrounded by a thick gelatinous mass, separating the lateral sets of muscles from each other. These muscles are attached to the external integument, each forming a thin flat angular band, the angle being directed forwards. However, specimens are frequently found in which the muscles are more developed, evidently at the expense of the gelatinous matter, which is diminished in quantity. They are attached to the chorda. and the entire fish has a more cylindrical form of the body (*Helmichthys*).

The nervous, circulatory, and respiratory organs are well developed. In those with a sub-cylindrical body the blood is red in those with a flat body the blood-corpuscles show but rarely a faint coloration. There are four branchial arches, and in some (*Tilurus*) pseudobranchiæ have been found. The gill-openings are more or less narrow. The nostrils are double on each side, and the posterior is close to the eye.

The stomach has a large blind sac, and in *Leptocephalus*

two lateral cæca. The intestine is straight, running close to the abdominal profile, with a small appendix directed forward and a larger one directed backwards. The vent is nearly always very small, and, in preserved examples at least, cannot always be discovered. Its position is variable, even in examples entirely similar in other points. Air-bladder none. No trace of generative organs.

The vertical fins, when present, are confluent, with more or less conspicuous traces of rays; sometimes they are merely a fold of the skin, without any rays. Pectoral fins sometimes present, sometimes rudimentary, sometimes entirely absent. Ventrals none.

Most examples have series of round black dots along each side of the abdominal profile, along the lateral line, and sometimes along the dorsal fin. They remind us of the luminous organs of many *Scopelidæ*, *Stomiatidæ*, and other pelagic fishes, but are composed entirely of pigmentary cells.

These fishes are found floating in the sea, frequently at a great distance from land. Their movements are slow and languid. The largest specimen of Leptocephalus observed was 10 inches, but specimens of that size are very rare.

[See Kölliker, Zeitschr. wiss. Zool. iv. 1852, p. 360; and Carus, Ueber die Leptocephaliden. Leipz. 1861. 4to.]

Taking into account all the various facts mentioned, we must come to the conclusion that the Leptocephalids are the offspring of various kinds of marine fishes, representing, not a normal stage of development (larvæ), but an arrest of development at a very early period of their life; they continue to grow to a certain size without corresponding development of their internal organs, and perish without having attained the characters of the perfect animal. The cause by which this abnormal condition is brought about is not known; but it is quite within the limits of probability that fishes usually spawning in the vicinity of land sometimes spawn in the open ocean, or that floating spawn is carried by currents to a great distance from land; and that such embryoes, which for their normal growth require the conditions afforded by the vicinity of the shore, if hatched in mid-ocean, grow into undeveloped hydropic creatures, such as the Leptocephales seem to be.

Abundance or scarcity of food, and other circumstances connected with the localities inhabited by fishes, affect considerably the colour of their muscles and integuments; the periodical changes of colour in connection with their sexual functions have been referred to above (p. 176). The flesh of many Teleostei is colourless, or but slightly tinged by the blood; that of Scombridæ, most Ganoids and Chondropterygians, is more or less red; but in badly-fed fishes, as well as in very young ones, the flesh is invariably white (anæmic). Many fishes, like the *Salmonidæ*, feed at times exclusively on Crustaceans, and the colouring substance of these Invertebrates, which by boiling and by the stomachic secretion turns red, seems to pass into the flesh of the fishes, imparting to it the well-known "salmon" colour. Further, the coloration of the integuments of many marine fish is dependent on the nature of their surroundings. In those which habitually hide themselves on the bottom, in sand, between stones or seaweeds, the colours of the body readily assimilate to those of the vicinity, and are thus an important element in the economy of their life. The changes from one set or tinge of colours to another may be rapid and temporary, or more or less permanent; in some fishes—as in the Pediculati, of which the Sea-Devil, or *Lophius*, and *Antennarius* are members—scarcely two individuals are found exactly alike in coloration, and only too frequently such differences in coloration are mistaken for specific characters. The changes of colours are produced in two ways: either by an increase or decrease of the black, red, yellow, etc., pigment-cells, or *chromatophors*, in the skin of the fish; or by the rapid contraction or expansion of the chromatophors which happen to be developed. The former change is gradual, like every kind of growth or development; the latter rapid, owing to the great sensitiveness of the cells, but certainly involuntary. In many bright-shining fishes—as Mackerels, Mullets—the colours appear to be brightest in the time intervening between the capture of the fish and its death: a phenomenon clearly due to the pressure of the convulsively-contracted muscles on the chromatophors. External irritation readily excites the chromatophors to expand—a fact unconsciously utilised by fishermen, who, by scaling the Red Mullet immediately before its death, produce the desired intensity of the red colour of the skin, without which the fish would not be saleable. However, it does not require such strong measures to prove the sensitiveness of the chromatophors to external irritation, the mere change of darkness into light is sufficient to induce them to contract, the fish appearing paler, and *vice versa*. In Trout which are kept or live in dark places, the black chromatophors are expanded, and, consequently, such specimens are very dark-coloured; when removed to the light they become paler almost instantaneously.

Total absence of chromatophors in the skin, or *Albinism*, is very rare among fishes; much more common is *incipient Albinism*, in which the dark chromatophors are changed into cells with a more or less intense yellow pigment. Fishes in a state of domestication, like the Crucian Carp of China, the Carp, Tench, and the Ide, are particularly subject to this abnormal coloration, and are known as the common Goldfish, the Gold-Tench, and the Gold-Orfe. But it occurs also not rarely in fishes living in a wild state, and has been observed in the Haddock, Flounder, Plaice, Carp, Roach, and Eel.

It will be evident, from the foregoing remarks, that the amount of variation within the limits of the same species—either due to the natural growth and development, or to external physical conditions, or to abnormal accidental circumstances—is greater in fishes than in any of the higher classes of Vertebrates. The amount of variation is greater in certain genera or families than in others, and it is much greater in Teleosteans and Ganoids than in Chondropterygians. Naturally, it is greatest in the few species which have been domesticated, and which we shall mention in the succeeding chapter.

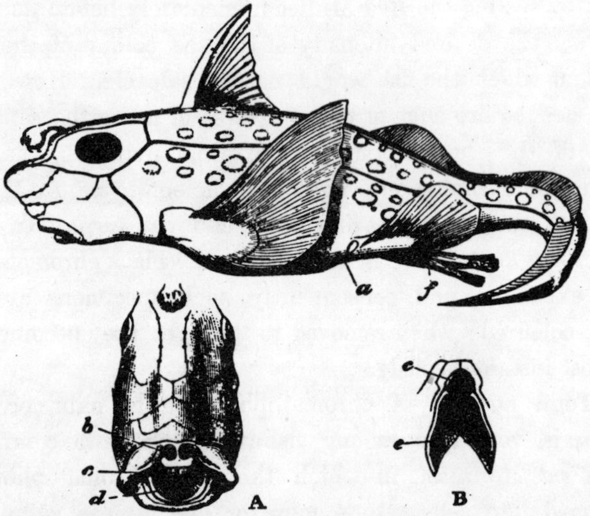

Fig. 96.—Chimæra colliei ♂, west coast of North America. A. Front view of head. B. Palate. *a*, Peritoneal aperture ; *b*, Nostrils ; *c*, Vomerine teeth ; *d*, Mandibular teeth ; *e*, Palatine teeth ; *f*, Claspers.

CHAPTER XIV.

DOMESTICATED AND ACCLIMATISED FISHES; ARTIFICIAL IMPREGNATION OF OVA—TENACITY OF LIFE AND REPRODUCTION OF LOST PARTS—HYBERNATION—USEFUL AND POISONOUS FISHES.

A FEW fishes only are thoroughly domesticated—that is, bred in captivity, and capable of transportation within certain climatic limits—viz. the Carp, Crucian Carp (European and Chinese varieties), Tench, Orfe or Ide, and the Goramy. The two former have accompanied civilised man almost to every place of the globe where he has effected a permanent settlement.

Attempts to acclimatise particularly useful species in countries in which they were not indigenous have been made from time to time, but were permanently successful in a few instances only; the failures being due partly to the choice of a species which did not yield the profitable return expected, partly to the utter disregard of the difference of the climatic and other physical conditions between the original and new homes of the fish. The first successful attempts of acclimatisation were made with domestic species, viz. the Carp and Gold-fish, which were transferred from Eastern Asia to Europe. Then, in the first third of the present century, the Javanese Goramy was acclimatised in Mauritius and Guiana, but no care seems to have been taken to insure permanent advantages from the successful execution of the experiment. In these cases fully developed individuals were transported to the country in which they were to be acclimatised. The most successful attempt of recent years is the acclimatisation of the Trout and Sea-Trout, and probably also of the Salmon, in Tasmania and New Zealand, and of the Californian Salmon (*Salmo quinnat?*), in Victoria, by means of artificially-impregnated ova. The ova were transported on ice, in order to retard their development generally, and thus to preserve them from destruction during the passage of the tropical zone.

Artificial impregnation of fish-ova was first practised by J. L. JACOBI, a native of Westphalia, in the years 1757-63, who employed exactly the same method which is followed now; and there is no doubt that this able observer of nature conceived and carried out his idea with the distinct object of advantageously restocking water-courses which had become unproductive, and increasing production by fecundating and preserving all ova, of which a great proportion, in the ordinary course of propagation, would be left unfecundated or accidentally perish. Physiology soon turned to account Jacobi's discovery, and artificial impregnation has proved to be one of the greatest helps to the student of embryology.

Fishes differ in an extraordinary degree with regard to tenacity of life. Some will bear suspension of respiration—caused by removal from water, or by exposure to cold or heat—for a long time, whilst others succumb at once. Nearly all marine fishes are very sensitive to changes in the temperature of the water, and will not bear transportation from one climate to another. This seems to be much less the case with some freshwater fishes of the temperate zones: the Carp may survive after being frozen in a solid block of ice, and will thrive in the southern parts of the temperate zone. On the other hand, some freshwater fishes are so sensitive to a change in the water that they perish when transplanted from their native river into another apparently offering the same physical conditions (Grayling, *Salmo hucho*). Some marine fishes may be abruptly transferred from salt into fresh water, like Sticklebacks, some Blennies, and *Cottus*, etc.; others survive the change when gradually effected, as many migratory fishes; whilst again, others cannot bear the least alteration in the composition of the salt water (all pelagic fishes). On the whole, instances of marine fishes voluntarily entering brackish or fresh water are very numerous, whilst freshwater fishes proper but rarely descend into salt water.

Abstinence from food affects different fishes in a similarly different degree. Marine fishes can endure hunger less than freshwater fishes, at least in the temperate zones, no observations having been made in this respect on tropical fishes. Goldfishes, Carps, Eels, are known to be able to subsist without food for months, without showing a visible decrease of bulk; whilst the Trigloids, Sparoids, and other marine fishes, survive abstinence from food for a few days only. In freshwater fishes the temperature of the water is of great influence on their vital functions generally, and consequently on their appetite,—many cease to feed altogether in the course of the winter; a few, like the Pike, are less inclined to feed during the heat of the summer than when the temperature is lowered.

Captivity is easily borne by most fishes, and the appliances introduced in our modern aquaria have rendered it possible to keep in confinement, and even to induce to propagate, fishes which formerly were considered to be intolerant of captivity.

Wounds affect fishes generally much less than higher Vertebrates. A Greenland Shark continues to feed whilst his head is pierced by a harpoon or by the knife, as long as the nervous centre is not touched; a Sea-perch or a Pike (Fig. 97) will survive the loss of a portion of its tail; a Carp that of half of its snout. However, some fishes are much more sensitive, and perish even from the superficial abrasion caused by the meshes of the net during capture (*Mullsn.*)

The power of *reproduction* of *lost parts* in Teleosteous fishes is limited to the delicate terminations of their fin-rays and the various tegumentary filaments with which some are provided. These filaments are sometimes developed in an extraordinary degree, mimicking the waving fronds of the sea-weed in which the fish hides. Both the ends of the fin-rays

Fig. 97.—Pike caught in the Thames, which, when young, had lost part of the tail with the caudal fin.

and the filaments are frequently lost, not only by accident, but merely by wear and tear; and as these organs are essential for the preservation of the fish, their reproduction is necessary.

In Dipnoi, *Ceratodus*, and *Protopterus*, the terminal portion of the tail has been found to have been reproduced, but without the notochord.

Hybernation has been observed in many Cyprinoids and Muraenoids of the temperate zones. They do not fall into a condition of complete torpidity, as Reptiles and Mammals, but their vital functions are simply lowered, and they hide in sheltered holes, and cease to go abroad in search of their food. Between the tropics a great number of fishes (especially Siluroids, Labyrinthici, Ophiocephaloids, the Dipnoi), are known to survive long-continued droughts by passing the dry season in a perfectly torpid state, imbedded in the hardened mud. Protopterus, and probably many of the other fishes mentioned, prepare for themselves a cavity large enough to hold them, and coated on the inside with a layer of hardened mucus, which preserves them from complete desiccation. It has been stated that in India fishes may survive in this condition for more than one season, and that ponds known to have been dry for several years, and to the depth of many feet, have swarmed with fishes as soon as the accumulation of water released them from their hardened bed.

The principal *use* derived by man from the class of Fishes consists in the abundance of wholesome and nourishing food which they yield. In the Polar regions especially, whole tribes are entirely dependent on this class for subsistence; and in almost all nations fishes form a more or less essential part of food, many being, in a preserved condition, most important articles of trade. The use derived by man from them in other respects is of but secondary importance. Cod-liver oil is prepared from the liver of some of the Gadoids of the Northern Hemisphere, and of Sharks; isinglass from the swim-bladder of Sturgeons, Sciænoids, and Polynemoids; shagreen from the skin of Sharks and Rays.

The flesh of some fishes is at times, or constantly, *poisonous.* When eaten, it causes symptoms of more or less intense irritation of the stomach and intestines, inflammation of the mucous membranes, and not rarely death. The fishes, the flesh of which appears always to have poisonous properties, are *Clupea thrissa*, *Clupea venenosa*, and some species of *Scarus*, *Tetrodon*, and *Diodon*. There are many others which have occasionally or frequently caused symptoms of poisoning Poey enumerates not less than seventy-two different kinds from Cuba; and various species of *Sphyræna*, *Balistes*, *Ostracion*, *Caranx*, *Lachnolæmus*, *Tetragonurus*, *Thynnus*, have been found to be poisonous in all seas between the tropics. All or nearly all these fishes acquire their poisonous properties from their food which consists of poisonous Medusæ, Corals, or decomposing substances. Frequently the fishes are found to be eatable if the head and intestines be removed immediately after capture. In the West Indies it has been ascertained that all the fishes living and feeding on certain coral banks are poisonous. In other fishes the poisonous properties are developed at certain seasons of the year only, especially the season of propagation: as the Barbel, Pike, and Burbot, whose roe causes violent diarrhœas when eaten during the season of spawning.

Poison-organs are more common in the class of Fishes than was formerly believed, but they seem to have exclusively the function of defence, and are not auxiliary in procuring food, as in venomous Snakes. Such organs are found in the Sting-rays, the tail of which is armed with one or more powerful barbed

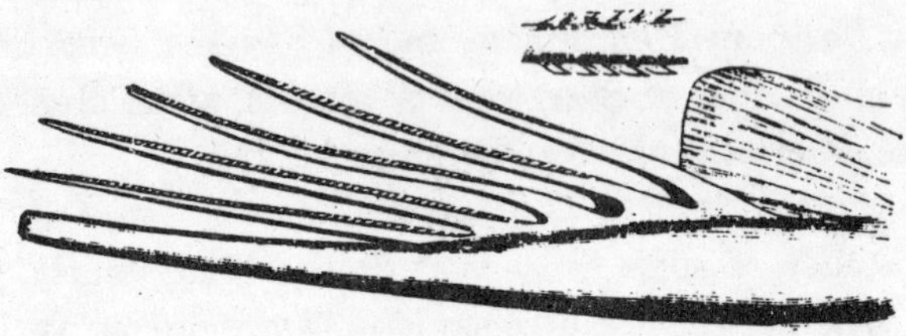

Fig. 98.—Portion of tail, with spines, of *Aëtobatis narinari*, a Sting-ray from the Indian Ocean. *a*, nat. size.

spines. Although they lack a special organ secreting poison, or a canal in or on the spine by which the venomous fluid is conducted, the symptoms caused by a wound from the spine of a Sting-ray are such as cannot be accounted for merely by the mechanical laceration, the pain being intense, and the subsequent inflammation and swelling of the wounded part terminating not rarely in gangrene. The mucus secreted from the surface of the fish and inoculated by the jagged spine evidently possesses venomous properties. This is also the case in many Scorpænoids, and in the Weaver (*Trachinus*); in which the dorsal and opercular spines have the same function as the caudal spines of the Sting-rays; however, in the Weavers the spines are deeply grooved, the groove

Fig. 99.—A dorsal spine, with poison-bags, of *Synanceia verrucosa*. Indian Ocean.

Fig. 100.—Opercular part of the Poison-apparatus of *Thalassophryne* (Panama).

1. Hinder half of the head, with the venom-sac* *in situ*. *a*, Lateral line and its branches; *b*, Gill-opening; *c*, Ventral fin; *d*, Base of Pectoral fin; *e*, Base of dorsal.
2. Operculum with the perforated spine.

being charged with a fluid mucus. In *Synanceia* the poison-organ (Fig. 99,) is still more developed: each dorsal spine is in its terminal half provided with a deep groove on each side, at the lower end of which lies a pear-shaped bag containing the milky poison; it is prolonged into a membranous duct, lying in the groove of the spine, and open at its point. The native fishermen, well acquainted with the dangerous nature of these fishes, carefully avoid handling them; but it often happens that persons wading with naked feet in the sea, step upon the fish, which generally lies hidden in the sand. One or more of the erected spines penetrate the skin, and the poison is injected into the wound by the pressure of the foot on the poison-bags. Death has not rarely been the result.

The most perfect poison-organs hitherto discovered in fishes are those of *Thalassophryne*, a Batrachoid genus of fishes from the coasts of Central America. In these fishes the operculum again and the two dorsal spines are the weapons. The former (Fig. 100, [2]) is very narrow, vertically styliform and very mobile; it is armed behind with a spine, eight lines long, and of the same form as the hollow venom-fang of a snake, being perforated at its base and at its extremity. A sac covering the base of the spine discharges its contents through the apertures and the canal in the interior of the spine. The structure of the dorsal spines is similar. There are no secretory glands imbedded in the membranes of the sacs; and the fluid must be secreted by their mucous membrane. The sacs are without an external muscular layer, and situated immediately below the thick loose skin which envelops the spines to their extremity; the ejection of the poison into a living animal, therefore, can only be effected, as in *Synanceia*, by the pressure to which the sac is subjected the moment the spine enters another body.

Finally, a singular apparatus found in many Siluroids may be mentioned in connection with the poison-organs, although its function is still problematical. Some of these fishes are armed with powerful pectoral spines and justly feared on account of the dangerous wounds they inflict; not a few of them possess, in addition to the pectoral spines, a sac with a more or less wide opening in the axil of the pectoral fin; and it does not seem improbable that it contains a fluid which may be introduced into a wound by means of the pectoral spine, which would be covered with it, like the barbed arrow-head of an Indian. However, whether this secretion is equally poisonous in all the species provided with that axillary sac, or whether it has poisonous qualities at all, is a question which can be decided by experiments only made with the living fishes.

CHAPTER XV.

DISTRIBUTION OF FISHES IN TIME.

Of what kind the fishes were which were the first to make their appearance on the globe; whether or not they were identical with, or similar to, any of the principal types existing at present; are questions which probably will for ever remain hidden in mystery and uncertainty. The supposition that the Leptocardii and Cyclostomes, the lowest of the vertebrate series, must have preceded the other sub-classes, is an idea which has been held by many Zoologists: and as the horny teeth of the Cyclostomes are the only parts of their body which under favourable circumstances might have been preserved, Palæontologists have ever been searching for this evidence.

Fig. 101. Right dental plate of Myxine affinis.

Indeed, in deposits belonging to the Lower Silurian and Devonian, in Russia, England, and North America, minute, slender, pointed horny bodies, bent like a hook, with sharp opposite margins, have been found and described under the name of *Conodonts.* More frequently they possess an elongated basal portion, in which there is generally a larger tooth with rows of similar but smaller denticles on one or both sides of the larger tooth, according as this is central or at one end of the base. In other examples there is no prominent central tooth, but a series of more or less similar teeth is implanted on a straight or curved base. Modifications of these arrangements are very numerous, and many Palæontologists entertain still doubts whether the origin of these remains is not rather from Annelids and Mollusks than from Fishes.

[See G. J. Hinde, in "Quarterly Journal of the Geological Society," 1879.]

The first undeniable evidence of a fish, or, indeed, of a vertebrate animal, occurs in the *Upper Silurian* Rocks, in a bone-bed of the Downton sandstone, near Ludlow. It consists of compressed, slightly curved, ribbed spines, of less than two inches in length (*Onchus*); of small shagreen-scales (*Thelodus*); the fragment of a jaw-like bar with pluricuspid teeth (*Plectrodus*); the cephalic bucklers of what seems to be a species of *Pteraspis*; and, finally, the coprolitic bodies of phosphate and carbonate of lime, including recognisable remains of the Mollusks and Crinoids inhabiting the same waters. But no vertebra or other part of the skeleton has been found. The spines and scales seem to have belonged to the same kind of fish, which probably was a Plagiostome. It is quite uncertain whether or not the jaw (if it be the jaw of a fish[1]) belonged to the buckler-bearing *Pteraspis*, the position of which among Ganoids, with which it is generally associated, is open to doubt.

No detached undoubted tooth of a Plagiostome or Ganoid scale has been discovered in the Ludlow deposits: but so much is certain that those earliest remains in Palæozoic rocks belonged to fishes closely allied to forms occurring in greater abundance in the succeeding formation, the Devonian, where they are associated with undoubted Palæichthyes, Plagiostomes as well as Ganoids.

These fish-remains of the *Devonian* or *Old Red Sandstone*, can be determined with greater certainty. They consist of spines or the so-called *Ichthyodorulites*, which show sufficiently distinctive characters to be referred to several genera, one of

[1] Ray Lankester considers it to be a portion of the long denticulated cornua of a genus *Eukeraspis* allied to *Cephalaspis*.

them, *Onchus*, still surviving from the Silurian epoch. All these spines are believed to be those of Chondropterygians, to which order some pluricuspid teeth (*Cladodus*) from the Old Red Sandstone in the vicinity of St. Petersburg have been referred likewise.

The remains of the Ganoid fishes are in a much more perfect state of preservation, so that it is even possible to obtain a tolerably certain idea of the general appearance and habits of some of them, especially of such as were provided with hard carapaces, solid scales, and ordinary or bony fin-rays. A certain proportion of them, as might have been expected, remind us, with regard to external form, of Teleosteous fishes rather than of any of the few still existing Ganoid types; but it is contrary to all analogy and to all palæontological evidence to suppose that those fishes were, with regard to their internal structure, more nearly allied to Teleosteans than to Ganoids. If they were not true Ganoids, they may be justly supposed to have had the essential characters of Palæichthyes. Other forms exhibit even at that remote geological epoch so unmistakably the characteristics of existing Ganoids, that no one can entertain any doubt with regard to their place in the system. In none of these fishes is there any trace of vertebral segmentation.

The Palæichthyes of the Old Red Sandstone, the systematic position of which is still obscure, are the *Cephalaspidæ* from the Lower Old Red Sandstone of Great Britain and Eastern Canada; *Pterichthys*, *Coccosteus*, and *Dinichthys*: genera which have been combined in one group—*Placodermi*; and *Acanthodes* and allied genera, which combined numerous branchiostegals with chondropterygian spines and a shagreen-like dermal covering.

Among the other Devonian fishes (and they formed the majority) two types may be recognised, both of which are unmistakably Ganoids. The first approaches the still living

Polypterus, with which some of the genera like *Diplopterus* singularly agree in the form and armature of the head, the lepidosis of the body, the lobate pectoral fins, and the termination of the vertebral column. Other genera, as *Holoptychius*, have cycloid scales; many have two dorsal fins (*Holoptychius*), and, instead of branchiostegals, jugular scutes; others one long dorsal confluent with the caudal (*Phaneropleuron*).

In the second type the principal characters of the *Dipnoi* are manifest, and some of them, for example *Dipterus, Palædaphus, Holodus*, approach so closely the Dipnoi which still survive, that the differences existing between them warrant a separation into families only.

Devonian fishes are frequently found under peculiar circumstances, enclosed in the so-called *nodules*. These bodies are elliptical flattened pebbles, which have resisted the action of water in consequence of their greater hardness, whilst the surrounding rock has been reduced to detritus by that agency. Their greater density is due to the dispersion in their substance of the fat of the animal which decomposed in them. Frequently, on cleaving one of these nodules with the stroke of the hammer, a fish is found embedded in the centre. At certain localities of the Devonian, fossil fishes are so abundant that the whole of the stratum is affected by the decomposing remains emitting a peculiar smell when newly opened, and acquiring a density and durability not possessed by strata without fishes. The flagstones of Caithness are a remarkable instance of this.

The fish-remains of the *Carboniferous* formation show a great similarity to those of the preceding. They occur throughout the series, but are very irregularly distributed, being extremely scarce in some countries, whilst in others entire beds (the so-called bone-beds) are composed of ichthyolites. In the ironstones they frequently form the nuclei of nodules, as in the Devonian.

Of Chondropterygians the spines of *Onchus* and others still occur, with the addition of teeth indicative of the existence of fishes allied to the Cestracion-type (*Cochliodus, Psammodus*): a type which henceforth plays an important part in the composition of the extinct marine fish faunæ. Another extinct Selachian family, that of Hybodontes, makes its appearance, but is known from the teeth only.

Of the Ganoid fishes, the family *Palæoniscidæ* (Traquair) is numerously represented; others are Cœlacanths (*Cœlacanthus, Rhizodus*), and *Saurodipteridæ* (*Megalichthys*). None of these fishes have an ossified vertebral column, but in some (*Megalichthys*) the outer surface of the vertebræ is ossified into a ring; the termination of their tail is heterocercal. The carboniferous *Uronemus* and the Devonian *Phaneropleuron* are probably generically the same; and the Devonian *Dipnoi* are continued as, and well represented by, *Ctenodus*.

The fishes of the *Permian* group are very similar to those of the Carboniferous. A type which in the latter was but very scantily represented, namely the *Platysomidæ*, is much developed. They were deep-bodied fish, covered with hard rhomboid scales possessing a strong anterior rib, and provided with a heterocercal caudal, long dorsal and anal, short nonlobate paired fins (when present), and branchiostegals. The *Palæoniscidæ* are represented by many species of *Palæoniscus, Pygopterus* and *Acrolepis*, and Cestracionts by *Janassa* and *Strophodus*.

The passage from the Palæozoic into the *Mesozoic* era is not indicated by any marked change as far as fishes are concerned. The more remarkable forms of the Trias are Shark-like fishes represented by ichthyodorulithes like *Nemacanthus, Liacanthus*, and *Hybodus*; and Cestracionts represented by species of *Acrodus* and *Strophodus.* Of the Ganoid genera *Cœlacanthus, Amblypterus* (*Palæoniscidæ*), *Saurichthys* persist from the Carboniferous epoch. *Ceratodus* appears for the first time (Muschel-Kalk of Germany).

Thanks to the researches of Agassiz, and especially Sir P. Egerton, the ichthyological fauna of the Lias is, perhaps, the best known of the Mesozoic era, 152 species having been described. Of the various localities, Lyme Regis has yielded more than any other, nearly all the Liassic genera being represented there by not less than seventy-nine species. The Hybodonts and Cestracionts continue in their fullest development. Holocephales (*Ischyodus*), true Sharks (*Palæoscyllium*), Rays (*Squaloraja, Arthropterus*), and Sturgeons (*Chondrosteus*) make their first appearance; but they are sufficiently distinct from living types to be classed in separate genera, or even families. The Ganoids, especially Lepidosteoids, predominate over all the other fishes: *Lepidotus, Semionotus, Pholidophorus, Pachycormus, Eugnathus, Tetragonolepis,* are represented by numerous species; other remarkable genera are *Aspidorhynchus, Belonostomus, Saurostomus, Sauropsis, Thrissonotus, Conodus, Ptycholepis, Endactis, Centrolepis, Legnonotus, Oxygnathus, Heterolepidotus, Isocolum, Osteorhachis, Mesodon.* These genera offer evidence of a great change since the preceding period, the majority not being represented in older strata, whilst, on the other hand, many are continued into the succeeding oolithic formations. The homocercal termination of the vertebral column commences to supersede the heterocercal, and many of the genera have well ossified and distinctly segmented spinal columns. Also the cycloid form of scales becomes more common: one genus (*Leptolepis*) being, with regard to the preserved hard portions of its organisation, so similar to the Teleosteous type that some Palæontologists refer it (with much reason) to that sub-class.

[See *E. Sauvage,* Essai sur la Faune Ichthyologique de la période Liasique. In "Bibl. de l'école des hautes études," xiii. art. 5. Paris 1875. 8º.]

As already mentioned, the *Oolithic* formations show a great similarity of their fish-fauna to that of the Lias; but still more apparent is its approach to the existing fauna. Teeth have been found which cannot even generically be distinguished from *Notidanus.* The Rays are represented by genera like *Spathobatis, Belemnobatis, Thaumas;* the *Holocephali* are more numerous than in the Lias (*Ischyodus, Ganodus*). The most common Ganoid genera are *Caturus, Pycnodus, Pholidophorus Lepidotus, Leptolepis,* all of which had been more or less fully represented in the Lias. Also *Ceratodus* is continued into it.

The *Cretaceous* group offers clear evidence of the further advance towards the existing fauna. Teeth of Sharks of existing genera *Carcharias* (*Corax*), *Scyllium, Notidanus,* and *Galeocerdo,* are common in some of the marine strata, whilst Hybodonts and Cestracionts are represented by a small number of species only; of the latter one new genus, *Ptychodus,* appears and disappears. A very characteristic Ganoid genus, *Macropoma,* comprises homocercal fishes with rounded ganoid scales sculptured externally and pierced by prominent mucous tubes. *Caturus* becomes extinct. Teeth and scales of *Lepidotus* (with *Sphærodus* as sub-genus), clearly a fresh-water fish, are widely distributed in the Wealden, and finally disappear in the chalk; its body was covered with large rhomboidal ganoid scales. *Gyrodus* and *Aspidorhynchus* occur in the beds of Voirons, *Coelodus* and *Amiopsis* (allied to Amra), in those of Comen, in Istria. But the Palæichthyes are now in the minority; undoubted Teleosteans have appeared, for the first time, on the stage of life in numerous genera, many of which are identical with still existing fishes. The majority are Acanthopterygians, but Physostomes and Plectognaths are likewise well represented, most of them being marine. Of Acanthopterygian families the first to appear are the *Bery-*

cidæ, represented by several very distinct genera: *Beryx*; *Pseudoberyx* with abdominal ventral fins; *Berycopsis* with cycloid scales; *Homonotus, Stenostoma, Sphenocephalus, Acanus, Hoplopteryx, Platycornus* with granular scales; *Podocys* with a dorsal extending to the neck; *Acrogaster, Macrolepis, Rhacolepis* from the chalk of Brazil. The position of *Pycnosterynx* is uncertain, it approaches certain Pharyngognaths. True *Percidæ* are absent, whilst the *Carangidæ, Sphyrænidæ, Cataphracti. Gobiidæ, Cottidæ,* and *Sparidæ* are represented by one or more genera. Somewhat less diversified are the Physostomes, which belong principally to the *Clupeidæ* and *Dercetidæ*, most of the genera being extinct; Clupea is abundant in some localities. *Scopelidæ* (*Hemisaurida* and *Saurocephalus*) occur in the chalk of Comen in Istria, and of Mæstricht. Of all cretaceous deposits none surpass those of the Lebanon with regard to the number of genera, species, and individuals; the forms are exclusively marine, and the remains in the most perfect condition.

In the *Tertiary* epoch the Teleosteans have almost entirely replaced the Ganoids; a few species only of the latter make their appearance, and they belong to existing genera, or, at least, very closely allied forms (*Lepidosteus, Amia, Hypamia, Acipenser*). The Chondropterygians merge more and more into recent forms; Holocephali continue, and still are better represented than in the present fauna. The Teleosteans show even in the Eocene a large proportion of existing genera, and the fauna of some localities of the Miocene (Oeningen) is almost wholly composed of them. On the whole, hitherto more than one-half have been found to belong to existing genera, and there is no doubt that the number of seemingly distinct extinct genera will be lessened as the fossils will be examined with a better knowledge of the living forms. The distribution of the fishes differed widely from that of our period, many of our tropical genera occurring in localities which are now included within our temperate zone, and being mixed with others, which nowadays are restricted to a colder climate: a mixture which continues throughout the Pliocene.

A few families of fishes, like the freshwater Salmonidæ, seem to have put in their appearance in *Post-pliocene* times; however, not much attention has been paid to fish-remains of these deposits; and such as have been incidentally examined offer evidence of the fact that the distribution of fishes has not undergone any further essential change down to the present period.

[See *E. Sauvage*, Mémoire sur la Faune Ichthyologique de la période Tertiaire. Paris 1873. 8°.]

Fig. 102.—*Pycnodus rhombus*, a Ganoid from the Upper Oolite.

CHAPTER XVI.

THE DISTRIBUTION OF EXISTING FISHES OVER THE EARTH'S SURFACE—GENERAL REMARKS.

In an account of the geographical distribution of fishes the *Freshwater* forms are to be kept separate from the *Marine*. However, when we attempt to draw a line between these two kinds of fishes, we meet with a great number of species and of facts which would seem to render that distinction very vague. There are not only species which can gradually accommodate themselves to a sojourn in either salt or fresh water, but there are also such as seem to be quite indifferent to a rapid change from one into the other: so that individuals of one and the same species (Gastrosteus, Gobius, Blennius, Osmerus, Retropinna, Clupea, Syngnathus, etc.), may be found at some distance out at sea, whilst others live in rivers far beyond the influence of the tide, or even in inland fresh waters without outlet to the sea. The majority of these fishes belong to forms of the fauna of the *brackish* water, and as they are not an insignificant portion of the fauna of almost every coast, we shall have to treat of them in a separate chapter.

Almost every large river offers instances of truly marine fishes (such as *Serranus, Sciænidæ, Pleuronectes, Clupeidæ, Tetrodon, Carcharias, Trygonidæ*), ascending for hundreds of miles of their course; and not periodically, or from any apparent physiological necessity, but sporadically throughout the year, just like the various kinds of marine Porpoises which are found all along the lower course of the Ganges, Yang-tse-

Kiang, the Amazons, the Congo, etc. This is evidently the commencement of a change in a fish's habits, and, indeed, not a few of such fishes have actually taken up their permanent residence in fresh waters (as species of Ambassis, Apogon Dules, Therapon, Sciæna, Blennius, Gobius, Atherina, Mugil, Myxus, Hemirhamphus, Clupea, Anguilla, Tetrodon, Trygon): all forms *originally marine.*

On the other hand, we find fishes belonging to fresh-water genera descending rivers and sojourning in the sea for a more or less limited period; but these instances are much less in number than those in which the reverse obtains. We may mention species of *Salmo* (the Common Trout, the Northern Charr), and Siluroids (as *Arius, Plotosus*). *Coregonus*, a genus so characteristic of the inland lakes of Europe, Northern Asia, and North America, nevertheless offers some instances of species wandering by the effluents into the sea, and taking up their residence in salt water, apparently by preference, as *Coregonus oxyrhynchus.* But of all the Fresh-water families none exhibit so great a capability of surviving the change from fresh into salt water, as the *Gastrosteidæ* (Stickle-backs), of the northern Hemisphere, and the equally diminutive *Cyprinodontidæ* of the tropics; not only do they enter into, and live freely in, the sea, but many species of the latter family inhabit inland waters, which, not having an outlet, have become briny, or impregnated with a larger proportion of salts than pure sea water. During the voyage of the "Challenger" a species of *Fundulus, F. nigrofasciatus*, which inhabits the fresh and brackish waters of the Atlantic States of North America, was obtained, with Scopelids and other pelagic forms, in the tow-net, midway between St. Thomas and Teneriffe.

Some fishes annually or periodically ascend rivers for the purpose of spawning, passing the rest of the year in the sea, as Sturgeons, many Salmonoids, some Clupeoids, Lampreys, etc. The two former evidently belonged originally to the freshwater series, and it was only in the course of their existence that they acquired the habit of descending to the sea, perhaps because their freshwater home did not offer a sufficient supply of food. These migrations of freshwater fishes have been compared with the migrations of birds; but they are much more limited in extent, and do not impart an additional element to the fauna of the place to which they migrate, as is the case with the distant countries to which birds migrate.

The distinction between freshwater and marine fishes is further obscured by geological changes, in consequence of which the salt water is gradually being changed into fresh, or *vice versa.* These changes are so gradual and spread over so long a time, that many of the fishes inhabiting such localities accommodate themselves to the new conditions. One of the most remarkable and best studied instances of such an alteration is the Baltic, which, during the second half of the Glacial period, was in open and wide communication with the Arctic Ocean, and evidently had the same marine fauna as the White Sea. Since then, by the rising of the land of Northern Scandinavia and Finland, this great gulf of the Arctic Ocean has become an inland sea, with a narrow outlet into the North Sea, and its water, in consequence of the excess of the fresh water pouring into it over the loss by evaporation, has been so much diluted as to be nearly fresh at its northern extremities: and yet nine species, the origin of which from the Arctic Ocean can be proved, have survived the changes, propagating their species, agreeing with their brethren in the Arctic Ocean in every point, but remaining comparatively smaller. On the other hand, fishes which we must regard as true freshwater fishes, like the Rudd, Roach, Pike, Perch, enter freely the brackish water of the Baltic.[1] Instances of marine fishes

[1] Ekström, Fische in den Scheeren von Mörkö.

being permanently retained in fresh water in consequence of geological changes are well known: thus *Cottus quadricornis* in the large lakes of Scandinavia; species of *Gobius, Blennius,* and *Atherina* in the lakes of Northern Italy; *Comephorus,* of the depths of the Lake of Baikal, which seems to be a dwarfed Gadoid. *Carcharias gangeticus* in inland lakes of the Fiji Islands, is another instance of a marine fish which has permanently established itself in fresh water.

In the miocene formation of Licata in Sicily, in which fish remains abound, numerous Cyprinoids are mixed with littoral and pelagic forms. Sauvage found in 450 specimens from that locality, not less than 266, which were Leucisci, Alburni, or Rhodei. Now, although it is quite possible that in consequence of a sudden catastrophe the bodies of those Cyprinoids were carried by a freshwater current into, and deposited on the bottom of, the sea, the surmise that they lived together with the littoral fishes in the brackish water of a large estuary, which was not rarely entered by pelagic forms, is equally admissible. And, if confirmed by other similar observations, this instance of a mixture of forms which are now strictly freshwater or marine, may have an important bearing on the question to what extent fishes have in time changed their original habitat.

Thus there is a constant exchange of species in progress between the freshwater and marine faunæ, and in not a few cases it would seem almost arbitrary to refer a genus or even larger group of fishes to one or the other; yet there are certain groups of fishes which entirely, or with but few exceptions are, and, apparently, during the whole period of their existence have been, inhabitants either of the sea or of fresh water; and as the agencies operating upon the distribution of marine fishes differ greatly from those influencing the dispersal of freshwater fishes, the two series must be treated separately. The most obvious fact that dry land, which intervenes between river systems, offers to the rapid spreading of a freshwater fish an obstacle which can be surmounted only exceptionally or by a most circuitous route, whilst marine fishes may readily and voluntarily extend their original limits, could be illustrated by a great number of instances. Without entering into details, it may suffice to state as the general result, that no species or genus of freshwater fishes has anything like the immense range of the corresponding categories of marine fishes; and that, with the exception of the Siluroids, no other freshwater family is so widely spread as the families of marine fishes. Surface temperature or climate which is, if not the most, one of the most important physical factors in the limitation of freshwater fishes, similarly affects the distribution of marine fishes, but in a less degree, and only those which live near to the shore or the surface of the ocean; whilst it ceases to exercise its influence in proportion to the depth, the true deep-sea forms being entirely exempt from its operation. Light, which is pretty equally distributed over the localities inhabited by freshwater fishes, cannot be considered as an important factor in their distribution, but it contributes towards constituting the impassable barrier between the surface and abyssal forms of marine fishes. Altitude has stamped the fishes of the various Alpine provinces of the globe with a certain character, and limited their distribution; but the number of these Alpine forms is comparatively small, ichthyic life being extinguished at great elevations even before the mean temperature equals that of the high latitudes of the Arctic region, in which some freshwater fishes flourish. On the other hand, the depths of the ocean, far exceeding the altitude of the highest mountains, still swarm with forms specially adapted for abyssal life. That other physical conditions of minor and local importance, under which fresh water fishes live, and by which their dispersal is regulated, are more complicated than similar ones of the ocean, is probable, though perhaps less so than is generally supposed: for the fact is that the former are more accessible to observation than the latter, and are, therefore, more generally and more readily comprehended and acknowledged. Thus, not only because many of the most characteristic forms of the marine and freshwater series are found, on taking a broader view of the subject, to be sufficiently distinct, but also because their distribution depends on causes different in their nature as well as the degree of their action, it will be necessary to treat of the two series separately. Whether the oceanic areas correspond in any way to the terrestrial will be seen in the sequel.

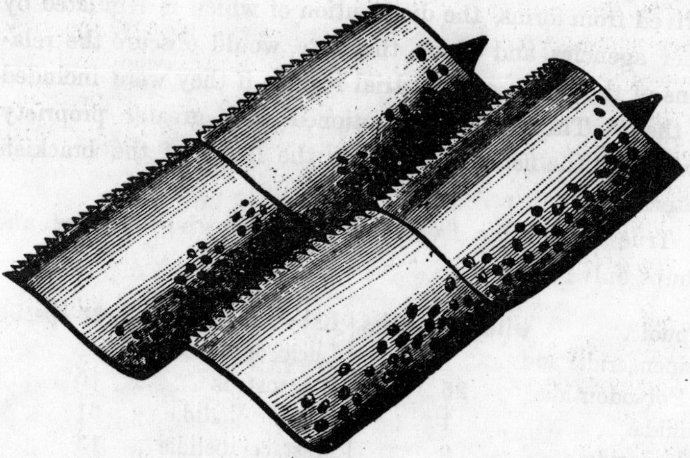

Fig. 103.—Ganoid scales of *Tetragonolepis*.

CHAPTER XVII.

THE DISTRIBUTION OF FRESHWATER FISHES.

HAVING shown above that numerous marine fishes enter fresh waters, and that some of them have permanently established themselves therein, we have to eliminate from the category of freshwater fishes all such adventitious elements. They are derived from forms, the distribution of which is regulated by other agencies, and which, therefore, would obscure the relations of the faunæ of terrestrial regions if they were included in them. They will be mentioned with greater propriety along with the fishes constituting the fauna of the brackish water.

True freshwater fishes are the following families and groups only :—

Dipnoi .	with	4	species.	Labyrinthici .	with	30	species.
Acipenseridæ and Polyodontidæ	„	26	„	Luciocephalidæ	„	1	„
Amiidæ .	„	1	„	Gastrosteus .	„	10	„
Polypteridæ .	„	2	„	Ophiocephalidæ	„	31	„
Lepidosteidæ .	„	3	„	Mastacembelidæ	„	13	„
Percina .	„	46	„	Chromides .	„	105	„
Grystina .	„	11	„	Comephoridæ	„	1	„
Aphredoderidæ	„	1	„	Gadopsidæ .	„	1	„
Centrarchina .	„	26	„	Siluridæ .	„	572	„
Dules .	„	10	„	Characinidæ .	„	261	„
Nandidæ .	„	7	„	Haplochitonidæ	„	3	„
Polycentridæ .	„	3	„	Salmonidæ (3 genera excepted) .	„	135	„

Percopsidæ .	with 1 species.	Kneriidæ .	with 2 species.
Galaxiidæ .	„ 15 „	Hyodontidæ .	„ 1 „
Mormyridæ (and Gymnarchidæ)	„ 52 „	Osteoglossidæ	„ 5 „
Esocidæ .	„ 8 „	Notopteridæ .	„ 5 „
Umbridæ .	„ 2 „	Gymnotidæ .	„ 20 „
Cyprinodontidæ	„ 112 „	Symbranchidæ	„ 5 „
Heteropygii .	„ 2 „	Petromyzontidæ	„ 12 „
Cyprinidæ .	„ 724 „	Total	2269 species.

As in every other class of animals, these freshwater genera and families vary greatly with regard to the extent of their geographical range; some extend over the greater half of the continental areas, whilst others are limited to one continent only, or even to a very small portion of it. As a general rule, a genus or family of freshwater fishes is regularly dispersed and most developed within a certain district, the species and individuals becoming scarcer towards the periphery as the type recedes more from its central home, some outposts being frequently pushed far beyond the outskirts of the area occupied by it. But there are not wanting those remarkable instances of closely allied forms occurring, almost isolated, at most distant points, without being connected by allied species in the intervening space; or of members of the same family, genus, or species inhabiting the opposite shores of an ocean, and separated by many degrees of abyssal depths. We mention of a multitude of such instances the following only:—

A. Species identical in distant continents—

1. A number of species inhabiting Europe and the temperate parts of eastern North America, as *Perca fluviatilis*, *Gastrosteus pungitius*, *Lota vulgaris*, *Salmo salar*, *Esox lucius*, *Acipenser sturio*, *Acipenser maculosus*, and several Petromyzonts.

2. *Lates calcarifer* is common in India as well as in Queensland.

3. *Galaxias attenuatus* inhabits Tasmania, New Zealand, the Falkland Islands, and the southernmost part of the South American continent.

4. Several Petromyzonts enter the fresh waters of Tasmania, South Australia, New Zealand, and Chili.

B. Genera identical in distant continents—

1. The genus *Umbra,* so peculiar a form as to be the type of a distinct family consisting of two most closely allied species only, one of which is found in the Atlantic States of North America, the other in the system of the Danube.

2. A very distinct genus of Sturgeons, *Scaphirhynchus,* consisting of two species only, one inhabiting fresh waters of Central Asia, the other the system of the Mississippi.

3. A second most peculiar genus of Sturgeons, *Polyodon,* consists likewise of two species only, one inhabiting the Mississippi, the other the Yang-tse-kiang.

4. *Amiurus,* a Siluroid, and *Catostomus,* a Cyprinoid genus, both well represented in North America, occur in a single species in temperate China.

5. *Lepidosiren* is represented by one species in tropical America, and by the second in tropical Africa (*Protopterus*).

6. *Notopterus* consists of three Indian and two West African species.

7. *Mastacembelus* and *Ophiocephalus,* genera characteristic of the Indian region, emerge severally by a single species in West and Central Africa.

8. *Symbranchus* has two Indian and one South American species.

9. *Prototroctes,* the singular antarctic analogue of *Coregonus,* consists of two species, one in the south of Australia the other in New Zealand

10. *Galaxias* is equally represented in Southern Australia, New Zealand, and the southern parts of South America.

C. Families identical in distant continents—

1. The *Labyrinthici*, represented in Africa by 5, and in India by 25 species.

2. The *Chromides*, represented in Africa by 25, and in South America by 80 species.

3. The *Characinidæ*, represented in Africa by 35, and in South America by 226 species.

4. The *Haplochitonidæ*, represented in Southern Australia by one, in New Zealand by one, and in Patagonia by a third species.

This list could be much increased from the families of *Siluridæ* and *Cyprinidæ*, but as these have a greater range than the other Freshwater fishes, they do not illustrate with equal force the object for which the list has been composed.

The ways in which the dispersal of Freshwater fishes has been effected were various; they are probably all still in operation, but most work so slowly and imperceptibly as to escape direct observation; perhaps, they will be more conspicuous, after science and scientific inquiry shall have reached to a somewhat greater age. From the great number of freshwater forms which we see at this present day acclimatised in, gradually acclimatising themselves in, or periodically or sporadically migrating into, the sea, we must conclude that, under certain circumstances, salt water may cease to be an impassable barrier at some period of the existence of freshwater species, and that many of them have passed from one river through salt water into another. Secondly, the headwaters of some of the grandest rivers, the mouths of which are at opposite ends of the continents which they drain, are sometimes distant from each other a few miles only; the intervening space may have been easily bridged over for the passage of fishes by a slight geological change affecting the level of the watershed, or even by temporary floods; and a communication of this kind, if existing for a limited period only, would afford the ready means of an exchange of a number of species previously peculiar to one or the other of those river or lake systems. Some fishes, provided with gill-openings so narrow that the water moistening the gills cannot readily evaporate; and endowed, besides, with an extraordinary degree of vitality, like many Siluroids (*Clarias*, *Callichthys*), Eels, etc., are enabled to wander for some distance over land, and may thus reach a watercourse leading them thousands of miles from their original home. Finally, fishes or their ova may be accidentally carried by waterspouts, by aquatic birds or insects, to considerable distances.

Freshwater fishes of the present fauna were already in existence when the great changes of the distribution of land and water took place in the tertiary epoch; and having stated that salt water is not an absolute barrier to the spreading of Freshwater fishes, we can now more easily account for those instances of singular disconnection of certain families or genera. It is not necessary to assume that there was a continuity of land stretching from the present coast of Africa to South America, or from South America to New Zealand and Australia, to explain the presence of identical forms at so distant localities; it suffices to assume that the distances were lessened by intervening archipelagoes, or that an oscillation has taken place in the level of the land area.

Dispersal of a type over several distant continental areas may be evidence of its great antiquity, but it does not prove that it is of greater antiquity than another limited to one region only. Geological evidence is the only proof of the antiquity of a type. Thus, although the *Dipnoi* occur on the continents of Africa, South America, and Australia, and their present distribution is evidently the consequence of their wide range in palæozoic and secondary epochs; the proof of their high antiquity can be found in their fossil remains only. For, though the Siluroids have a still greater range, their wide distribution is of comparatively recent date, as the few fossil remains that have been found belong to the tertiary epoch. The rapidity of dispersal of a type depends entirely on its facility to accommodate itself to a variety of physical conditions, and on the degree of vitality by which it is enabled to survive more or less sudden changes under unfavourable conditions; proof of this is afforded by the family of Siluroids, many of which can suspend for some time the energy of their respiratory functions, and readily survive a change of water.

To trace the geological sequence of the distribution of an ichthyic type, and to recognise the various laws which have governed, and are still governing its dispersal, is one of the ultimate tasks of Ichthyology. But the endeavour to establish by means of our present fragmentary geological knowledge the divisions of the fauna of the globe, leads us into a maze of conflicting evidence; or, as Mr. Wallace truly observes, "any attempt to exhibit the regions of former geological ages in combination with those of our own period must lead to confusion." Nevertheless, as the different types of animals found at the present day within a particular area have made their appearance therein at distant periods, we should endeavour to decide as far as we can, in an account of the several zoo-geographical divisions, the following questions:—

1. Which of the fishes of an area should be considered to be the remnants of *ancient* types, probably spread over much larger areas in preceding epochs?

2. Which of them are to be considered to be *autochthont* species, that is, forms which came in the tertiary epoch or later into existence within the area to which they are still limited, or from which they have since spread?

3. Which are the forms which must be considered to be *immigrants* from some other region?

The mode of division of the earth's surface into zoological regions or areas now generally adopted, is that proposed by Mr. Sclater, which recommends itself as most nearly agreeing with the geographical divisions. These regions are as follows:—

I. PALÆOGÆA.

1. The *Palæarctic* region; including Europe, temperate Asia, and North Africa.
2. The *Ethiopian* region; including Africa, south of the Sahara, Madagascar, and the Mascarene Islands; also Southern Arabia.
3. The *Indian* region; including India south of the Himalayas, to Southern China, Borneo, and Java.
4. The *Australian* region; including Australia, the Pacific Islands, Celebes, and Lombock.

II. NEOGÆA.

5. The *Nearctic* region; including North America to Northern Mexico.
6. The *Neotropical* region; including South America, the West Indies, and Southern Mexico.

Comparatively few classes and orders of animals have been carefully studied with regard to their geographical distribution, but the majority of those which have been examined show that the difference of latitude is accompanied by a greater dissimilarity of indigenous species than that of longitude, and that a main division into an old world and new world fauna is untenable. More especially the Freshwater fishes, with which we are here solely concerned, have been spread in *circumpolar* zones, and in a but limited degree from north to south. No family, much less a genus, ranges from the north to the south, whilst a number of families and genera make the entire circuit, and some species more than half of the circuit round the globe within the zone to which they belong. Not even the Cyprinoids and Siluroids, which are most characteristic of the freshwater fauna of our period, are an exception to this. Temperature and climate, indeed, are the principal factors by which the character of the freshwater fauna is determined; they form the barriers which interfere with the unlimited dispersal of an ichthyic type, much more than mountain ranges, deserts, or oceans. Hence the tropical zone is an impassable barrier to the northern Freshwater fish in its progress towards the south; where a similarly temperate climate obtains in the southern hemisphere, fish-forms appear *analogous* to those of the north, but *genetically* and *structurally distinct*.

The similarity which obtains in fishes at somewhat distant points of the same degree of longitude, rarely extends far, and is due to the natural tendency of every animal to spread as far as physical conditions will permit. Between two regions situated north and south of each other there is always a debateable border ground, in parts of which sometimes the fishes of the one, sometimes those of the other, predominate, and which is, in fact, a *band* of demarcation. Within this band the regions overlap each other; therefore, their border *lines* are rarely identical, and should be determined by the northern and southernmost extent of the most characteristic types of each region. Thus, for instance, in China, a broad band intervenes between temperate and tropical Asia, in which these two faunæ mix, and the actual northern border line of the tropical fauna is north of the southern border line of temperate Asia.

It is the aim of every philosophical classification to indicate the degree of affinity which obtains between the various divisions; but the mode of division into six equivalent regions, as given above, does not fulfil this aim with regard to Freshwater fishes, the distribution of which allows of further generalisation and subdivision. The two families, *Cyprinidæ* and *Siluridæ*, of which the former yields a contingent of one-third, and the latter of one-fourth of all the freshwater species known of our period, afford most valuable guidance for the valuation of the degrees of affinity between the various divisions The Cyprinoids may be assumed to have taken their origin in the Alpine region, dividing the temperate and tropical parts of Asia; endowed with a greater capability of acclimatising themselves in a temperate as well as tropical climate than any other family of freshwater fishes, they spread north and south as well as east and west; in the preglacial epoch they reached North America, but they have not had time to penetrate into South America, Australia, or the islands of the Pacific. The Siluroids, principally fishes of the sluggish waters of the plains, and well adapted for surviving changes of the water in which they live, for living in mud or sea-water, flourish most in the tropical climate, in which this type evidently had its origin. They came into existence after the Cyprinoids, fossil remains being known only from tertiary deposits in India, none from Europe. They rapidly spread over the areas of land within the tropical zone, reaching northern Australia from India, and one species, even immigrated into the Sandwich Islands, probably from South America. The Coral Islands of the Pacific still remain untenanted by them. Their progress into temperate regions was evidently slow, only very few species penetrating into the temperate parts of Asia and Europe; and the North American species, although more numerous, showing no great variety of structure, all belonging to the same group (*Amiurina*). Towards the south their progress was still slower, Tasmania, New Zealand, and Patagonia being without representatives, whilst the streams of the Andes of Chili are inhabited by a few dwarfed forms identical with such as are characteristic of similar localities in the more northern and warmer parts of the South American continent.

After these preliminary remarks we propose the following division of the fauna of Freshwater fishes :—

I. THE NORTHERN ZONE.— Characterised by Acipenseridæ. Few Siluridæ. Numerous Cyprinidæ. Salmonidæ, Esocidæ.

1. *Europo-Asiatic or Palæarctic Region.*—Characterised by absence of osseous Ganoidei ; Cobitidæ and Barbus numerous.

2. *North American Region.*—Characterised by osseous Ganoidei, Amiurina, and Catostomina ; but no Cobitidæ or Barbus.

II. THE EQUATORIAL ZONE.—Characterised by the development of Siluridæ.

A. *Cyprinoid Division.* — Characterised by presence of Cyprinidæ and Labyrinthici.

1. *Indian Region.*—Characterised by [absence of Dipnoi [1]] Ophiocephalidæ, Mastacembelidæ. Cobitidæ numerous.

2. *African Region.*—Characterised by presence of Dipnoi and Polypteridæ. Chromides and Characinidæ numerous. Mormyridæ. Cobitidæ absent.

1 Will probably be found.

B. *Acyprinoid Division.*—Characterised by absence of Cyprinidæ and Labyrinthici.

1. *Tropical American Region.*—Characterised by presence of Dipnoi. Chromides and Characinidæ numerous. Gymnotidæ.
2. *Tropical Pacific Region.*—Characterised by presence of Dipnoi. Chromides and Characinidæ absent.

III. The Southern Zone.—Characterised by absence of Cyprinidæ, and scarcity of Siluridæ. Haplochitonidæ and Galaxiidæ represent the Salmonoids and Esoces of the Northern zone. One region only.

1. *Antarctic Region.*—Characterised by the small number of species; the fishes of—

   a. The Tasmanian sub-region;
   b. The New Zealand sub-region;
   c. The Patagonian sub-region;

   being almost identical.[1]

In the following detailed account we begin with a description of the equatorial zone, this being the one from which the two principal families of freshwater fishes seem to have spread.

I. Equatorial Zone.

Roughly speaking, the borders of this zoological zone coincide with the geographical limits of the tropical zone, the tropics of the Cancer and Capricorn; its characteristic forms, however, extend in undulating lines several degrees north and southwards. Commencing from the west coast of

[1] We distinguish these sub-regions, because their distinction is justified by other classes of animals; as regards freshwater fishes their distinctness is even less than that between Europe and Northern Asia.

Africa the desert of the Sahara forms a well-marked boundary between the equatorial and northern zones; as the boundary approaches the Nile it makes a sudden sweep towards the north as far as Northern Syria (*Mastacembelus*, near Aleppo, and in the Tigris; *Clarias* and *Chromides*, in the lake of Galilee); crosses through Persia and Afghanistan (*Ophiocephalus*), to the southern ranges of the Himalayas, and follows the course of the Yang-tse-Kiang, which receives its contingent of equatorial fishes through its southern tributaries. Its continuation through the North Pacific may be considered to be indicated by the tropic which strikes the coast of Mexico at the southern end of the Gulf of California. Equatorial types of South America are known to extend so far northwards; and by following the same line the West India Islands are naturally included in this zone.

Towards the south the equatorial zone embraces the whole of Africa and Madagascar, and seems to extend still farther south in Australia, its boundary probably following the southern coast of that continent; the detailed distribution of the freshwater fishes of South-Western Australia has been but little studied, but the few facts which we know show that the tropical fishes of Queensland follow the principal water-course of that country, the Murray River, far towards the south and probably to its mouth. The boundary-line then stretches northwards of Tasmania and New Zealand, coinciding with the tropic until it strikes the western slope of the Andes, on the South American Continent, where it again bends southwards to embrace the system of the Rio de la Plata.

The equatorial zone is divided into four regions:—

A. The Indian region.

B. The African region.

C. The Tropical American region.

D. The Tropical Pacific region.

These four regions diverge into two well-marked divisions, one of which is characterised by the presence of Cyprinoid fishes, combined with the development of Labyrinthici; whilst in the other both these types are absent. The boundary between the Cyprinoid and Acyprinoid division seems to follow Wallace's line, a line drawn from the south of the Philippines between Borneo and Celebes, and farther south between Bali and Lombock. Borneo abounds in Cyprinoids; from the Philippine Islands a few only are known at present, and in Bali two species have been found; but none are known from Celebes or Lombock, or from islands situated farther east of them.[1]

Taking into consideration the manner in which Cyprinoids and Siluroids have been dispersed, we are obliged to place the Indian region as the first in the order of our treatment; and indeed the number of its freshwater fishes, which appear to have spread from it into the neighbouring regions, far exceeds that of the species which it has received from them.

A. The Indian Region comprises the whole continent of Asia south of the Himalayas and the Yang-tse-kiang; it includes the islands to the west of Wallace's line. Towards the north-east the island of Formosa, which also by other parts of its fauna leans more towards the equatorial zone, has received some characteristic Japanese Freshwater fishes, for instance, the singular Salmonoid *Plecoglossus*. Within the geographical boundaries of China the Freshwater fishes of the tropics pass gradually into those of the northern zone, both being separated by a broad debateable ground. The affluents of the great river tra-

[1] Martens (Preuss. Exped. Ostas. Zool. i. p. 356), has already drawn attention that a Barbel, said to have been obtained by Ida Pfeiffer in Amboyna (Günth. Fish. vii. p. 123), cannot have come from that locality.

versing this district are more numerous from the south than from the north, and carry the southern fishes far into the temperate zone. The boundary of this region towards the north-west is scarcely better defined. Before Persia passed through the geological changes by which its waters were converted into brine and finally dried up, it seems to have been inhabited by many characteristic Indian forms, of which a few still survive in the tract intervening between Afghanistan and Syria; *Ophiocephalus* and *Discognathus* have each at least one representative, *Macrones* has survived in the Tigris, and Mastacembelus has penetrated as far as Aleppo. Thus, Freshwater fishes belonging to India, Africa, and Europe, are intermingled in a district which forms the connecting link between the three continents. Of the freshwater fishes of Arabia we are perfectly ignorant; so much only being known that the Indian *Discognathus lamta* occurs in the reservoirs of Aden, having, moreover, found its way to the opposite African coast; and that the ubiquitous Cyprinodonts flourish in brackish pools of Northern Arabia.

The following is the list of the forms of freshwater fishes inhabiting this region:[1]—

Percina—		
Lates[2] [Africa, Australia]	1	species.
Nandina	7	,,
Labyrinthici [Africa]	25	,,
Luciocephalidæ	1	,,
Ophiocephalidæ [1 species in Africa]	30	,,
Mastacembelidæ [3 species in Africa]	10	,,
Chromides [Africa, South America]		
Etroplus	2	,,

[1] In the following and succeeding lists, those forms which are peculiar to and exclusively characteristic of, the region, are printed in italics; the other regions, in which the non-peculiar forms occur, are mentioned within brackets [ ].

[2] Lates calcarifer in India as well as Australia.

Siluridæ—		
Clariina [Africa] . . .	12	species.
Chacina	3	"
Silurina [Africa, Palæarct.] . .	72	"
Bagrina [Africa] . . .	50	"
Ariina [Africa, Australia, South America]	40	"
Bagariina	20	"
Rhinoglanina [Africa] . . .	1	"
Hypostomatina [South America] . .	5	"
Cyprinodontidæ—		
Carnivoræ [Palæarct., North America, Africa, South America] . .		
Haplochilus [Africa, South America, North America, Japan] . .	4	"
Cyprinidæ [Palæarct., N. America, Africa]—		
Cyprinina [Palæarct., N. America, Africa]	190	"
Rasborina [Africa, 1 species] . .	20	"
Semiplotina	4	"
Danionina [Africa] . . .	30	"
Abramidina [Palæarct., N. Amer., Africa]	30	"
Homalopterina	10	"
Cobitidina [Palæarct.] . . .	50	"
Osteoglossidæ [Africa, Australia, S. America]	1	"
Notopteridæ [Africa] . . .	3	"
Symbranchidæ—		
Amphipnous	1	"
Monopterus	1	"
Symbranchus [1 species in S. America] .	2	"
	625	species.

In analysing this list we find that out of 39 families or groups of freshwater fishes 12 are represented in this region, and that 625 species are known to occur in it; a number equal to two-sevenths of the entire number of freshwater fishes known. This large proportion is principally due to the development of numerous local forms of Siluroids and

Cyprinoids, of which the former show a contingent of about 200, and the latter of about 330 species. The combined development of those two families, and their undue preponderance over the other freshwater types, is therefore the principal characteristic of the Indian region. The second important character of its fauna is the apparently total absence of Ganoid and Cyclostomous fishes. Every other region has representatives of either Ganoids or Cyclostomes, some of both. However, attention has been directed to the remarkable coincidence of the geographical distribution of the *Sirenidæ* and *Osteoglossidæ*, and as the latter family is represented in Sumatra and Borneo, it may be reasonably expected that a Dipnoous form will be found to accompany it. The distribution of the *Sirenidæ* and *Osteoglossidæ* is as follows :—

Tropical America.

Lepidosiren paradoxa	Osteoglossum bicirrhosum. Arapaima gigas.

Tropical Australia.

Ceratodus forsteri. Ceratodus miolepis.	Osteoglossum leichardti.

East Indian Archipelago.

	Osteoglossum formosum.

Tropical Africa.

Protopterus annectens.	Heterotis niloticus.

Not only are the corresponding species found within the same region, but also in the same river systems ; and although such a connection may and must be partly due to a similarity of habit, yet the identity of this singular distribution is so striking that it can only be accounted for by assuming that the *Osteoglossidæ* are one of the earliest Teleosteous types which have been contemporaries of and have accompanied the present Dipnoi since or even before the beginning of the tertiary epoch.

Of the *autochthont* freshwater fishes of the Indian region, some are still limited to it, viz., the *Nandina*, the *Luciocephalidæ* (of which one species only exists in the Archipelago), of Siluroids the *Chacina* and *Bagariina*, of Cyprinoids the *Semiplotina* and *Homalopterina*; others very nearly so, like the *Labyrinthici*, *Ophiocephalidæ*, *Mastacembelidæ*, of Siluroids the *Silurina*, of Cyprinoids the *Rasborina* and *Danionina*, and *Symbranchidæ*.

The regions with which the Indian has least similarity are the North American and Antarctic, as they are the most distant. Its affinity to the other regions is of a very different degree:—

1. Its affinity to the Europo-Asiatic region is indicated almost solely by three groups of Cyprinoids, viz., the *Cyprinina*, *Abramidina*, and *Cobitidina*. The development of these groups north and south of the Himalayas is due to their common origin in the highlands of Asia; but the forms which descended into the tropical climate of the south are now so distinct from their northern brethren that most of them are referred to distinct genera. The genera which are still common to both regions are only the true Barbels (*Barbus*), a genus which, of all Cyprinoids, has the largest range over the old world, and of which some 160 species have been described; and, secondly, the Mountain Barbels (*Schizothorax*, etc.), which, peculiar to the Alpine waters of Central Asia, descend a short distance only towards the tropical plains, but extend farther into rivers within the northern temperate districts. The origin and the laws of the distribution of the *Cobitidina* appear to have been identical with those of *Barbus*, but they have not spread into Africa.

If, in determining the degree of affinity between two

regions, we take into consideration the extent in which an exchange has taken place of the faunæ originally peculiar to each, we must estimate that obtaining between the freshwater fishes of the Europo-Asiatic and Indian regions as very slight indeed.

2. There exists a great affinity between the Indian and African regions; seventeen out of the twenty-six families or groups found in the former are represented by one or more species in Africa, and many of the African species are not even generically different from the Indian. As the majority of these groups have many more representatives in India than in Africa, we may reasonably assume that the African species have been derived from the Indian stock; but this is probably not the case with the Siluroid group of *Clariina*, which with regard to species is nearly equally distributed between the two regions, the African species being referable to three genera (*Clarias, Heterobranchus, Gymnallabes*, with the subgenus *Channallabes*), whilst the Indian species belong to two genera only, viz. *Clarias* and *Heterobranchus.* On the other hand, the Indian region has derived from Africa one freshwater form only, viz. *Etroplus*, a member of the family of *Chromides*, so well represented in tropical Africa and South America. *Etroplus* inhabits Southern and Western India and Ceylon, and has its nearest ally in a Madegasse Freshwater fish, *Paretroplus.* Considering that other African Chromides have acclimatised themselves at the present day in saline water, we think it more probable that Etroplus should have found its way to India through the ocean than over the connecting land area; where, besides, it does not occur.

3. A closer affinity between the Indian and Tropical American regions than is indicated by the character of the equatorial zone generally, does not exist. No genus of Freshwater fishes occurs in India and South America without being found in the intermediate African region, with two exceptions.

Four small Indian Siluroids (*Sisor, Erethistes, Pseudecheneis,* and *Exostoma*) have been referred to the South American *Hypostomatina*; but it remains to be seen whether this combination is based upon a sufficient agreement of their internal structure, or whether it is not rather artificial. On the other hand, the occurrence and wide distribution in tropical America of a fish of the Indian family Symbranchidæ (*Symbranchus marmoratus*), which is not only congeneric with, but also most closely allied to, the Indian *Symbranchus bengalensis*, offers one of those extraordinary anomalies in the distribution of animals of which no satisfactory explanation can be given at present.

4. The relation of the Indian region to the Tropical Pacific region consists only in its having contributed a few species to the poor fauna of the latter. This immigration must have taken place within a recent period, because some species now inhabit fresh waters of tropical Australia and the South Sea Islands without having in any way changed their specific characters, as *Lates calcarifer*, species of *Dules, Plotosus anguillaris*; others (species of *Arius*) are but little different from Indian congeners. All these fishes must have migrated by the sea; a supposition which is supported by what we know of their habits. We need not add that India has not received a single addition to its freshwater fish-fauna from the Pacific region.

Before concluding these remarks on the Indian region, we must mention that peculiar genera of Cyprinoids and Siluroids inhabit the streams and lakes of its alpine ranges in the north. Some of them, like the Siluroid genera *Glyptosternum, Euglyptosternum, Pseudecheneis,* have a folded disk on the thorax between their horizontally spread pectoral fins; by means of this they adhere to stones at the bottom of the mountain torrents, and without it they would be swept away into the lower courses of the rivers. The Cyprinoid genera inhabiting similar localities, and the lakes into which the alpine rivers pass, such as *Oreinus, Schizothorax, Ptychobarbus, Schizopygopsis, Diptychus, Gymnocypris*, are distinguished by peculiarly enlarged scales near the vent, the physiological use of which has not yet been ascertained. These alpine genera extend far into the Europo-Asiatic region, where the climate is similar to that of their southern home. No observations have been made by which the altitudinal limits of fish life in the Himalayas can be fixed, but it is probable that it reaches the line of perpetual snow, as in the European Alps which are inhabited by Salmonoids. Griffith found an *Oreinus* and a Loach, the former in abundance, in the Helmund at Gridun Dewar, altitude 10,500 feet; and another Loach at Kaloo at 11,000 feet.

B. The AFRICAN REGION comprises the whole of the African continent south of the Atlas and the Sahara. It might have been conjectured that the more temperate climate of its southern extremity would have been accompanied by a conspicuous difference of the fish-fauna. But this is not the case; the difference between the tropical and southern parts of Africa consists simply in the gradual disappearance of specifically tropical forms, whilst Siluroids, Cyprinoids, and even Labyrinthici penetrate to its southern coast; no new form has entered to impart to South Africa a character distinct from the central portion of the continent. In the north-east the African fauna passes the Isthmus of Suez and penetrates into Syria; the system of the Jordan presenting so many African types that it has to be included in a description of the African region as well as of the Europo-Asiatic. This river is inhabited by three species of *Chromis*, one of *Hemichromis*, and *Clarias macracanthus*, a common fish of the Upper Nile. This infusion of African forms cannot be accounted for by any one of those accidental means of dispersal, as *Hemichromis* is not represented in the north-eastern parts of Africa proper, but chiefly on the west coast and in the Central African lakes.

Madagascar clearly belongs to this region. Besides some Gobies and *Dules*, which are not true freshwater fishes, four *Chromides* are known. To judge from general accounts, its Freshwater fauna is poorer than might be expected; but, singular as it may appear, collectors have hitherto paid but little attention to the Freshwater fishes of this island. The fishes found in the freshwaters of the Seychelles and Mascarenes are brackish-water fishes, such as *Fundulus*, *Haplochilus*, *Elops*, *Mugil*, etc.

The following is the list of the forms of Freshwater fishes inhabiting this region :—

Dipnoi [Australia, Neotrop.]—		
Lepidosiren annectens	1	species.
Polypteridæ	2	„
Percina (Cosmopol.)—		
Lates [India, Australia]	1	„
Labyrinthici [India]	5	„
Ophiocephalidæ [India]	1	„
Mastacembelidæ [India]	3	„
Chromides [South America]—		
Chromis	23	„
Hemichromis	5	„
Paretroplus	1	„
Siluridæ—		
Clariina [India]	14	„
Silurina [India, Palæarct.]	11	„
Bagrina [India]	10	„
Pimelodina [South America]	2	„
Ariina[1] [India, Australia, S. Amer., Patagonia]	4	„
Doradina [South America]—		
Synodontis	15	„

[1] One species (*Arius thalassinus*) found in Indian and African rivers.

Rhinoglanina [India]	2 species.
Malapterurina	3 „
Characinidæ [South America]—	
Citharinina	2 „
Nannocharacina	2 „
Tetragonopterina—	
Alestes	14 „
Crenuchina—	
Xenocharax	1 „
Hydrocyonina—	
Hydrocyon	4 „
Distichodontina	10 „
Ichthyborina	2 „
Mormyridæ (*Gymnarchidæ*)	51 „
Cyprinodontidæ—	
Carnivoræ [Palæarct., India, S. America—	
Haplochilus [India, South America]	7 ,
Fundulus [Palæarct., Nearct.]	1 „
Cyprinidæ [Palæarct., India, North America]—	
Cyprinina [Palæarct., India, N. America—	
Labeo [India]	6 „
Barynotus [India]	2 „
Abrostomus	2 „
Discognathus lamta[1] [India]	1 „
Barbus [Palæarct., India]	35 „
Rasborina [India]	1 „
Danionina [India]—	
Barilius [India]	3 „
Abramidina [Palæarct., India, N. America]—	
Pelotrophus	2 „
Kneriidæ	2 „
Osteoglossidæ [India, Australia, South America]—	
Heterotis	1 „
Pantodontidæ	1 „
Notopteridæ [India]	2 „
	255 species.

[1] This species extends from India into East Africa.

Out of the 39 families or groups of freshwater fishes 15 are represented in the African region, or three more than in the Indian region; however of two of them, viz., the *Ophiocephalidæ* and *Mastacembelidæ*, a few species only have found their way into Africa. On the other hand, the number of species is much less, viz. 255, which is only two-fifths of that of the known Indian species. The small degree of specialisation and localisation is principally due to the greater uniformity of the physical conditions of this continent, and to the almost perfect continuity of the great river systems, which take their origin from the lakes in its centre. This is best shown by a comparison of the fauna of the Upper Nile with that of the West African rivers. The number of species known from the Upper Nile amounts to 56, and of these not less than 25 are absolutely identical with West African species. There is an uninterrupted continuity of the fish-fauna from west to the north-east, and the species known to be common to both extremities may be reasonably assumed to inhabit also the great reservoirs of water in the centre of the continent. A greater dissimilarity is noticeable between the west and north-east fauna on the one hand, and that of the Zambezi on the other; the affinity between them is merely generic; and all the fishes hitherto collected in Lake Nyassa have proved to be distinct from those of the Nile, and even from those of other parts of the system of the Zambezi.

Africa, unlike India, does not possess either alpine ranges or outlying archipelagoes, the fresh waters of which would swell the number of its indigenous species; but at a future time, when its fauna is better known than at present, it is possible that the great difference in the number of species between this and the Indian regions may be somewhat lessened.

The most numerously-represented families are the Siluroids, with 61 species; the Cyprinoids, with 52; the Mormyridæ, with 51; the Characinidæ, with 35; and the Chromides, with 29. There is not, therefore, that great preponderance of the two first families over the remaining, which we noticed in the Indian region; in Africa there is a comparatively greater variety of distinct Freshwater types, imparting to the study of its fauna an unflagging pleasure such as is scarcely gained by the study of the other region. With the forms peculiar to it there are combined those of India as well as South America.

In Tropical Africa there are still remnants of Ganoids: *Protopterus* (*Lepidosiren*) *annectens* and *Polypterus bichir*, with the singularly modified *Calamoichthys*. The two former range from east to west, and are accompanied by an Osteoglossoid (*Heterotis*) which has hitherto been found in the Nile and on the West Coast only.

Autochthont and limited to this region are the *Mormyridæ*, *Pantodontidæ*, and *Kneriidæ*, a singular type, somewhat akin to the Loaches. Of Siluroid genera the most characteristic are *Synodontis*, *Rhinoglanis*, and the electric *Malapterurus*; of Characinoids, *Citharinus*, *Alestes*, *Xenocharax*, *Hydrocyon*, *Distichodon*, *Ichthyborus*.

The regions with which Africa (like India) has least similarity are, again, the North American and Antarctic. Its affinity with the Europo-Asiatic region consists only in having received, like this latter, a branch of the Cyprinoids, the African Carps and Barbels resembling, on the whole, more Indian than Europo-Asiatic forms. Its similarity to Australia is limited to the two regions possessing Dipnoous and Osteoglossoid types. But its relations to the two other regions of the equatorial zone are near and of great interest.

1. Africa has, in common with India, the Siluroid group of *Clariina*, the *Silurina*, and *Bagrina*; and more especially the small but very natural family of *Notopteridæ*, represented by three species in India, and by two on the *west coast* of Africa. It would be hazardous to state at present in which

of the two regions these fishes first made their appearance, but the discovery of remains of *Notopteridæ* and *Silurina* in tertiary deposits of Sumatra points to the Indian region as their original home. We can have less doubt about the other fishes common to both regions; they are clearly immigrants into Africa from the East, and it is a remarkable fact that these immigrants have penetrated to the most distant limits of Africa in the west as well as in the south,—viz. the *Labyrinthici*, represented by two genera closely allied to the Indian *Anabas;* the *Ophiocephalidæ* and *Mastacembelidæ*, a few species of which have penetrated to the west coast, singularly enough being absent from the eastern rivers; the *Ariina*, represented by several species, of which one or two are identical with Indian, having extended their range along the intervening coasts to the east coast of Africa. The Cyprinoids also afford an instance of an Indian species ranging into Africa, viz. *Discognathus lamta*, which seems to have crossed at the southern extremity of the Red Sea, as it is found in the reservoirs at Aden and the hill-streams of the opposite coast-region of Abyssinia.

2. No such direct influx of species and genera has occurred from South America into Africa. Yet the affinity of their Freshwater fishes is striking. Two of the most natural families of fishes, the *Chromides* and *Characinidæ*, are peculiar, and (with the exception of *Etroplus*) restricted to them. The African and South American Dipnoi are closely allied to each other. The *Pimelodina*, so characteristic of Tropical America, have three representatives in Africa, viz., *Pimelodus platychir*, *P. balayi*, and *Auchenoglanis biscutatus;* the *Doradina* are another Siluroid group restricted to these two continents.[1] Yet, with all these points of close resem-

[1] We have left out from these considerations the Ariina and Cyprinodonts, which can pass with impunity through salt water, and are spread over much larger areas.

blance, the African and South American series are, with the exception of the two species of Pimelodus, *generically* distinct; which shows that the separation of the continents must have been of an old date. On the other hand, the existence of so many similar forms on both sides of the Atlantic affords much support to the supposition that at a former period the distance between the present Atlantic continents was much less, and that the fishes which have diverged towards the East and West are descendants of a common stock which had its home in a region now submerged under some intervening part of that ocean. Be this as it may, it is evident that the physical conditions of Africa and South America have remained unchanged for a considerable period, and are still sufficiently alike to preserve the identity of a number of peculiar freshwater forms on both sides of the Atlantic. Africa and South America are, moreover, the only continents which have produced in Freshwater fishes, though in very different families, one of the most extraordinary modifications of an organ—the conversion, that is, of muscle into an apparatus creating electric force.

C. The boundaries of the Tropical American (*Neotropical*) Region have been sufficiently indicated in the definition of the Equatorial zone. A broad and most irregular band of country, in which the South and North American forms are mixed, exists in the north; offering some peculiarities which deserve fuller attention in the subsequent description of the relations between the South and North American faunæ. The following Freshwater fishes inhabit this region:—

Dipnoi [Australia, Africa]—

Lepidosiren paradoxa . . .	1	species.
Polycentridæ	3	„
Chromides [Africa]—		
Heros, Acara, Cichla, etc. . .	80	„
(*Lucifuga*	2	„)

Siluridæ—		
Hypophthalmina	5	species.
Pimelodina [Africa, 2 species]	70	„
Ariina [Africa, India, Australia, Fuegian]	35	„
Doradina [Africa]	60	„
Hypostomatina [India]	90	„
Aspredinina	9	„
Nematogenyina [Fuegian]—	2	„
Trichomycterina [Fuegian]	2	„
Stegophilina	3	„
Characinidæ [Africa]—		
Erythrinina	15	„
Curimatina	40	„
Anastomatina	25	„
Tetragonopterina	80	„
Hydrocyonina	30	„
Crenuchina	1	„
Serrasalmonina	35	„
Cyprinodontidæ—		
Carnivoræ [Europe, Asia, N. America, India, Africa]	30	„
Limnophagæ	31	„
Osteoglossidæ [Africa, India, Australia]	2	„
Gymnotidæ	20	„
Symbranchidæ [India]	1	„
	672	species.

Out of the 39 families or groups of Freshwater fishes, 9 only are represented in the Tropical American region. This may be accounted for by the fact that South America is too much isolated from the other regions of the Equatorial zone to have received recent additions to its fauna. On the other hand, the number of species exceeds that of every other region, even of the Indian, with which, in regard to the comparative development of families, the Neotropical region shows great analogy, as will be seen from the following Table:—

INDIAN.		NEOTROPICAL.	
Siluridæ .	200 sp.	Siluridæ .	276 sp.
Cyprinidæ .	330 sp.	Characinidæ .	226 sp.
Labyrinthici .	25 sp.	Chromides .	80 sp.
Ophiocephalidæ	30 sp.	Cyprinodontidæ	60 sp.
Mastacembelidæ	10 sp.	Gymnotidæ .	20 sp.

In both regions the great number of species is due to the development of numerous local forms of two families, the *Characinidæ* taking in the New World the place of the *Cyprinidæ* of the Old World. Thereto are added a few smaller families with a moderately large number of species, which, however, is only a fraction of that of the leading families, the remainder of the families being represented by a few species only. The number of genera within each of the two regions of the two principal families is also singularly alike; the Indian region having produced about 45 Siluroid and as many Cyprinoid genera, whilst the Neotropical region is tenanted by 54 Siluroid and 40 Characinoid genera. These points of similarity between the two regions cannot be accidental; they indicate that agreement in their physical and hydrographical features which in reality exists.

Of Ganoids, we find in Tropical America one species only, *Lepidosiren paradoxa*, accompanied by two Osteoglossoids (*Osteoglossum bicirrhosum* and *Arapaima gigas*).

Autochthont and limited to this region are the *Polycentridæ*, all the non-African genera of *Chromides* and *Characinidæ*; of Siluroids, the *Hypophthalmina*, *Aspredinina*, and *Stegophilina*, and the majority of *Pimelodina*, *Hypostomatina*, and *Doradina*; the herbivorous Cyprinodonts or *Limnophagæ*, and numerous insectivorous Cyprinodonts or *Carnivoræ*; and the *Gymnotidæ* (Electric eel).

The relations to the other regions are as follows:—

1. The resemblances to the Indian and Tropical Pacific regions partly date from remote geological epochs, or are partly

due to that similarity of physical conditions to which we have already referred. We have again to draw attention to the unexplained presence in South America of a representative of a truly Indian type (not found in Africa), viz. *Symbranchus marmoratus.* On the other hand, a direct genetic affinity exists between the Neotropical and African regions, as has been noticed in the description of the latter, a great part of their freshwater fauna consisting of descendants from a common stock.

2. A comparison of the specifically Neotropical with the specifically North American types shows that no two regions can be more dissimilar. It is only in the intervening borderland, and in the large West Indian Islands, that the two faunæ mix with each other. We need not enter into the details of the physical features of Central America and Mexico —the broken ground, the variety of climate (produced by different altitudes) within limited districts, the hot and moist alluvial plains surrounding the Mexican Gulf, offer a diversity of conditions most favourable to the intermixture of the types from the north and the south. But yet the exchange of peculiar forms appears to be only beginning; none have yet penetrated beyond the debateable ground, and it is evident that the land-connection between the two continents is of comparatively recent date: a view which is confirmed by the identity of the marine fishes on both sides of Central America.

Cuba—and this is the only island in the West Indies which has a number of freshwater fishes sufficient for the determination of its zoogeographical relations—is inhabited by several kinds of a perch (*Centropomus*), freshwater mullets, Cyprinodonts, one species of Chromid (an *Acara*), and *Symbranchus marmoratus.* All these fishes are found in Central America, and as they belong to forms known to enter brackish water more or less freely, it is evident that they have crossed from the mainland of South America or from Central

America. But with them there came a remarkable North American type, *Lepidosteus*. *Lepidosteus viridis*, which is found in the United States, has penetrated on the mainland to the Pacific coast of Guatemala, where it is common at the mouth of the rivers and in brack-water lakes along the coast; it probably crossed into Cuba from Florida. A perfectly isolated type of fishes inhabits the subterranean waters of the caves of Cuba (two species of *Lucifuga*). The eyes are absent or quite rudimentary, as in most other cave animals. Singularly, it belongs to a family (*Ophidiidæ*), the members of which are strictly marine; and its nearest ally is a genus, *Brotula*, the species of which are distributed over the Indo-Pacific Ocean, one only occurring in the Caribbean Sea. This type must have witnessed all the geological changes which have taken place since Cuba rose above the surface of the sea.

A similar mixture of forms of the Tropical and Temperate types of Freshwater fishes takes place in the south of South America; its details have not yet been so well studied as in the north; but this much is evident that, whilst in the East Tropical forms follow the Plate river far into the Temperate region, in the West the Temperate Fauna finds still a congenial climate in ranges of the Andes, situated close to, or even north of, the Tropic.

Like the Indian region, the Tropical American has a peculiar Alpine Fauna, the Freshwater fishes of which, however, belong to the Siluroids and Cyprinodonts. The former are small, dwarfed forms (*Arges*, *Stygogenes*, *Brontes*, *Astroblepus*, *Trichomycterus*, *Eremophilus*), and have a perfectly naked body, whilst the representatives in the lowlands of, at least, the first four genera are mailed. The Alpine Cyprinodonts, on the other hand, (*Orestias*) exceed the usual small size of the other members of this family, are covered with thick scales, but have lost their ventral fins. Some of these Alpine forms, like *Trichomycterus*, follow the range of the Andes far into the southern temperate region. The majority reach to a height of 15,000 feet above the level of the sea, and a few are found still higher.

D. The TROPICAL PACIFIC REGION includes all the islands east of Wallace's Line, New Guinea, Australia—with the exception of its south-eastern portion,—and all the islands of the Tropical Pacific to the Sandwich group. Comparing the area of this region with that of the others, we find it to be not only the poorest in point of the number of its species generally, but also in that of the possession of peculiar forms, as will appear from the following list:—

Dipnoi [Neotrop., Africa.]	
Ceratodus	2 species.
Percidæ [Cosmopol.]—	
Lates (calcarifer) [India] . .	1 ,,
Nannoperca	1 ,,
Oligorus [New Zealand] . . .	1 ,,
Dules [India]	8 ,,
(*Macquaria*)	1 ,,
Labyrinthici—	
Anabas (scandens) [India] . .	1 ,,
Ophiocephalidæ—	
Ophiocephalus (striatus) [India] . .	1 ,,
Atherinidæ [Brack-water]—	
Atherinichthys	2 ,,
Osteoglossidæ [India, Africa, Neotrop.] .	1 ,,
Siluridæ—	
Plotosina [India] . . .	9 ,,
Ariina [India, Africa, Neotrop.] . .	7 ,,
Symbranchidæ—	
Monopterus (javanicus) [India] . .	1 ,,
Total .	36 species.

The paucity of freshwater fishes is due, in the first place, to the arid climate and the deficiency of water in the Australian continent, as well as to the insignificant size of the fresh-water courses in the smaller islands. Still this cannot be the only cause : the large island of Celebes, which, by its mountainous portions, as well as by its extensive plains and lowlands, would seem to offer a favourable variety of conditions for the development of a freshwater Fauna, is, as far as has been ascertained, tenanted by seven Freshwater fishes only, viz. 2 *Arius*, 2 *Plotosus*, 1 *Anabas*, 1 *Ophiocephalus*, 1 *Monopterus*, all of which are the commonest species of the Indian region. New Guinea has not yet been explored, but, from the faunæ nearest to this island, we expect its fresh-water fishes will prove to be equally few in number, and identical with those of Celebes and North Australia ; a supposition confirmed by the few small collections which have reached Europe. Finding, then, that even those parts of this region, which are favourable to the development of Fresh-water fishes, have not produced any distinct forms, and that the few species which inhabit them, are unchanged, or but slightly modified Indian species, we must conclude that the whole of this area has remained geologically isolated from the other regions of this zone since the commencement of the existence of Teleostei; and that, with the exception of *Ceratodus* and *Osteoglossum*, the immigration of the other species is of very recent date.

Fossil remains of *Ceratodus* have been found in Liassic and Triassic formations of North America, England, Germany, and India ; and it is, therefore, a type which was widely spread in the Mesozoic epoch. Although it would be rash to conclude that its occupation of Australia dates equally far back, for it may have reached that continent long afterwards ; yet it is evident that, as it is one of the most ancient of the existing types, so it is certainly the first of the Freshwater fishes which appeared in Australia. *Osteoglossum*, of which no fossil remains yet have been found, is proved by its distribution to be one of the oldest Teleosteous types. There must have been a long gap of time before these ancient types were joined by the other Teleostei. All of them migrated through the intervening parts of the ocean from India. Most of the *Plotosina*, some of the *Arii*, *Dules*, and the *Atherinichthys*, also *Nannoperca* (allied to *Apogon*), were among the earliest arrivals, being sufficiently differentiated to be specifically or even generically (*Cnidoglanis*, *Nannoperca*) distinguished; but some others, like *Anabas scandens*, *Lates calcarifer*, *Dules marginatus*, must have reached the Australian continent quite recently, for they are indistinguishable from Indian specimens.

In South-western Australia a mingling of the scanty fauna with that of the southern temperate parts takes place. *Oligorus macquariensis* (The Murray Cod), which has a congener on the coast of New Zealand, ascends high up the Murray river, so that we cannot decide whether this Percoid should be located in the Tropical or Temperate part of Australia. Several *Galaxias* also extend to the confines of Queensland, and will probably some day be found members of this region.

In the smaller Pacific islands the Freshwater fishes exhibit a remarkable sameness: two or three species of *Dules*, several Eels, an Atherine, or some Gobies, Mullets, and other fishes which with equal readiness exchange fresh for salt water, and which would at once reach and occupy any streams or freshwater lakes that may be formed on an island.

The Sandwich Islands are the only group among the smaller islands which are tenanted by a Siluroid, a species of *Arius*, which is closely allied to Central American species, and, therefore, probably immigrated from Tropical America.

II. Northern Zone.

The boundaries of the Northern Zone coincide in the

main with the northern limit of the Equatorial Zone; but at three different points they overlap the latter, as has been already indicated. This happens in, and east of, Syria, where the mixed faunæ of the Jordan and the rivers of Mesopotamia demand the inclusion of this territory into the Northern Zone as well as the Equatorial; in the island of Formosa, where a Salmonoid and several Japanese Cyprinoids flourish; and in Central America, where a *Lepidosteus*, a Cyprinoid (*Sclerognathus meridionalis*), and an Amiurus (*A. meridionalis*) represent the North American fauna in the midst of a host of tropical forms.

A separate *Arctic* Zone does not exist for Freshwater fishes; ichthyic life becomes extinct towards the pole as soon as the fresh water remains frozen throughout the year, or thaws for a few weeks only; and the few fishes which extend into high latitudes, in which lakes are open for two or three months in the year, belong to types in no wise differing from those of the more temperate south. The highest latitude at which fishes have been obtained is 82° lat. N., whence the late Arctic Expedition brought back specimens of Charr (*Salmo arcturus* and *Salmo naresii*).

The ichthyological features of this zone are well marked: the Chondrosteous Ganoids or Sturgeons, and the families of *Salmonidæ* and *Esocidæ* are limited to, and characteristic of, it; Cyprinoids flourish with the Salmonoids, both families preponderating in numbers over the others, whilst the Siluroids are few in number and in variety.

The two regions in which this zone is divided are very closely related to one another, and their affinity is not unlike that which obtains between the sub-regions of the Southern Zone. The subjoined list will show their close agreement with regard to families as well as species. Several of the latter are common to both, viz.—*Acipenser sturio*, *A. maculatus*, *Perca fluviatilis*, *Gastrosteus pungitius*, *Salmo salar*,

Esox lucius, *Lota vulgaris*, *Petromyzon marinus*, *P. fluviatilis*, and *P. branchialis*; and all recent investigations have resulted in giving additional evidence of the affinity, and not of the diversity of the two regions.

In Europe and temperate Asia, as well as in North America, mountain ranges elevated beyond the line of perpetual snow would seem to offer physical conditions favourable for the development of a distinct alpine fauna. But this is not the case, because the difference of climate between the mountain districts and the lowlands is much less in this zone than in the Equatorial. Consequently the alpine freshwater fishes do not essentially differ from those of the plains; they are principally Salmonoids; and in Asia, besides, mountain-barbels and Loaches. *Salmo orientalis* was found by Griffith to abound in the tributaries of the Bamean river at an altitude of about 11,000 feet.

	Europe-Asiatic.	N. American.
Acipenseridæ—		
Acipenser . . .	9 species.	12 species.
Scaphirhynchus . .	2 „	1 „
Polyodon	1 „	1 „
Lepidosteidæ	0 „	3 „
Amiidæ	0 „	1 „
Percina [Cosmopol.] . .	10 „	30 „
Grystina [Australia, New Zealand]	0 „	2 „
Centrarchina . .	0 „	26 „
Aphredoderidæ . . .	0 „	1 „
Cottidæ [partly marine]—		
Cottus	3 „	8 „
Ptyonotus . . .	0 „	1 „
Gastrosteidæ	5 „	5 „
Comephoridæ	1 „	0 „
Gadidæ [marine]—		
Lota	1 „	1 „
Siluridæ—		
Silurina [India, Africa] .	5 „	0 „

	Europo-Asiatic.	N. American.
Bagrina	2 species.	0 species.
Amiurina	1 "	17 "
Salmonidæ	90 "	45 "
Percopsidæ	0 "	1 "
Esocidæ	1 "	7 "
Umbridæ	1 "	1 "
Cyprinodontidæ Carnivoræ [India, Africa, Neotrop.]	9 "	30 "
Heteropygii	0 "	2 "
Cyprinidæ—		
Catostomina	1 "	25 "
Cyprinina [India, Africa]	80 "	30 "
Leuciscina	60 "	70 "
Rhodeina	10 "	0 "
Abramidina [India, Africa]	44 "	10 "
Cobitidina [India]	20 "	0 "
Hyodontidæ	0 "	1 "
Petromyzontidæ [Southern Zone]	4 "	8 "
	360 species.	339 species.

A. The Europo-Asiatic (Palæarctic) Region.—Its western and southern boundaries coincide with those of the Northern Zone, so that only those which divide it from North America have to be indicated. Behring's Strait and the Kamtschatka Sea have been conventionally taken as the boundary, but this is shown to be artificial by the fact that the animals of both coasts, as far as they are known at present, are not sufficiently distinct to be referred to two distinct regions. As to the freshwater fishes those of North-western America and of Kamtschatka are but imperfectly known, but there can be little doubt that the same agreement exists between them as is the case with other classes of animals. The Japanese islands exhibit a decided Palæarctic fish-fauna, which includes Barbus and Cobitioids, forms strange to the North American fauna. A slight influx of tropical forms is perceived in the south of Japan, where two Bagrina (*Pseudobagrus aurantiacus* and *Liocassis longirostris*) have established themselves for a considerable period, for both are peculiar to the island, and have not been found elsewhere.

In the east, as well as in the west, the distinction between the Europo-Asiatic and North American regions disappears almost entirely the farther we advance towards the north. Of four species of the genus Salmo known from Iceland, one (*S. salar*) is common to both regions, two are European (*S. fario* and *S. alpinus*), and one is a peculiarly Icelandic race (*S. nivalis*). As far as we know the Salmonoids of Greenland and Baffin's Land they are all most closely allied to European species, though they may be distinguished as local races.

Finally, as we have seen above, the Europo-Asiatic fauna mingles with African and Indian forms in Syria, Persia, and Afghanistan. *Capoëta*, a Cyprinoid genus, is characteristic of this district, and well represented in the Jordan and rivers of Mesopotamia.

Assuming that the distribution of Cyprinoids has taken its origin from the alpine tract of country dividing the Indian and Palæarctic regions, we find that this type has found in the temperate region as equally favourable conditions for its development as in the tropical. Out of the 360 species known to exist in the Palæarctic regions, no less than 215 are Cyprinoids. In the countries and on the plateaus immediately joining the Himalayan ranges those mountain forms which we mentioned as peculiar to the Indian Alps abound and extend for a considerable distance towards the west and east, mixed with other *Cyprinina* and *Cobitidina*. The representatives of these two groups are more numerous in Central and Eastern Asia than in Europe and the northern parts of Asia, where the *Leuciscina* predominate. *Abramidina* or Breams are more numerous in the south and east of Asia, but they spread to the extreme north-western and northern limits, to which the Cyprinoid type reaches. The *Rhodeina* are a small family especially characteristic of the East, but with one or two off-shoots in Central Europe. Very significant is the appearance in China of a species of the *Catostomina*, a group otherwise limited to North America.

The Cyprinoids, in their dispersal from the south northwards, are met from the opposite direction by the Salmonoids. These fishes are, without doubt, one of the youngest families of *Teleostei*, for they did not appear before the Pliocene era; they flourished at any rate during the glacial period, and, as is testified by the remnants which we find in isolated elevated positions, like the Trout of the Atlas, of the mountains of Asia-Minor, and of the Hindu Kush, they spread to the extreme south of this region. At the present day they are most numerously represented in its northern temperate parts; towards the south they become scarcer, but increase again in numbers and species, wherever a great elevation offers them the snow-fed waters which they affect. In the rivers of the Mediterranean Salmonoids are by no means scarce, but they prefer the upper courses of those rivers, and do not migrate to the sea.

The Pike, Umbra, several species of Perch and Stickleback, are also clearly autochthont species of this region. Others belong to marine types, and seem to have been retained in fresh water at various epochs: thus the freshwater Cottus (Miller's Thumb); *Cottus quadricornis*, which inhabits lakes of Scandinavia, whilst other individuals of the same species are strictly marine; the Burbot (*Lota vulgaris*); and the singular *Comephorus*, a dwarfed and much-changed Gadoid which inhabits the greatest depths of Lake Baikal.

Remnants of the Palæichthyic fauna are the *Sturgeons* and *Lampreys*. The former inhabit in abundance the great rivers of Eastern Europe and Asia, periodically ascending them from the sea; their southernmost limits are the Yang-tse-kiang in the east, and rivers flowing into the Adriatic, Black and Caspian Seas, and Lake Aral, towards the centre of this region. None are known to have gone beyond the boundaries of the Northern Zone. If the Lampreys are justly reckoned among Freshwater fishes, their distribution is unique and exceptional. In the Palæarctic region some of the species descend periodically to the sea, whilst others remain stationary in the rivers; the same has been observed in the Lampreys of North America. They are entirely absent in the Equatorial Zone, but reappear in the Temperate Zone of the Southern Hemisphere. Many points of the organisation of the Cyclostomes indicate that they are a type of great antiquity.

The remaining Palæarctic fishes are clearly immigrants from neighbouring regions: thus *Silurus*, *Macrones*, and *Pseudobagrus* from the Indian region; *Amiurus* (and, as mentioned above, *Catostomus*) from North America. The Cyprinodonts are restricted to the southern and warmer parts; all belong to the carnivorous division. The facility with which these fishes accommodate themselves to a sojourn in fresh, brackish, or salt water, and even in thermal springs, renders their general distribution easily comprehensible, but it is impossible to decide to which region they originally belonged; their remains in tertiary deposits round the Mediterranean are not rare.

B. The boundaries of the NORTH AMERICAN OR NEARCTIC REGION have been sufficiently indicated. The main features and the distribution of this fauna are identical with those of the preceding region. The proportion of Cyprinoid species to the total number of North-American fishes (135 : 339) appears to be considerably less than in the Palæarctic region, but we cannot admit that these figures approach the truth, as the Cyprinoids of North America have been much less studied than those of Europe; of many scarcely more than the name is known. This also applies in a great measure to the Salmonoids, of which only half as many as are found in the Palæarctic region have been sufficiently described to be worthy of consideration. North America will, without doubt, in the end show as many distinct races as Europe and Asia.

Cyprinoids, belonging to genera living as well as extinct, existed in North America in the tertiary period. At present, *Cyprinina*, *Leuciscina*, and *Abramidina* are well represented, but there is no representative of the Old World genus *Barbus*, or of the *Cobitidina*[1]; *Rhodeina* are also absent. On the other hand, a well-marked Cyprinoid type is developed—the *Catostomina*, of which one species has, as it were, returned into Asia. Very characteristic is the group of *Centrarchina*, allied to the Perch, of which there are some thirty species; two *Grystina*. Of the Sticklebacks there are as many species as in Europe, and of Pike not less than seven species have been distinguished. *Umbra* appears to be as local as in Europe. Some very remarkable forms, types of distinct families, though represented by one or two species only, complete the number of North American autochthont fishes—viz., *Aphredoderus*, *Percopsis*, *Hyodon*, and the *Heteropygii* (*Amblyopsis* and *Chologaster*). The last are allied to the Cyprinodonts, differing from them in some points of the structure of their intestines. The two genera are extremely similar, but *Chologaster*, which is found in ditches of the rice-fields of South Carolina, is provided with eyes, and lacks the ventral fins. *Amblyopsis* is the celebrated Blind Fish of the Mammoth Cave of Kentucky: colourless, eyeless, with rudimentary ventral fins, which may be occasionally entirely absent.

[1] Cope has discovered in a tertiary freshwater-deposit at Idaho an extinct genus of this group, *Diastichus*. He considers this interesting fact to be strongly suggestive of continuity of territory of Asia and North America.—"Proc. Am. Phil. Soc. 1873," p. 55.

A peculiar feature of the North American Fish Fauna is that it has retained, besides the Sturgeons and Lampreys, representatives of two Ganoid families, *Lepidosteus* and *Amia*. Both these genera existed in tertiary times: the former occurs in tertiary deposits of Europe as well as North America, whilst fossil remains of *Amia* have been found in the Western Hemisphere only.

It is difficult to account for the presence of the *Amiurina* in North America. They form a well-marked division of the *Bagrina*, which are well represented in Africa and the East Indies, but absent in South America; it is evident, therefore, they should not be regarded as immigrants from the south, as is the case with the Palæarctic Siluroids. Nor, again, has the connection between South and North America been established sufficiently long to admit of the supposition that these Siluroids could have spread in the interval from the south to the northern parts of the continent, for some of the species are found as far north as Pine Islands Lake (54° lat. N.)[1]

III. Southern Zone.

The boundaries of this zone have been indicated in the description of the Equatorial Zone; they overlap the southern boundaries of the latter in South Australia and South America, but we have not at present the means of exactly defining the limits to which southern types extend northwards. This zone includes Tasmania with at least a portion of South-eastern Australia (*Tasmanian sub-region*), New Zealand and the Auckland Islands (*New Zealand sub-region*), and Chili, Patagonia, Terra del Fuego, and the Falkland Islands (*Fuegian sub-region*) No freshwater fishes are known

[1] Leidy describes a Siluroid (*Pimelodus*) from tertiary deposits of Wyoming Territory. "Contrib. to the Extinct Vert. Fauna of the Western Territ. 1873," p. 193.

from Kerguelen's Land, or from islands beyond 55° lat. S. The southern extremity of Africa has to be excluded from this zone so far as Freshwater fishes are concerned.

This zone is, with regard to its extent as well as to the number of species, the smallest of the three; yet its ichthyological features are well marked; they consist in the presence of two peculiar families, each of which is analogous to a northern type, viz. the *Haplochitonidæ*, which represent the *Salmonidæ*, *Haplochiton* being the analogue of *Salmo*, and *Prototroctes* that of *Coregonus*; and the *Galaxiidæ*, which are the Pikes of the Southern Hemisphere.

Although geographically widely separate from each other, the Freshwater fishes of the three divisions are nevertheless so closely allied that conclusions drawn from this group of animals alone would hardly justify us in regarding these divisions as sub-regions. One species of *Galaxias* (*G. attenuatus*) and the three Lampreys are found in all three, or at least two, sub-regions.

Freshwater Fishes of the Southern Zone.

	Tasmanian.	N. Zealand.	Fuegian.
Percichthys . .	...	..	3
Siluridæ—			
Diplomystax . . .	...	...	1
Nematogenys . . .	...	...	1
Trichomycterina [Neotrop.]	...	...	5
Gadopsidæ	1	...	...
(*Retropinna* . . .	...	1	...)
Haplochitonidæ . . .	1	1	1
Galaxiidæ	6	5	4
Petromyzontidæ .	3	1	3
	11	8	18

But little remains to be added in explanation of this list; *Percichthys* is in Chili the autochthont form of the cosınopolitan group of *Percina*. *Diplomystax*, an Arioid fish of Chili, and *Nematogenys* seem to have crossed the Andes from Tropical America at a comparatively early period, as these genera are not represented on the eastern side of South America; the *Trichomycterina* occur on both sides of the Andes, which they ascend to a considerable height. *Retropinna* is a true Salmonoid, allied to, and representing in the Southern Hemisphere the Northern Smelt, *Osmerus*. In both these genera a part of the specimens live in the sea, and ascend rivers periodically to spawn; another part remain in rivers and lakes, where they propagate, never descending to the sea, this freshwater race being constantly smaller than their marine brethren. That this small Teleostean of the Northern Hemisphere should reappear, though in a generically modified form, in New Zealand, without having spread over other parts of the Southern Zone, is one of the most remarkable, and at present inexplicable facts of the geographical distribution of freshwater fishes.

Fig. 104.—*Haplochiton zebra*, Straits of Magelhæn.

CHAPTER XVIII.

THE FISHES OF THE BRACKISH WATER.

On such parts of a coast at which there is a mixture of fresh and salt water, either in consequence of some river emptying its water into the sea or from an accumulation of land surface-water forming lagunes, which are in uninterrupted or temporary communication with the sea, there flourishes a peculiar brackish water fauna which is characterised by the presence of fishes found sometimes in sea-, sometimes in pure fresh-water.

This fauna can be rather sharply defined if a limited district only is taken into consideration; thus, the species of the brackish water fauna of Great Britain, the Pacific coast of Central America, of the larger East India Islands, etc., can be enumerated without much hesitation. But difficulties arise when we attempt to generalise in the enumeration of the forms referable to the brackish water fauna; because the genera and families enumerated include certain species and genera which have habituated themselves exclusively either to a freshwater or marine existence; and, besides, because a species of fish may be at one locality an inhabitant of brackish water, at another of the sea, and at a third of fresh water. The circumstance that these fishes can live in sea and fresh water has enabled them to spread readily over the globe, a few only being limited to particular regions; therefore, for the purposes of dividing the earth's surface into natural zoological regions the brackish water forms are useless. The following fishes may be referred to this Fauna :—

1. Species of *Rajidæ* (*Raja, Trygon*) prefer the mouths of rivers, probably because the muddy or sandy bottom offers the most suitable conditions for fishes which can feed on the bottom only; such brackish water species belong chiefly to the Equatorial Zone, some having taken up their abode entirely in fresh water (South American Trygons).

2. *Ambassis*, a Percoid genus, consisting of numerous small species, inhabiting the shores of the tropical parts of the Indian Ocean and the coasts of Tropical Australia. Many species enter, and all seek the neighbourhood of, fresh water; hence they disappear in the islands of the Pacific, and are scarce in the Red Sea.

3. *Therapon*, with the same distribution as the former

4. Numerous *Sciænidæ* of the Equatorial Zone.

5. The *Polynemidæ*, chiefly inhabitants of brackish water of the Equatorial Zone, most developed in the Indian region, and scarce in the Tropical Pacific.

6. Numerous species of *Caranx* (or Horse Mackerels) of the Equatorial Zone.

7. Nearly all species of *Gastrosteus* enter brackish water, *G. spinachia* being almost exclusively confined to it: Northern Zone.

8. The most important genera of the Gobies (*Gobiina*): *Gobius* (nearly cosmopolitan), *Sicydium, Boleophthalmus, Periophthalmus, Eleotris* (equatorial). Many of the species are entirely confined to fresh water.

9. The *Amblyopina*, similar to the Gobies, but with more elongated body: Tropical Indo-Pacific.

10. The *Trypauchenina:* Coasts of the Indian region.

11. Many species of *Blennius*, of which several are found far inland in fresh waters—for instance in North Italy, in the Lake of Galilee, in the eastern parts of Asia Minor.

12. The majority of *Atherinidæ*, and

13. The *Mugilidæ:* both families being most numerous and abundant in brackish water, and almost cosmopolitan.

14. Many *Pleuronectidæ* prefer the mouths of rivers for the same reason as the Rays; some ascend rivers, as the Flounder, *Cynoglossus*, etc.

15. Several *Siluridæ*, as especially the genera *Plotosus, Cnidoglanis, Arius,* which attain their greatest development in brackish water.

16. The *Cyprinodontidæ* are frequently found in brackish water.

17. Species of *Clupea*, some of which ascend rivers, and become acclimatized in fresh water, as *Clupea finta*, which has established itself in the lakes of northern Italy.

18. *Chatoessus*, a genus of Clupeoid fishes of the Equatorial Zone, of which some species have spread into the Northern Zone.

19. *Megalops:* Equatorial Zone.

20. *Anguilla.* The distribution, no less than the mode of propagation, and the habits generally, of the so-called Freshwater-eels still present us with many difficult problems. As far as we know at present their birthplace seems to be the coast in the immediate neighbourhood of the mouths of rivers. They are much more frequently found in fresh water than in brackish water, but the distribution of some species proves that they at times migrate by sea as well as by land and river. Thus *Anguilla mauritiana* is found in almost all the fresh and brackish waters of the islands of the Tropical Indian Ocean and Western Pacific, from the Comoros to the South Sea; *Anguilla vulgaris* is spread over temperate Europe (exclusive of the system of the Danube, the Black and Caspian Seas), in the Mediterranean district (including the Nile and rivers of Syria), and on the Atlantic coast of North America; *Anguilla bostoniensis*, in Eastern North America, China, and Japan; *Anguilla lati-*

rostris, in Temperate Europe, the whole Mediterranean district, the West Indies, China, and New Zealand. The other more local species are found, in addition to localities already mentioned, on the East Coast of Africa, South Africa, on the continent of India, various East Indian Islands, Australia, Tasmania, Auckland Islands; but none have ever been found in South America, the West Coast of North America, and the West Coast of Africa: surely one of the most striking instances of irregular geographical distribution.

21. Numerous *Syngnathidæ* have established themselves in the Northern Zone as well as in the Equatorial, in the vegetation which flourishes in brackish water.

This list could be considerably increased if an enumeration of species, especially of certain localities, were attempted; but this is more a subject of local interest, and would carry us beyond the scope of a general account of the distribution of Fishes.

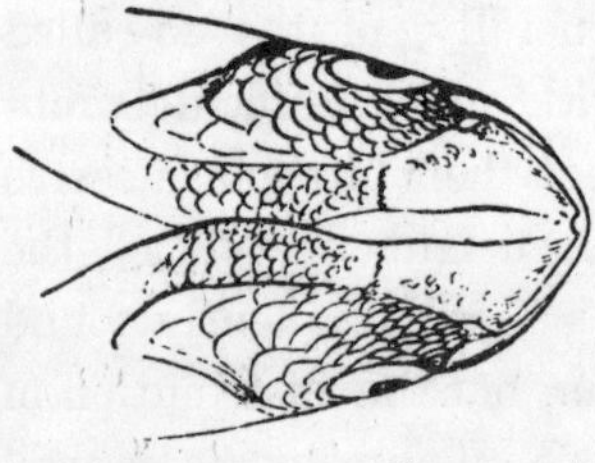

Fig. 105.—*Mugil octo-radiatus.*

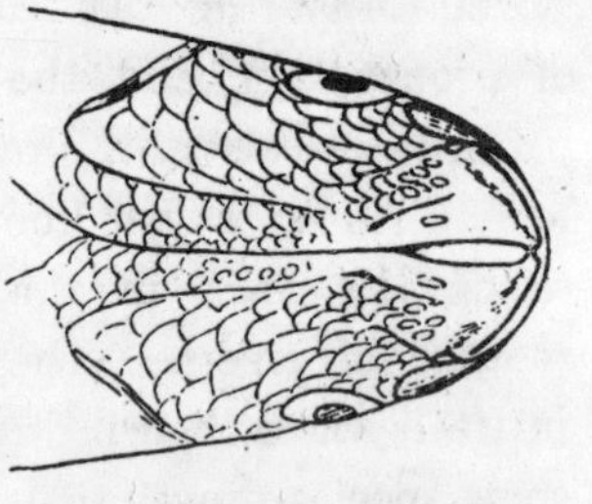

Fig. 106.—*Mugil auratus.*

Fig. 107.—*Mugil septentrionalis.*

Heads of Grey Mullets, fishes of Brackish water.

CHAPTER XIX.

THE DISTRIBUTION OF MARINE FISHES.

MARINE fishes fall, with regard to their mode of life and distribution, into three distinct categories :—

1. *Shore Fishes*—That is, fishes which inhabit chiefly parts of the sea in the immediate neighbourhood of land either actually raised above, or at least but little submerged below, the surface of the water. They do not descend to any great depth,—very few to 300 fathoms, and the majority live close to the surface. The distribution of these fishes is determined not only by the temperature of the surface water but also by the nature of the adjacent land, and its animal and vegetable products ; some of these fishes being confined to flat coasts with soft or sandy bottoms, others to rocky and fissured coasts, others to living coral formations. If it were not for the frequent mechanical and involuntary removals to which these fishes are exposed, their distribution within certain limits, as it no doubt originally existed, would resemble still more that of freshwater fishes than we find it actually does at the present period.

2. *Pelagic Fishes*—that is, fishes which inhabit the surface and uppermost strata of the open ocean, which approach the shores only accidentally, or occasionally (in search of prey), or periodically (for the purpose of spawning). The majority spawn in the open sea, their ova and young being always found at great distance from the shore. With regard to their distribution, they are still subject to the influences of light and the temperature of the surface water ; but they are

independent of the variable local conditions which tie the shore fish to its original home, and therefore roam freely over a space which would take a freshwater or shore fish thousands of years to cover in its gradual dispersal. Such as are devoid of rapidity of motion are dispersed over similarly large areas by the oceanic currents, more slowly than, but as surely as, the strong swimmers. Therefore, an accurate definition of their distribution within certain areas equivalent to the terrestrial regions is much less feasible than in the case of shore fishes.

3. *Deep-sea Fishes*—that is, fishes which inhabit such depths of the ocean as to be but little or not influenced by light or the surface temperature; and which, by their organisation are prevented from reaching the surface stratum in a healthy condition. Living almost under identical tellurian conditions, the same type, the same species, may inhabit an abyssal depth under the equator as well as one near the arctic or antarctic circle; and all we know of these fishes points to the conclusion that no separate horizontal regions can be distinguished in the abyssal fauna, and that no division into bathymetrical strata can be attempted on the base of generic much less of family characters.

It must not be imagined that these three categories are more sharply defined than Freshwater and Marine Fishes. They gradually pass into each other, and there are numerous fishes about which uncertainty exists whether they should be placed in the Shore or Pelagic series, or in the Pelagic or Deep-sea series; nay, many facts favour the view that changes in the mode of life and distribution of fishes are still in progress.

The change in habitat of numerous fishes is regulated by the distribution of their favourite food. At certain seasons the surface of the sea in the vicinity of land swarms with mollusks, larval Crustaceans, Medusæ, attracting shoals of fishes from the open ocean to the shores; and these are again pursued by fishes of larger size and predacious habits, so that all these fishes might be included, with equal propriety, in the littoral or pelagic series. However, species which are known to normally spawn in the open ocean must be always referred to the latter division.

Chondropterygii, Acanthopterygii, Anacanths, Myxinoids, and Pharyngobranchii furnish the principal contingents to the Marine Fauna; whilst the majority of Malacopterygians the Ganoids, and Cyclostomes are Freshwater Fishes.

I.—Distribution of Shore Fishes.

The principal types of Shore-fishes are the following:—

CHONDROPTERYGII—		
Holocephala	4	species.
Plagiostomata—		
Carchariidæ (part.)	12	„
Scylliidæ	30	„
Cestraciontidæ	4	„
Spinacidæ (part.)	8	„
Rhinidæ	1	„
Pristiophoridæ	4	„
Pristidæ	5	„
Rhinobatidæ	14	„
Torpedinidæ	15	„
Rajidæ	34	„
Trygonidæ	47	„
ACANTHOPTERYGII—		
Percidæ (part. incl. Pristipomatidæ)	625	„
Mullidæ	35	„
Sparidæ	130	„
Squamipinnes	130	„
Cirrhitidæ	40	„

Heterolepidina	12	species.
Scorpænidæ	120	„
Cottidæ (part.)	100	„
Cataphracti (part.)	20	„
Trachinidæ	100	„
Sciænidæ	100	„
Sphyrænidæ	15	„
Trichiuridæ	17	„
Elacate	1	„
Nomeidæ (part.)	5	„
Cyttidæ	8	„
Stromateus	9	„
Mene	1	„
Carangidæ (part.)	130	„
Kurtidæ	7	„
Gobiodon	7	„
Callionymina	30	„
Discoboli	11	„
Batrachidæ	14	„
Pediculati (part.)	11	„
Blenniidæ	90	„
Acanthoclinidæ	1	„
Teuthididæ	30	„
Acronuridæ	60	„
Hoplognathidæ	3	„
Malacanthidæ	3	„
Plesiopina	4	„
Trichonotidæ	2	„
Cepolidæ	7	„
Gobiesocidæ	21	„
Psychrolutidæ	2	„
Centriscidæ	7	„
Fistulariidæ	4	„

ACANTHOPTERYGII PHARYNGOGNATHI—

Pomacentridæ	150	„
Labridæ	400	„
Embiotocidæ	17	„

ANACANTHINI—		
Gadopsidæ	1	species.
Lycodidæ	15	,,
Gadidæ (part.)	50	,,
Ophidiidæ (part.)	40	,,
Pleuronectidæ	160	,,
PHYSOSTOMI—		
Saurina (part.)	16	,,
Salmonidæ (part.)	7	,,
Clupeidæ (part.)	130	,,
Chirocentridæ	1	,,
Chilobranchus	1	,,
Murænidæ (part.)	200	,,
Pegasidæ	4	,,
LOPHOBRANCHII	120	,,
PLECTOGNATHI—		
Sclerodermi	95	,,
Gymnodontes	83	,,
CYCLOSTOMATA—		
MYXINIDÆ	5	,,
LEPTOCARDII	2	,,
	3587	species.

These types of Shore fishes are divided among the following oceanic areæ:—

I. The Arctic Ocean.

II. The Northern Temperate Zone.

A. The Temperate North Atlantic.

1. The British district
2. The Mediterranean district.
3. The North American district

B. The Temperate North Pacific.

1. The Kamtschatkan district.
2. The Japanese district.
3. The Californian district.

III. The Equatorial Zone.

A. The Tropical Atlantic.

B. The Tropical Indo-Pacific.

C. The Pacific Coast of Tropical America.

1. The Central American district.
2. The Galapagoes district.
3. The Peruvian district.

IV. The Southern Temperate Zone.

1. The Cape of Good Hope district.
2. The South Australian district.
3. The Chilian district.
4. The Patagonian district.

V. The Antarctic Ocean.

As with freshwater fishes, the main divisions of the Shore-fish faunæ are determined by their distance from the equator, the equatorial zone of the Freshwater series corresponding entirely to that of the Shore-fish series. But as Marine fishes extend farther towards the Poles than Freshwater fishes, and as the polar types are more specialised, a distinct Arctic and Antarctic fauna may be separated from the faunæ of the temperate zones. The two subdivisions of the Northern temperate zone in the Freshwater series are quite analogous to the corresponding divisions in the Coast series. In the Southern Hemisphere the Shore-fishes of the extremity of Africa form a separate district of the temperate zone, whilst the Freshwater fishes of South Africa were found to be tropical types The Marine series of the Southern temperate zone is also much more diversified than the Freshwater series, and admits of further subdivision, which, although in some degree indicated in the Freshwater series, does not entirely correspond to that proposed for the latter.

I. Shore Fishes of the Arctic Ocean.

The Shore fishes clearly prove a continuity of the Arctic circumpolar fauna, as the southern limit of which we may indicate the southern extremity of Greenland and the Aleutian Archipelago, or 60° of lat. N.

Towards the North, fishes become less in variety of species and fewer in number of individuals, and only very few genera are restricted to this fauna.

The highest latitude at which Shore fishes have been observed is 83° N. lat. The late Arctic Expedition collected at and near that latitude specimens of *Cottus quadricornis, Icelus hamatus, Cyclopterus spinosus, Liparis fabricii, Gymnelis viridis*, and *Gadus fabricii*. This number probably would have been larger if the difficulties of collecting fishes in those high latitudes were not almost insuperable for the greater part of the year.

As far as we know, the fishes north and south of Behring's Straits belong to the same generic or family types as those of the corresponding latitudes of the Eastern Hemisphere, though the majority are specifically distinct. But the information we possess of the fishes of the northernmost extremity of the Pacific is extremely scanty and vague. Farther south, whence now and then a collection reaches Europe, we meet with some European species, as the Herring, Holibut, Hake.

The Chondropterygians are very scarce, and it is doubtful whether another Chondropterygian, beside the pelagic *Læmargus* or Greenland Shark, crosses the Arctic circle. In the more temperate latitudes of South Greenland, Iceland, and Northern Scandinavia, *Acanthias, Centroscyllium*, and a species of *Raja*, also *Chimæra*, are met with.

Of Acanthopterygians the families of *Cottidæ, Cataphracti, Discoboli*, and *Blenniidæ* are well represented, and several of the genera are characteristic of the Arctic fauna: marine species of *Cottus; Centridermichthys, Icelus, Triglops; Agonus, Aspidophoroides; Anarrhichas, Centronotus, Stichæus; Cyclopterus* and *Liparis.* Two species of *Sebastes* are rather common.

Characteristic is also the development of Gadoid fishes, of which some thirteen species, belonging to *Gadus, Merluccius,* and *Molva,* form one of the principal articles of food to the inhabitants of the coasts of the Arctic Ocean. The Blennioid Anacanthini or *Lycodidæ,* are limited to the Arctic and Antarctic coasts. *Ammodytes* and a few Flat-fishes (*Hippoglossoides* and *Pleuronectes*) are common in the more temperate parts.

Labroids only exceptionally penetrate so far towards the north.

Physostomes are very scarce, and represented only by a few species of *Clupea* and by *Mallotus;* the latter is an ancient inhabitant of the Greenland coasts, fossil remains, indistinguishable from the species of the present day, being frequently found in nodules of clay of comparatively recent formation.

The Arctic climate is still less favourable to the existence of Lophobranchs, only a few *Syngnathus* and *Nerophis* being present in the more southern latitudes, to which they have been carried by oceanic currents from their more congenial home in the south. Scleroderms and Plectognaths are entirely absent.

The Gadoids are accompanied by *Myxine,* which parasitically thrives in them.

II. The Northern Temperate Zone.

A. *Shore Fishes of the Temperate North Atlantic.*

This part of the fauna may be subdivided into three districts:—

1. The fishes of the north-eastern shores, viz. of the British islands, of Scandinavia so far as it is not included in the Arctic fauna, and of the continent of Europe southwards to about 40° of lat. N.—*British* district.

2. The fishes of the Mediterranean shores and of the adjoining shores of the Atlantic, including the Azores, Madeira, and the Canary Islands—*Mediterranean* district.

3. The fishes of the western shores, from 60° lat. N. to about 30° lat. N.—the *North American* district.

1. The *British* district shows scarcely any marked distinctive features; the character of its fauna is simply intermediate between that of the Arctic Ocean and the Mediterranean district; truly Arctic forms disappear, while such as are also found in the Mediterranean make their appearance. Also with regard to the abundance of individuals and variety of fishes this district forms a transition from the north towards the south.

Besides the few Arctic Chondropterygians, all of which extend into this district, the small shore Dog-fishes are well represented (*Mustelus, Galeus, Scyllium, Pristiurus*); the ubiquitous *Rhina* or Monk-fish is common; of Rays, *Raja* predominates in a variety of species over *Torpedo* and *Trygon*, which are still scarce.

Of Acanthopterygians, *Centridermichthys, Icelus, Triglops*, and *Aspidophoroides*, do not extend from the north into this district; and *Cottus. Anarrhichas, Centronotus, Stichæus*, the *Discoboli* disappear within its limits. Nearly all the remainder are genera which are also found in the Mediterranean districts. The following are the principal forms, and known to propagate on these shores: *Labrax; Serranus, Polyprion, Dentex; Mullus; Cantharus, Pagrus, Pagellus; Sebastes; Cottus, Trigla, Agonus; Trachinus; Sciæna* (?); *Zeus; Trachurus, Capros; Callionymus; Discoboli; Lophius; Anarrhichas, Centronotus, Stich-*

œus; Blenniops, Zoarces (not in Mediterranean); *Cepola; Lepadogaster.*

Of the Anacanthini the Gadoids are as numerous as in the Arctic Ocean, most being common to both districts; they are represented by *Gadus, Gadiculus, Merluccius, Phycis, Molva, Motella, Raniceps,* and *Brosmius;* but, whilst the majority show their northern origin by not extending into the Mediterranean, *Ammodytes* and most *Pleuronectidæ* prove themselves to be the more southern representatives of this order. In the British district we find *Hippoglossus, Hippoglossoides, Rhombus, Phrynorhombus, Pleuronectes, Solea,* and only the two first are not met with in the Mediterranean.

Labroids are common; with the exception of the North American *Tautoga,* all the other genera are met with.

Physostomes are not well represented, viz. by one species of *Osmerus,* one of *Engraulis,* one of *Conger,* and about five of *Clupea.*

Syngnathus and *Nerophis* become more common as we proceed southwards; but the existence of Sclerodems and Plectognaths is indicated by single individuals only, stragglers from their southern home, and unable to establish themselves in a climate ungenial to them.

The Gadoids are accompanied by *Myxine;* and *Branchiostoma* may be found in all suitable localities.

2. The *Mediterranean* district is distinguished by a great variety of forms; yet, with the exception of a few genera established for single species, none of the forms can be considered peculiar to it; and even that small number of peculiar genera is more and more diminished as our knowledge of the distribution of fishes advances. Some genera are identical with those found on the western coasts of the Atlantic and in the West Indies; but a most remarkable and unexpected affinity obtains with another very distant

fauna, viz. that of Japan. The number of genera common to the Mediterranean district and the Japanese coasts is larger than that of the genera common to the Mediterranean and the opposite American coasts.

The Chondropterygians found in the British district continue in the Mediterranean, their number being increased by *Centrina, Spinax, Pteroplatea*, and some species of *Rhinobatus*, a genus more numerously represented in the Tropics. *Torpedo* and *Trygon* are common.

The greatest variety belong to the Acanthopterygians, as will be seen from the following list:—*Labrax; Anthias, Serranus, Polyprion, Apogon, Pomatomus, Pristipoma, Diagramma* (an Indian genus with two Mediterranean species, and otherwise not represented in the Atlantic), *Dentex, Mæna, Smaris; Mullus; Cantharus, Box, Scatharxs, Oblata, Sargus, Pagrus, Pagellus, Chrysophrys; Sebastes, Scorpæna; Hoplostethus, Beryx, Polymixia; Trigla, Lepidotrigla, Agonus, Peristethus; Trachinus, Uranoscopus; Umbrina, Sciæna; Sphyræna; Aphanopus, Lepidopus, Nesiarchus, Trichiurus, Thyrsites; Cubiceps; Zeus, Cyttus; Stromateus; Trachurus, Caranx, Capros, Diretmus, Antigonia; Callionymus; Batrachus; Lophius; Cristiceps, Tripterygium; Cepola; Lepadogaster; Centriscus; Notacanthus.*

The *Labridæ* are as common as, or even more so than, in the British district, and represented by the same genera. But, besides, some other Pharyngognaths, properly belonging to the Tropical Atlantic, have fully established themselves, though only by a few species, viz. *Glyphidodon* and *Heliastes; Cossyphus, Novacula, Julis, Coris*, and *Scarus*.

The Gadoids show a marked decrease of development; and the species of *Gadus, Gadiculus, Mora, Strinsia, Phycis*, and *Molva*, which are peculiar to the Mediterranean, seem to inhabit rather the colder water of moderate depths, than the surface near the shore. *Motella*, however, proves to be a true

Shore fish also in the Mediterranean, at least in its adult state. *Ophidium* and *Fierasfer* appear now besides *Ammodytes.* As the Gadoids decrease, so the *Pleuronectidæ* increase, the genera of the Mediterranean district being *Rhombus, Phrynorhombus, Arnoglossus, Citharus, Rhomboidichthys, Pleuronectes* (a northern genus not extending farther southwards), *Solea, Synaptura,* and *Ammopleurops.*

The variety of Physostomes is small; the following only being superadded to those of the British district:—*Saurus* (a tropical genus), *Aulopus; Congromuræna, Heteroconger, Myrus, Ophichthys, Muræna.*

The Lophobranchs are more numerous in species and individuals than in the British district; and, besides *Syngnathus* and *Nerophis,* several species of *Hippocampus* are common. Also a few species of *Balistes* occur.

Myxine is lost in this district; whilst *Branchiostoma* is abundant.

3. The shore fishes of the *North American* district consist, as on the eastern coasts of the North Atlantic, of northern and southern elements; but they are still more mixed with each other than on the European coasts, so that a boundary line cannot be drawn between them. The affinity to the fauna of the eastern shores is great, but almost entirely limited to the genera composing the fauna of the British district. British genera not found on the American coasts are—*Galeus, Scyllium, Chimæra, Mullus, Pagellus, Trigla, Trachinus, Zeus, Callionymus.* The southern elements of North America are rather derived from the West Indies, and have no special affinity to Mediterranean forms; very few of the non-British Mediterranean forms extend across the Atlantic; instead of a Mediterranean we find a West Indian element. Many of the British *species* range across the Atlantic, and inhabit in an unchanged condition the northern parts of

this district; and from the frequent occurrence of isolated specimens of other British species on the North American coast, we may presume that many more occasionally cross the Atlantic, but without being able to obtain a permanent footing.

The genera peculiar to this district are few in number, and composed of very few species, viz. *Hemitripterus*, *Pammelas*, *Chasmodes*, *Cryptacanthodes*, and *Tautoga*.

The close resemblance of what must be considered northern forms to those of Europe will be evident from the following list:—

Mustelus, *Rhina*, *Torpedo*, *Raja*, *Trygon*.

Labrax, *Centropristis*, *Serranus*; *Pagrus*, *Chrysophrys*; *Sebastes*, *Hemitripterus*; *Cottus*, *Aspidophoroides*; *Uranoscopus*; *Micropogon*, *Pogonias*, *Sciæna*; *Trachurus*, *Pammelas*; *Cyclopterus*, *Liparis*; *Lophius*; *Anarrhichas*, *Chasmodes*, *Stichæus*, *Centronotus*, *Cryptacanthodes*, *Zoarces*.

Tautoga, *Ctenolabrus*.

Gadus, *Merluccius*, *Phycis*, *Molva*, *Motella*, *Brosmius*; *Ophidium* (one species, perhaps identical with a Mediterranean species); *Ammodytes*; *Hippoglossus*, *Hippoglossoides*, *Rhombus*, *Pleuronectes*.

Osmerus, *Mallotus*; *Engraulis*, *Clupea*; *Conger*.

Syngnathus—*Myxine*—*Branchiostoma*.

West Indian genera, or at least genera which are more developed within the tropics, and which extend more or less northwards in the North American district, are:—

Pteroplatea (also in the Mediterranean).

Gerres, *Dules* (*auriga*), *Lobotes*, *Ephippus*; *Sargus*; *Prionotus*; *Umbrina*, *Otolithus*, *Larimus*; *Sphyræna* (Mediterr.); *Trichiurus* (Mediterr.); *Elacate*; *Cybium*, *Trachynotus*; *Stromateus* (Mediterr.); *Caranx*; *Batrachus* (Mediterr.); *Malthe*.

Pseudorhombus, *Solea* (Mediterr.)

Saurus (Mediterr.); *Etrumeus*, *Albula*, *Elops*, *Megalops*.

Hippocampus (Mediterr.)
Balistes; Monacanthus.

B. *Shore Fishes of the Temperate North Pacific.*

This fauna shows a great affinity to that of the temperate North Atlantic, not only in including a considerable proportion of identical genera, and even of species, but also in having its constituent parts similarly distributed. However, our knowledge of the ichthyology of this fauna is by no means complete. Very few collections have been made in Northern Japan, and on the coasts farther north of it; and, again, the ichthyology of the coasts of Southern California is but little known. Southern Japan has been well searched, but very little attention has been paid to the extent of the northward range of the species. In collections made by Mr. Swinhoe at Chefoo, in lat. 37° N., the proportions of temperate and tropical fishes were found to be about equal. Thus, the details of the distribution of the fishes of these shores have still to be worked out; nevertheless, three divisions may be recognised which, for the present, may be defined as follows:—

1. The fishes of the north-western shores, to about 37° lat. N., including the corresponding northern parts of Japan—*Kamtschatkan* district; this corresponds to the British district of the Atlantic.

2. The fishes of Southern Japan and the corresponding shores of the continent of Asia, between 37° and 30° lat. N.—*Japanese* district, which corresponds to the Mediterranean.

3. The fishes of the eastern shores southwards to the latitude of San Francisco—*Californian* district; this corresponds to the North American district of the Atlantic.

Too little is known of the shore fishes of the coasts between San Francisco and the tropic to enable us to treat of it as a separate division.

The Shore fishes of the North Pacific generally are composed of the following elements:—

a. Arctic forms which extend into the Arctic Ocean, and the majority of which are also found in the British district.

b. Peculiar forms limited to the North Pacific, like the *Heterolepidina*, *Embiotocidæ*, and certain Cottoid and Blennioid genera.

c. Forms identical with fishes of the Mediterranean.

d. Peculiar forms limited to the southern parts of Japan.

e. Tropical forms which have entered the North Pacific from the south.

1. The small list of fishes which we can assign to the *Kamtschatkan* district is due rather to the imperfect manner in which its fauna has been explored than to its actual poverty of fishes; thus, although we may be sure that sooner or later the small kinds of Dog-fishes of the British district will be found there also, at present we have positive knowledge of the occurrence of only two Chondropterygians, viz. *Chimæra* and *Raja*. The species of the latter genus seem to be much less numerous than in the Atlantic.

Of Acanthopterygians the following are known:—*Sebastes; Chirus, Agrammus; Podabrus, Blepsias, Cottus, Centridermichthys, Hemilepidotus, Agonus; Trichodon; Callionymus; Liparis; Dictyosoma, Stichæus, Centronotus.*

Labroids are absent; they are clearly a type unable to endure great cold; of the Embiotocoids which represent them in the Pacific, one species only (a species of *Ditrema*) is known from this district.

The Gadoids are, so far as we know at present, sparsely represented, viz. by isolated species of *Gadus*, *Motella*, and *Lotella*, the latter being an inhabitant of moderate depths rather than of the surface. *Hippoglossus*, *Pleuronectes*, and *Parophrys*, seem to occur everywhere at suitable localities.

The Physostomes are nearly the same as in the British district, viz. a Smelt (*Hypomesus*), probably also the Arctic *Mallotus*, an Anchovy, several species of *Clupea*, and the Conger-eel. A very singular Salmonoid fish, *Salanx*, which is limited to the north-western Pacific, occurs in great abundance.

Also, the Lophobranchs correspond in their development to those of the British district, *Nerophis* being replaced by *Urocampus*.

Neither Myxinoids nor *Branchiostoma* have as yet been found.

2. The *Japanese* district is, like the Mediterranean, distinguished by a great variety of forms; some of them are peculiar to it (marked *J.* in the following list); others occur in the Mediterranean, though also in other districts (*M.*) The resemblance to the Mediterranean is even greater than would appear from the following list of genera, inasmuch as a considerable number of species are identical in both districts. Three of the Berycoid genera have hitherto been found in the Japanese and Mediterranean districts only, and nowhere else. Another very singular fact is that some of the most characteristic genera, like *Mullus, Zeus, Callionymus, Centriscus*, inhabit the Mediterranean and Japanese districts, *but have never reached the opposite American coasts, either in the Atlantic or Pacific;* although, at least in the latter, the oceanic currents would rather favour than obstruct their dispersal in the direction towards America. Bold as the hypothesis may appear, we can only account for the singular distribution of these shore fishes by assuming that the Mediterranean and Japanese seas were in direct and open communication with each other within the period of the existence of the present Teleosteous Fauna.

Gadoids have disappeared, or are represented by forms

inhabiting moderate depths. Neither *Myxine* nor *Branchiostoma* are known to have as yet been found.

List of Japanese Shore Fishes.

Chimæra (M.)

Galeus (M.), *Mustelus* (M.), *Triacis*, *Scyllium* (M.), *Crossorhinus*, *Pristiophorus*, *Cestracion*; *Rhina* (M.); *Rhinobatus* (M.), *Narcine*, *Raja* (M.), *Trygon* (M.), *Pteroplatea* (M.)

Percalabrax (J.), *Niphon* (J.), *Centropristis*, *Anthias* (M.), *Serranus* (M.), *Apogon* (M.), *Scombrops* (J.), *Acropoma*, *Anoplus* (J.), *Pristipoma* (M.), *Hapalogenys* (J.), *Histiopterus*, *Velifer* (J.), *Dentex* (M.), *Erythrichthys*—*Mullidæ* (M.)—*Girella*, *Pagrus* (M.), *Chrysophrys* (M.)—*Chilodactylus*—*Sebastes* (M.), *Scorpæna* (M.), *Aploactis*, *Trichopleura*, *Pelor*—*Monocentris* (J.), *Hoplostethus* (M.), *Beryx* (M.), *Polymixia* (M.)—*Platycephalus*, *Hoplichthys* (J.), *Bembras* (J.), *Prionotus*, *Lepidotrigla* (M.), *Trigla* (M.), *Peristethus* (M.)—*Uranoscopus* (M.), *Percis*, *Sillago*, *Latilus*.—*Sciæna* (M.), *Otolithus*—*Sphyræna* (M.)—*Lepidopus* (M.), *Trichiurus* (M.)—*Zeus* (M.)—*Caranx*, *Trachurus* (M.)—*Callionymus* (M.)—*Lophius* (M.), *Halieuthæa* (J.)—*Hoplognathus*—*Cepola* (M.)—*Centriscus* (M.), *Fistularia*.

Heliastes (M.)—*Labrichthys*, *Duymæria*, *Platyglossus*, *Novacula* (M.), *Julis* (M.), *Coris* (M.)

Sirembo (J.)—*Motella* (M.)—*Ateleopus* (J.)

Pseudorhombus, *Pleuronectes* (M.), *Solea* (M.), *Synaptura* (M.)

Saurus (M.), *Harpodon*.—*Salanx* (J.)—*Engraulis* (M.), *Clupea* (M.), *Etrumeus*—*Conger* (M.), *Congromuræna* (M.), *Murænesox* (M.), *Oxyconger*, *Myrus* (M.), *Ophichthys* (M.), *Muræna* (M.)

Syngnathus (M.), *Hippocampus* (M.), *Solenognathus*.

Triacanthus, *Monacanthus*, *Ostracion*.

3. The *Californian* district includes a marked northern element, the principal constituents of which are identical with types occurring in the corresponding district of the Atlantic, viz. the North American, as exemplified by *Discoboli, Anarrhichas, Centronotus, Cottus, Hippoglossus, Clupea* (*harengus*), etc. But it possesses also, in the greatest degree of development, some types almost peculiar to itself, as the *Heterolepidina*, some remarkable Cottoid and Blennioid genera, and more especially the Embiotocoids—viviparous Pharyngognaths—which replace the Labroids of the other hemisphere. Gadoids are much less numerous than in the North American district. The southern forms are but little known, but it may be anticipated that, owing to the partial identity of the Faunæ of the two coasts of the Isthmus of Panama, a fair proportion of West Indian forms will be found to have entered this district from the south. The following are the principal genera :—

Chimæra, Galeus, Mustelus, Triacis, Cestracion, Rhina, Raja.

Serranus ; Chirus, Ophiodon, Zaniolepis ; Sebastes ; Nautichthys, Scorpænichthys, Cottus, Centridermichthys, Hemilepidotus, Artedius, Prionotus, Agonus ; Cyclopterus, Liparis ; Anarrhichas, Neoclinus, Cebidichthys, Stichæus, Centronotus, Apodichthys ; Psychrolutes ; Auliscops.

Embiotocidæ.

Gadus. Hippoglossus, Psettichthys, Citharichthys, Paralichthys, Pleuronectes, Parophrys.

Osmerus, Thaleichthys, Hypomesus ; Engraulis, Clupea.

Syngnathus.

III.—The Equatorial Zone.

As we approach the Tropic from the north, the tribes characteristic of the Arctic and Temperate zones become scarcer, and disappear altogether: to be replaced by the greater variety of Tropical types. Of Chondropterygians, the *Chimæridæ, Spinacidæ, Mustelus,* and *Raja,* do not pass the

Tropic, or appear in single species only; and of Teleosteans, the *Berycidæ*, *Pagrus*, the *Heterolepidina*, *Cottus* and allied genera, *Lophius*, *Anarrhichas*, *Stichæus*, *Lepadogaster*, *Psychrolutes*, *Centriscus*, *Notacanthus*, the *Labridæ* and *Embiotocidæ*, the *Lycodidæ*, *Gadidæ*, and marine *Salmonidæ* disappear either entirely, or retire from the shores and surface into the depths of the ocean.

With regard to variety of forms, as well as to number of individuals, this zone far surpasses either of the temperate zones; in this respect, the life in the sea is as that on the land. Coast fishes are not confined to the actual coast-line, but abound on the coral reefs, with which some parts of the Atlantic and Pacific are studded, and many of which are submerged below the water. The abundance of animal and vegetable life which flourishes on them renders them the favourite pasture-grounds for the endless variety of coral-fishes (*Squamipinnes*, *Acronuridæ*, *Pomacentridæ*, *Julidæ*, *Plectognathi*, etc.), and for the larger predatory kinds. The colours and grotesque forms of the Fishes of the Tropics have justly excited the admiration of the earliest observers. Scarlet, black, blue, pink, red, yellow, etc., are arranged in patterns of the most bizarre fashion, mingling in spots, lines, bands; and reminding us of the words of Captain Cook when describing the coral-reefs of Palmerston Island: "The glowing appearance of the Mollusks was still inferior to that of the multitude of fishes that glided gently along, seemingly with the most perfect security. The colours of the different sorts were the most beautiful that can be imagined—the yellow, blue, red, black, etc., far exceeding anything that art can produce. Their various forms, also, contributed to increase the richness of this sub-marine grotto, which could not be surveyed without a pleasing transport."

Of Chondropterygians the *Scylliidæ*, *Pristis* (Saw-fishes), *Rhinobatidæ*, and *Trygonidæ* attain to the greatest development. Of Acanthopterygians *Centropristis*, *Serranus*, *Plectropoma*, *Mesoprion*, *Priacanthus*, *Apogon*, *Pristipoma*, *Hæmulon*, *Diagramma*, *Gerres*, *Scolopsis*, *Synagris*, *Cæsio*, *Mullidæ*, *Lethrinus*, *Squamipinnes*, *Cirrhites*, some genera of *Scorpænidæ*, *Platycephalus*, *Sciænidæ*, *Sphyræna*, *Caranx* *Equula*, *Callionymus*, *Teuthis*, *Acanthurus*, *Naseus*, are represented by numerous species; and the majority of these genera and families are limited to this zone. Of Pharyngognaths the *Pomacentridæ*, *Julidina*, and *Scarina*, are met with near every coral formation in a living condition. Of Gadoids, a singular minute form, *Bregmaceros*, is almost the only representative, the other forms belonging to deep water, and rarely ascending to the surface. Flat-fishes (*Pleuronectidæ*) are common on sandy coasts, and the majority of the genera are peculiar to the Tropics. Of *Physostomi* only the *Saurina*, *Clupeidæ*, and *Murænidæ* are represented, the *Clupeidæ* being exceedingly numerous in individuals, whilst the *Murænidæ* live more isolated, but show a still greater variety of species. Lophobranchii and Sclerodermi are generally distributed. Branchiostoma has been found on several coasts.

Geographically it is convenient to describe the Coast fauna of the tropical Atlantic separately from that of the Indo-Pacific ocean. The differences between them, however, are far less numerous and important than between the freshwater or terrestrial faunæ of continental regions. The majority of the principal types are found in both, many of the species being even identical; but the species are far more abundant in the Indo-Pacific than in the Atlantic, owing to the greater extent of the archipelagoes in the former. But for the broken and varied character of the coasts of the West Indies, the shores of the tropical Atlantic would, by their general uniformity, afford but a limited variety of conditions to the development of specific and generic forms, whilst the deep inlets of the

Indian ocean, with the varying configuration of their coasts, and the different nature of their bottom, its long peninsulas, and its archipelagoes, and the scattered islands of the tropical Pacific, render this part of the globe the most perfect for the development of fish-life. The fishes of the Indian and Pacific oceans (between the Tropics) are almost identical, and the number of species ranging from the Red Sea and east coast of Africa to Polynesia, even to its westernmost islands, is very great indeed. However, this Indo-Pacific fauna does not reach the Pacific coast of South America. The wide space devoid of islands, east of the Sandwich Islands and the Marquesas group, together with the current of cold water which sweeps northwards along the South American coast, has proved to be a very effectual barrier to the eastward extension of the Indo-Pacific fauna of coast fishes; and, consequently, we find an assemblage of fishes on the American coast and at the Galapagoes Islands, sufficiently distinct to constitute a distinct zoological division.

The following list, which contains only the principal genera and groups of coast fishes, will give an idea of the affinity of the tropical Atlantic and Indo-Pacific:—[1]

	Trop.-Atl.	Ind.-Pac.
Scylliidæ	—	13
Pristis	3	4
Rhinobatidæ	4	8
Torpedinidæ	1	8
Trygonidæ	14	24
Etelis	1	1
Aprion	—	1
Apsilus	1	—
Centropristis	15	—
Anthias	4	5
Serranus	30	85
Plectropoma	11	5

[1] The genera peculiar to the Equatorial zone are printed in italics.

	Trop.-Atl.	Indo-Pac.
Grammistes	—	2
Rhypticus	3	—
Diploprion	—	1
Myriodon	—	1
Mesoprion	15	50
Priacanthus	4	12
Apogon and *Chilodipterus*	2	75
Pristipoma	12	14
Hæmulon	15	—
Diagramma	—	30
Gerres	12	16
Scolopsis	—	20
Dentex and *Symphorus*	—	7
Synagris and *Pentapus*	—	24
Cæsio	—	12
Mullidæ	5	22
Sargus	7	2
Lethrinus	1	18
Chrysophrys	1	[illegible]
Pimelepterus	1	5
Squamipinnes	13	110
Toxotes	—	2
Cirrhites	—	20
Scorpænidæ	2	65
Myripristis	3	15
Holocentrum	6	25
Platycephalus	—	25
Prionotus	1	—
Trigla	—	4
Peristethus	2	6
Uranoscopina	[illegible]	8
Champsodon	—	1
Percis	—	10
Sillago	—	5
Latilus	1	2
Opisthognathus	2	5
Pseudochromis	—	8
Cichlops and *Pseudoplesiops*	—	2

	Trop. Atl.	Ind.-Pac.
Sciænidæ	44	43
Sphyræna	1	10
Trichiuridæ	6	5
Caranx	20	60
Chorinemus	4	7
Trachynotus	6	4
Psettus	1	2
Platax	—	7
Zanclus	—	1
Equula and *Gazza*	—	20
Teuthis	—	30
Acanthurus	3	42
Naseus	—	12
Kurtidæ	1	6
Gobiodon	—	7
Callionymus	—	17
Batrachidæ	5	4
Tetrabrachium	—	1
Malthe	1	—
Petroscirtes	—	30
Clinus	6	—
Dactyloscopus	1	—
Malacanthus	1	2
Cepola	—	1
Gobiesocidæ	5	1
Amphisile	—	3
Fistulariidæ	3	3
Pomacentridæ	17	120
Lachnolæmus	1	—
Julidina	36	190
Pseudodax	—	1
Scarina	21	65
Pseudophycis	—	1
Bregmaceros	—	1
Ophidiidæ	3	7
Fierasfer	—	6
Pleuronectidæ	21	56
Saurina	5	9

	Trop.-Atl.	Ind.-Pac.
Clupeidæ	33	84
Chirocentrus	—	1
Murænidæ	47	130
Pegasus	—	3
Solenostoma	—	2
Syngnathidæ	7	41
Sclerodermi	16	67
Gymnodontes	23	40

A. *Shore Fishes of the Tropical Atlantic.*

The boundaries of the tropical Atlantic extend zoologically a few degrees beyond the Northern and Southern Tropics, but as the mixture with the types of the temperate zone is very gradual, no distinct boundary line can be drawn between the tropical and temperate faunæ.

Types, almost exclusively limited to it, and not found in the Indo-Pacific, are few in nmmber, as *Centropristis, Rhypticus, Hæmulon, Malthe.* A few others preponderate with regard to the number of species, as *Plectropoma, Sargus, Trachynotus, Batrachidæ,* and *Gobiesocidæ.* The Sciænoids are equally represented in both oceans. All the remainder are found in both; but in the minority in the Atlantic, where they are sometimes represented by one or two species only (for instance, *Lethrinus*).

B. *Shore Fishes of the Tropical Indo-Pacific Ocean.*

The ichthyological boundaries of this part of the tropical zone may be approximately given as 30° of lat. N. and S.; on the Australian coasts it should probably be placed still farther south, viz., to 34°; it includes, as mentioned above, the Sandwich Islands, and all the islands of the South Sea, but not the American coasts.

Some eighty genera of Shore fishes are peculiar to the Indo-Pacific, but the majority consists of one or a few species only; comparatively few have a plurality of species, as *Diagramma, Lethrinus, Equula, Teuthis, Amphiprion, Dascyllus, Choerops, Chilinus, Anampses, Stethojulis, Coris, Coiris.*

The Sea-perches, large and small, which feed on Crustaceans and other small fishes, and the coral-feeding Pharyngognaths are the types which show the greatest generic and specific variety in the Indo-Pacific. Then follow the *Squamipinnes* and *Murænidæ*, the *Clupeidæ* and *Carangidæ* families in which the variety is more that of species than of genus. The *Scorpænidæ, Pleuronectidæ, Acronuridæ, Sciænidæ, Syngnathidæ*, and *Teuthyes*, are those which contribute the next largest contingents. Of shore-loving Chondropterygians the *Scylliidæ* and *Trygonidæ* only are represented in moderate numbers, though they are more numerous in this ocean than in any other.

C. *Shore Fishes of the Pacific Coasts of Tropical America.*

As boundaries within which this fauna is comprised, may be indicated 30° lat. N. and S.. as in the Indo-Pacific. Its distinction from the Indo-Pacific lies in the almost entire absence of coral-feeding fishes. There are scarcely any Squamipinnes, Pharyngognaths or Acronuridæ, and the Teuthyes are entirely absent. The genera that remain are such as are found in the tropical zone generally, but the species are entirely different from those of the Indo-Pacific. They are mixed with a sprinkling of peculiar genera, consisting of one or two species, like *Discopyge, Hoplopagrus, Doydixodon*, but they are too few in number to give a strikingly peculiar character to this fauna.

Three districts are distinguishable :—

a. The *Central American district*, in which we include, for the present, Lower California, shows so near an affinity to the tropical Atlantic that, if it were not separated from it by the neck of land uniting the two American Continents, it would most assuredly be regarded as a portion of the Fauna of the tropical Atlantic. With scarcely any exceptions the genera are identical, and of the species found on the Pacific side nearly one-half have proved to be the same as those of the Atlantic. The explanation of this fact has been found in the existence of communications between the two oceans by channels and straits which must have been open till within a recent period. The isthmus of Central America was then partially submerged, and appeared as a chain of islands similar to that of the Antilles; but as the reef-building corals flourished chiefly north and east of those islands, and were absent south and west of them, reef-fishes were excluded from the Pacific shores when the communications were destroyed by the upheaval of the land.

b. The *Galapagoes district* received its coast fauna principally from the Central American district, a part of the species being absolutely the same as on the coast of the Isthmus of Panama, or as in the West Indies. Yet the isolation of this group has continued a sufficiently long period to allow of the development of a number of distinct species of either peculiarly Atlantic genera (such as *Centropristis, Rhypticus, Gobiesox, Prionotus*), or at least tropical genera (such as *Chrysophrys, Pristipoma, Holacanthus, Caranx, Balistes*). A few other types from the Peruvian coast (*Doydixodon*), or even from Japan (*Prionurus*), have established themselves in this group of islands. A species of *Cestracion* has also reached the Galapagoes, but whether from the south, north, or west, cannot be determined.

The presence of the Atlantic fauna on the Pacific side is felt still farther west than the Galapagoes, some Atlantic species having reached the Sandwich Islands, as *Chætodon humeralis* and *Blennius brevipinnis.*

c. The *Peruvian district* possesses a very limited variety of shore fishes, which belong, with few exceptions, like *Discopyge, Hoplognathus, Doydixodon,* to genera distributed throughout the tropical zone, or even beyond it. But the species, so far as they are known at present, are distinct from those of the Indo-Pacific, as well as of the tropical Atlantic; and therefore this district cannot be joined either to the Central American or the Galapagoes.

IV.—The Southern Temperate Zone.

This zone includes the coasts of the southern extremity of Africa, from about 30° lat. S., of the south of Australia with Tasmania, of New Zealand, and the Pacific and Atlantic coasts of South America between 30° and 50° lat. S.

The most striking character of this fauna is the reappearance of types inhabiting the corresponding latitudes of the Northern Hemisphere, and not found in the intervening tropical zone. This interruption of the continuity in the geographical distribution of Shore-fishes is exemplified by species as well as genera, for instance—*Chimæra monstrosa, Galeus canis, Acanthias vulgaris, Acanthias blainvillii, Rhina squatina, Zeus faber, Lophius piscatorius, Centriscus scolopax, Engraulis encrasicholus, Clupea sprattus, Conger vulgaris.* Instances of genera are still more numerous—*Cestracion, Spinax, Pristiophorus, Raja; Callanthias, Polyprion, Histiopterus, Cantharus, Box, Girella, Pagellus, Chilodactylus, Sebastes, Aploactis, Agonus, Lepidopus, Cyttus, Psychrolutidæ, Notacanthus; Lycodes, Merluccius, Lotella, Phycis, Motella; Aulopus; Urocampus, Solenognathus; Myxine.*

Naturally, where the coasts of the tropical zone are continuous with those of the temperate, a number of tropical genera enter the latter, and genera which we have found between the tropics as well as in the temperate zone of the Northern Hemisphere, extend in a similar manner towards the south. But the truly tropical forms are absent; there are no *Squamipinnes*, scarcely any *Mullidæ*, no *Acronuri*, no *Teuthyes*, no *Pomacentridæ* (with a single exception on the coast of Chili), only one genus of *Julidina*, no *Scarina*, which are replaced by another group of Pharyngognaths, the *Odacina*. The *Labrina*, so characteristic of the temperate zone of the Northern Hemisphere, reappear in a distinct genus (*Malacopterus*) on the coast of Juan Fernandez.

The family of *Berycidæ*, equally interesting with regard to their distribution in time and in space, consists of temperate and tropical genera. The genus by which this family is represented in the southern temperate zone (*Trachichthys*) is much more nearly allied to the northern than to the tropical genera.

The true *Cottina* and *Heterolepidina* (forms with a bony stay of the præoperculum, which is generally armed) have not crossed the tropical zone; they are replaced by fishes extremely similar in general form, and having the same habits, but lacking that osteological peculiarity. Their southern analogues belong chiefly to the family *Trachinidæ*, and are types of genera peculiar to the Southern Hemisphere.

The *Discoboli* of the Northern Hemisphere have likewise not penetrated to the south, where they are represented by *Gobiesocidæ*. These two families replace each other in their distribution over the globe.

Nearly all the *Pleuronectidæ* (but they are not numerous) belong to distinct genera, some, however, being remarkably similar in general form to the northern *Pleuronectes*.

With Gadoids *Myxinidæ* reappear, one species being extremely similar to the European Myxine. *Bdellostoma* is a genus peculiar to the southern temperate zone.

As in the northern temperate zone, so in the southern, the number of individuals and the variety of forms is much less than between the tropics. This is especially apparent on comparing the numbers of species constituting a genus. In this zone genera composed of more than ten species are the exception, the majority having only from one to five.

The proportion of genera limited to this zone is rather high; they will be indicated under the several districts, which we distinguish on geographical rather than zoological grounds.

1. The *Cape of Good Hope* district.

The principal genera found in this district are the following (those limited to the entire zone being marked with a single (*) and those peculiar to this district with a double (**) asterisk):—

Chimæra, **Callorhynchus*, *Galeus*, ***Leptocarcharias*, *Scyllium*, *Acanthias*, *Rhinobatus*, *Torpedo*, *Narcine*, *Astrape*, *Raja*.

Serranus, *Dentex*, *Pristipoma*; *Cantharus*, *Box*, ***Dipterodon*, *Sagrus*, *Pagrus*, *Pagellus*, *Chrysophrys*; **Chilodactylus*; *Sebastes*, **Agriopus*; *Trigla*; *Sphyræna*; *Lepidopus*, *Thyrsites*; *Zeus*; *Caranx*; *Lophius*; *Clinus* (10 species), *Cristiceps*; ***Chorisochismus*.

***Halidesmus*, **Genypterus*, *Motella*.

Syngnathus.—**Bdellostoma*.

This list contains many northern forms, which in conjunction with the peculiarly southern types (*Callorhynchus*, *Chilodactylus*, *Agriopus*, *Clinus*, *Genypterus*, *Bdellostoma*) leave no doubt that this district belongs to the southern temperate zone, whilst the Freshwater fishes of South Africa are members of the tropical fauna. Only a few (*Rhinobatus*, *Narcine*, *Astrape*, and *Sphyræna*) have entered from the neighbouring tropical coasts. The development of Sparoids is greater than in any of the other districts of this zone, and may be regarded as one of its distinguishing features.

2. The *South Australian* district comprises the southern coasts of Australia (northwards, about to the latitude of

Sydney), Tasmania, and New Zealand. It is the richest in the southern temperate zone, partly in consequence of a considerable influx of tropical forms on the eastern coast of Australia, where they penetrate farther southwards than should have been expected from merely geographical considerations; partly in consequence of the thorough manner in which the ichthyology of New South Wales and New Zealand has been explored. On the other hand, the western half of the south coast of Australia is still almost a *terra incognita.*

The shore-fishes of New Zealand are not so distinct from those of south-eastern Australia as to deserve to be placed in a separate district. Beside the genera which enter this zone from the Tropics, and which are more numerous on the Australian coast than on that of New Zealand, and beside a few very local genera, the remainder are identical. Many of the South Australian species, besides, are found also on the coasts of New Zealand. The principal points of difference are the extraordinary development of Monacanthus on the coast of South Australia, and the apparently total absence in Australia of Gadoids, which in the New Zealand Fauna are represented by six genera.

Shore-fishes of the South Australian district.

	South Australia and Tasmania.	New Zealand.
*Callorhynchus (antarcticus) .	1	1
Galeus (canis) . .	1	1
Scyllium . . .	2	1
**Parascyllium . .	1	—
Crossorhinus . .	1	—
Cestracion . . .	2	1
Mustelus (antarcticus) .	1	1
Acanthias (vulgaris and blainvillii)	2	1
Rhina . .	1	—
Pristiophorus . .	1	—

	South Australia and Tasmania.	New Zealand.
**Trygonorhina (fasciata)	1	1
Rhinobatus	1	1
Torpedo	—	1
Narcine	1	—
Raja	3	1
Trygon (Urolophus)	3	2
**Enoplosus	1	—
Anthias (richardsonii)	1	1
Callanthias	1	—
Serranus	x[1]	—
Plectropoma	4	—
**Lanioperca	1	—
**Arripis	3	1
Histiopterus	1	—
Erythrichthys	—	1
*Haplodactylus	2	2
Girella	4	—
**Tephræops	1	—
Pagrus	1	1
*Scorpis	2	1
**Atypichthys	1	—
**Trachichthys	—	1
**Chironemus	1	1
**Holoxenus	1	—
Chilodactylus	9	4
**Nemadactylus	1	—
**Latris	2	2
Scorpæna	4	2
**Glyptauchen	1	—
Centropogon	2	—
*Agriopus	1	1
*Aploactis	1	—
**Pentaroge	1	—
Platycephalus	5	—
Lepidotrigla	3	1
Trigla	3	1

[1] Number of species uncertain.

	South Australia and Tasmania.	New Zealand.
**Anema	—	1
**Crapatalus	—	1
**Kathetostoma	1	2
**Leptoscopus	1	3
Percis	2	1
*Aphritis	1	—
Sillago	2	—
*Bovichthys	1	1
*Notothenia	—	1
Sphyræna	1	—
Lepidopus	—	1
Trichiurus	1	—
Thyrsites	1	1
**Platystethus	—	2
Zeus (faber)	1	1
Cyttus	1	1
Trachurus (trachurus)	1	1
Caranx	x	2
*Seriolella	—	1
Pempheris	1	—
Callionymus	3	—
Batrachus	1	—
**Brachionichthys	2	—
**Saccarius	—	1
Clinus	1	1
**Lepidoblennius	1	—
Cristiceps and Tripterygium	4	5
**Patæcus	3	—
**Acanthoclinus	—	1
**Diplocrepis	—	1
**Crepidogaster	3	1
**Trachelochismus	—	1
**Neophrynichthys	—	1
Centriscus	2	1
Notacanthus (sexspinis)	1	1
**Labrichthys	8	2
**Odax	5	1

	South Australia and Tasmania.	New Zealand.
**Coridodax	—	1
**Olistherops	1	—
**Siphonognathus	1	—
Gadus	—	1
Merluccius	—	1
Lotella	—	1
**Pseudophycis	—	1
Motella	—	1
Bregmaceros	—	1
*Genypterus	1	1
**Lophonectes	1	—
**Brachypleura	—	1
Pseudorhombus	—	1
**Ammotretis	1	1
**Rhombosolea	3	3
**Peltorhamphus	—	1
Solea	1	—
Aulopus	1	—
Gonorhynchus (greyi)	1	1
Engraulis (encrasicholus)	1	1
Clupea	1	1
**Chilobranchus	1	—
Conger (vulgaris)	1	1
Ophichthys	1	1
Muræníchthys	1	—
Congromuræna	—	1
Syngnathus	5	2
Ichthyocampus	—	1
**Nannocampus	1	—
Urocampus	1	—
**Stigmatophora	2	1
Solenognathus	2	1
**Phyllopteryx	2	—
Monacanthus	15	1
Ostracion	3	1
*Bdellostoma	—	1
Branchiostoma	1	1

3. The coast-line of the *Chilian district* extends over 20 degrees of latitude only, and is nearly straight. In its northern and warmer parts it is of a very uniform character, and exposed to high and irregular tides, and to remarkable and sudden changes of the levels of land and water, which must seriously interfere with fishes living and propagating near the shore. No river of considerable size interrupts the monotony of the physical conditions, to offer an additional element in favour of the development of littoral animals. In the southern parts, where the coast is lined with archipelagoes, the climate is too severe for the majority of fishes. All these conditions combine to render this district comparatively poor as regards variety of Shore fishes, as will be seen from the following list:—

*Callorhynchus; Scyllium, Acanthias, Spinax; Urolophus.

Serranus, Plectropoma, Polyprion, Pristipoma, Erythrichthys; *Haplodactylus; *Scorpis; Chilodactylus, **Mendosoma; Sebastes, *Agriopus; Trigla, Agonus; *Aphritis, *Eleginus, Pinguipes, Latilus, Notothenia (1 sp.) Umbrina; Thyrsites; Trachurus, Caranx, *Seriolella; Porichthys; **Myxodes, Clinus, Sicyases, Gobiesox.

Heliastes; **Malacopterus; Labrichthys.

Merluccius; *Genypterus, Pseudorhombus.

Engraulis, Clupea; Ophichthys, Muræna.

Syngnathus.—*Bdellostoma.

Of these genera six only are not found in other districts of this zone. Three are peculiar to the Chilian district; *Porichthys* and *Agonus* have penetrated so far southwards from the Peruvian and Californian districts; and *Polyprion* is one of those extraordinary instances in which a very specialised form occurs at almost opposite points of the globe, without having left a trace of its previous existence in, or of its passage through, the intermediate space.

4. The *Patagonian district* is, with the exception of the neighbourhood of the mouth of the Rio de la Plata, almost unknown. In that estuary occur *Mustelus vulgaris*, two *Raja*, two *Trygon*, several Sciænoids, *Paropsis signata* and *Percophis brasilianus* (two fishes peculiar to this coast), *Prionotus punctatus*, *Lœmonema longifilis* (a Gadoid), a *Pseudorhombus*, two Soles, *Engraulis olidus*, a *Syngnathus*, *Conger vulgaris*, and *Ophichthys ocellatus*; and if we notice the occurrence of a *Serranus* and *Caranx*, of *Aphritis* and *Pinguipes*, and of two or three *Clupea*, we shall have enumerated all that is known of this fauna. The fishes of the southern part, viz. the coast of Patagonia proper, southwards to Magelhæn's Straits, are unknown; which is the more to be regretted, as it is most probably the part in which the characteristic types of this district are most developed.

V.—Shore Fishes of the Antarctic Ocean.

To this fauna we refer the shore fishes of the southernmost extremity of South America, from 50° lat. S., with Terra del Fuego and the Falkland Islands, and those of Kerguelen's Land, with Prince Edward's Island. No fishes are known from the other oceanic islands of these latitudes.

In the Southern Hemisphere surface fishes do not extend so far towards the Pole as in the Northern; none are known from beyond 60° lat. S., and the Antarctic Fauna, which is analogous to the Arctic Fauna, inhabits coasts more than ten degrees nearer to the equator. It is very probable that the shores between 60° and the Antarctic circle are inhabited by fishes sufficiently numerous to supply part of the means of subsistence for the large Seals which pass there at least some season of the year, but hitherto none have been obtained by naturalists; all that the present state of our knowledge justifies us in saying is, that the general character of the Fauna of Magelhæn's Straits and Kerguelen's Land is extremely similar to that of Iceland and Greenland.

As in the arctic Fauna, Chondropterygians are scarce, and represented by *Acanthias vulgaris* and species of *Raja*. *Holocephali* have not yet been found so far south, but *Callorhynchus*, which is not uncommon near the northern boundary of this fauna, will prove to extend into it.

As to Acanthopterygians, *Cataphracti* and *Scorpænidæ* are represented as in the arctic Fauna, two of the genera (*Sebastes* and *Agonus*) being identical. The *Cottidæ* are replaced by six genera of *Trachinidæ*, remarkably similar in form to arctic types; but *Discoboli* and the characteristic Arctic Blennioids are absent.

Gadoid Fishes reappear, but are less developed; as usual they are accompanied by *Myxine*. The reappearance of so specialised a genus as *Lycodes* is most remarkable. Flatfishes are scarce as in the North, and belong to peculiar genera.

Physostomes are probably not entirely absent, but hitherto none have been met with so far south. Lophobranchs are scarce, as in the Arctic zone; however, it is noteworthy that a peculiar genus, with persistent embryonic characters (*Protocampus*), is rather common on the shores of the Falkland Islands.

The following are the genera known from this zone. Those with a single asterisk (*) are known to extend into the Temperate zone, but not beyond it; those with a double asterisk (**) are limited to the Antarctic shores:—

	Magelhæn's and Falkland.	Kerguelen.
Acanthias vulgaris . .	1	—
Raja . . .	1	2
Psammobatis . .	1	—
Sebastes . . .	1	—
**Zanclorhynchus . .	—	1

	Magelhæn's and Falkland.	Kerguelen.
*Agriopus . . .	1	—
Agonus . . .	1	—
*Aphritis . . .	1	—
*Eleginus . . .	1	—
**Chænichthys . .	1	1
*Bovichthys . . .	2	—
*Notothenia . . .	8	7
**Harpagifer . . .	1	1
Lycodes . . .	4	—
**Magnea . . .	1	—
Lotella . . .	1	—
Merluccius . . .	1	—
**Lepidopsetta . .	—	1
**Thysanopsetta . .	1	—
Syngnathus . .	1	—
**Protocampus . .	1	—
Myxine . .	1	—
	31	13

Fig. 108.—*Chænichthys rhinoceratus*, shores of the Antarctic Ocean

CHAPTER XX.

DISTRIBUTION OF PELAGIC FISHES.

Pelagic Fishes,—that is, fishes inhabiting the surface of mid-ocean (see p. 255), belong to various orders, viz. Chondropterygians, Acanthopterygians, Physostomes, Lophobranchs, and Plectognaths. But neither Anacanths nor Pharyngognaths contribute to this series of the Marine Fauna. The following genera and families are included in it:—

Chondropterygii: Carcharias, Galeocerdo, Thalassorhinus, Zygæna, Triænodon, Lamnidæ, Rhinodon, Notidanidæ, Læmargus, Euprotomicrus, Echinorhinus, Isistius; Myliobatidæ.

Acanthopterygii: Dactylopterus, Micropteryx, Scombrina, Gastrochisma, Nomeus, Centrolophus, Coryphænina, Seriola, Temnodon, Naucrates, Psenes, Xiphiidæ, Antennarius.

Physostomi: Sternoptychidæ, Scopelus, Astronesthes, Scombresocidæ (majority).

Lophobranchii: Hippocampus.

Plectognathi: Orthagoriscus and some other Gymnodonts.

Pelagic fishes differ much from one another in their mode of life. The majority are excellent swimmers, which not only can move with great rapidity, but also are possessed of great powers of endurance, and are thus enabled to continue their course for weeks, apparently without the necessity of rest: such are many Sharks, Scombroids, Dolphins, Pilot-fish, Sword-fishes. In some, as in *Dactylopterus* and *Exocœtus*, the ability of taking flying leaps out of the water is superadded to the power of swimming (Flying-fishes). But in others the power of swimming is greatly reduced, as in *Antennarius, Hippocampus*, and Gymnodonts; they frequent places in the ocean covered with floating seaweed, or drift on the surface without resistance, at the mercy of wind and current. The *Echeneis* or Sucking-fishes attach themselves to other large fish, ships, or floating objects, and allow themselves to be carried about, unless change of climate or want of food obliges them to abandon their temporary carrier. Finally, another class of Pelagic fishes come to the surface of the ocean during the night only; in the day time they descend to some depth, where they are undisturbed by the rays of the sun or the agitation of the surface-water: such are *Brama*, the *Sternoptychidæ, Scopelus, Astronesthes*; fishes, the majority of which are provided with those extraordinary luminary organs that we find so much developed in the true Deep-sea fishes. Indeed, this last kind of Pelagic fishes forms a passage to the Deep-sea forms.

Pelagic fishes, like shore fishes, are most numerous in the Tropical Zone; and, with few exceptions (*Echinorhinus, Psenes, Sternoptychidæ, Astronesthes*), the same genera are represented in the tropical Atlantic as well as in the Indo-Pacific. The number of identical species occurring in both these oceans is great, and probably still greater than would appear from systematic lists, in which there are retained many specific names that were given at a time when species were believed to have a very limited range. The Pelagic fauna of the tropics gradually passes into that of the temperate zones, only a few genera, like *Cybium, Psenes, Antennarius*, being almost entirely confined to the tropics. All the other tropical genera range into the temperate zones, but their representatives become scarcer with the increasing distance from the equator. North of 40° lat. N. many genera have disappeared, or are met with in isolated examples only, as *Carcharias, Zygæna, Notidanus, Myliobatidæ, Dactylopterus, Echeneis,*

Nomeus, Coryphæna, Schedophilus, Seriola, Temnodon, Antennarius, Sternoptychidæ, Astronesthes, Exocoetus, Tetrodon, Diodon; and only one genus of Sharks, *Galeocerdo*, approaches the Arctic circle. Some few species, like *Antennarius, Scopelus*, are carried by currents near to the northern confines of the temperate zones; but such occurrences are accidental, and these fishes must be regarded as entirely foreign to the fauna of those latitudes. On the other hand, some Pelagic fishes inhabit the temperate zones, whilst their occurrence within the tropics is very problematical; thus, in the Atlantic, *Thalassorhinus, Selache, Læmargus, Centrolophus, Diana, Ausonia, Lampris* (all genera composed of one or two species only). Beside the Shark mentioned, no other Pelagic fishes are known from the Arctic Ocean.

We possess very little information about the Pelagic fish-fauna of the Southern oceans. So much only is certain, that the tropical forms *gradually* disappear; but it would be hazardous, in the present state of our knowledge, to state even approximately, the limits of the southward range of a single genus Scarcely more is known about the appearance of types peculiar to the Southern temperate zone; for instance, the gigantic Shark (*Rhinodon*), representing the Northern Selache, near the coasts of South Africa, and the Scombroid genus, *Gastrochisma*, in the South Pacific.

The largest of marine fishes, *Rhinodon, Selache, Carcharodon, Myliobatidæ, Thynnus, Xiphiidæ, Orthagoriscus*, belong to the Pelagic Fauna. Young fishes are frequently found in mid-ocean, which are the offspring of shore-fishes normally depositing their spawn near the coast The manner, in which this fry passes into the open sea, is unknown; for it has not yet been ascertained whether it is carried by currents from the place where it was deposited originally, or whether shore-fishes sometimes spawn at a distance from the coast. We may remember that shore-fishes inhabit not only coasts but also submerged banks with some depth of water above, and that, by the action of the water, spawn deposited on these latter localities is very liable to be dispersed over wide areas of the ocean. Embryoes of at least some shore-fishes hatched under abnormal conditions seem to have an abnormal growth up to a certain period of their life, when they perish. The *Leptocephali* must be regarded as such abnormally developed fish (see p. 179). Fishes of a similar condition are the so-called Pelagic *Plagusiæ*, young Pleuronectoids, the origin of which is still unknown. As mentioned before, Flat-fishes, like all the other Anacanths, are otherwise not represented in the Pelagic fauna.

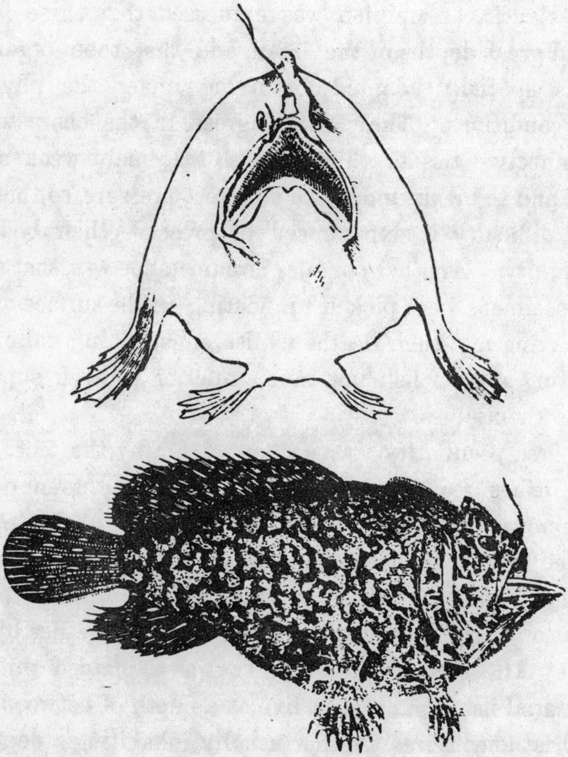

Figs. 109 and 110.—*Antennarius caudimaculatus*, a pelagic fish, from the Indian Ocean.

CHAPTER XXI.

THE FISHES OF THE DEEP SEA.

THE knowledge of the existence of deep-sea fishes is one of the recent discoveries of ichthyology. It is only about twenty years ago that, from the evidence afforded by the anatomical structure of a few singular fishes obtained in the North Atlantic, an opinion was expressed that these fishes inhabited great depths of the ocean, and that their organisation was specially adapted for living under the physical abyssal conditions. These fishes agreed in the character of their connective tissue, which was so extremely weak as to yield to, and to break under, the slightest pressure, so that the greatest difficulty is experienced to preserve their body in its continuity. Another singular circumstance was, that some of the specimens were picked up floating on the surface of the water, having met their deaths whilst engaged in swallowing or digesting another fish not much inferior or even superior in size to themselves.

The first peculiarity was accounted for by the fact that, if those fishes really inhabited the great depths supposed, their removal from the enormous pressure under which they lived would be accompanied by such an expansion of gases within their tissues as to rupture them, and to cause a separation of the parts which had been held together by the pressure. The second circumstance was explained thus :— A raptatorial fish organised to live at a depth of between 500 and 800 fathoms seizes another usually inhabiting a depth of between 300 and 500 fathoms. In its struggles to escape, the fish seized, nearly as large or strong as the attacking fish, carries the latter out of its depth into a higher stratum, where the diminished pressure causes such an expansion of gases as to make the destroyer with its victim rise with increasing rapidity towards the surface, which they reach dead or in a dying condition. Specimens in this condition are not rarely picked up; and as, of course, comparatively few can by accident fall into the hands of naturalists, occurrences of the kind related must happen very often.

Thus, the existence of fishes peculiarly adapted for the deep sea has been a fact maintained and admitted for some time in Ichthyology; and as the same genera and species were found at very distant parts of the ocean, it was further stated that those Deep-sea fishes were not limited in their range, and that, consequently, the physical conditions of the depths of the ocean must be the same or nearly the same over the whole globe. That Deep-sea fishes were not of a peculiar order, but chiefly modified forms of surface types, was another conclusion arrived at from the sporadic evidence collected during the period which preceded systematic deep-sea dredging.

However, nothing was positively known as to the exact depths inhabited by those fishes until observations were made during the voyage of H.M.S. "Challenger." The results obtained by this expedition afforded a surer and more extended basis for our knowledge of Deep-sea fishes.

The physical conditions of the deep sea, which must affect the organisation and distribution of fishes, are the following:—

1. Absence of sunlight. Probably the rays of the sun do not penetrate to, and certainly do not extend beyond, a depth of 200 fathoms, therefore we may consider this to be the depth where the Deep-sea fauna commences. Absence of light is, of necessity, accompanied by modifications of the organs of vision and by simplification of colours.

2. The absence of sunlight is in some measure compensated for by the presence of phosphorescent light, produced by many marine animals, and also by numerous Deep-sea fishes.

3. Depression and equality of the temperature. At a depth of 500 fathoms the temperature of the water is already as low as 40° Fahr., and perfectly independent of the temperature of the surface-water; and from the greatest depths upwards to about 1000 fathoms the temperature is uniformly but a few degrees above freezing-point. Temperature, therefore, ceases to offer an obstacle to the unlimited dispersal of Deep-sea fishes.

4. The increased pressure by the water. The pressure of the atmosphere on the level of the sea amounts to fifteen pounds per square inch of the surface of the body of an animal; but the pressure amounts to a ton weight for every 1000 fathoms of depth.

5. With the sunlight, vegetable life ceases in the depths of the sea All Deep-sea fishes are therefore carnivorous; the most voracious feeding frequently on their own offspring, and the toothless kinds being nourished by the animalcules which live on the bottom, or which, "like a constant rain," settle down from the upper strata towards the bottom of the sea.

6. The perfect quiet of the water at great depths. The agitation of the water, caused by the disturbances of the air does not extend beyond the depth of a few fathoms; below this surface-stratum there is no other movement except the quiet flow of ocean-currents, and near the bottom of the deep sea the water is probably in a state of almost entire quiescence

The effect upon fishes of the physical conditions described is clearly testified by the modification of one or more parts of their organisation, so that every Deep-sea fish may be recognised as such, without the accompanying positive evidence that it has been caught at a great depth; and *vice versa*, fishes reputed to have been obtained at a great depth, and not having any of the characteristics of the dwellers of the deep sea, must be regarded as surface-fishes.

The most striking characteristic, found in many Deep-sea fishes, is in relation to the tremendous pressure under which they live. Their osseous and muscular systems are, as compared with the same parts of surface-fishes, very feebly developed. The bones have a fibrous, fissured, and cavernous texture; are light, with scarcely any calcareous matter, so that the point of a needle will readily penetrate them without breaking. The bones, especially the vertebræ, appear to be most loosely connected with one another; and it requires the most careful handling to prevent the breaking of the connective ligaments. The muscles, especially the great lateral muscles of the trunk and tail, are thin, the fascicles being readily separated from one another or torn, the connective tissue being extremely loose, feeble, or apparently absent. This peculiarity has been observed in the *Trachypteridæ*, *Plagyodus*, *Chiasmodus*, *Melanocetus*, *Saccopharynx*. But we cannot assume that it actually obtains whilst those fishes exist under their natural conditions. Some of them are most rapacious creatures which must be able to execute rapid and powerful movements to catch and overpower their prey; and for that object their muscular system, thin as its layers may be, must be as firm, and the chain of the segments of their vertebral column as firmly linked together as in surface-fishes. Therefore, it is evident that the change which the body of those fishes has undergone on their withdrawal from the pressure under which they live is a much aggravated form of the affection that is experienced by persons reaching great altitudes in their ascent of a mountain or in a balloon. In every living organism with an intestinal tract there are accumulations of free gases; and, moreover, the blood and other fluids, which permeate every part of the body, contain gases in solution. Under greatly diminished pressure these gases expand, so that, if the withdrawal from a depth is not an extremely slow and gradual process, the various tissues must be distended, loosened, ruptured; and what is a vigorous fish at a depth of 500 or more fathoms, appears at the surface as a loosely-jointed body which, if the skin is not of sufficient toughness, can only be kept together with difficulty. At great depths a fibrous osseous structure and a thin layer of muscles suffices to obtain the same results for which, at the surface, thickness of muscle and firm osseous or cartilaginous tissue are necessary.

The muciferous system of many Deep-sea fishes is developed in an extraordinary degree. We find already in fishes which are comparatively little removed from the surface (that is to depths of 100-200 fathoms), the lateral line much wider than in their congeners or nearest allies which live on the surface, as in *Trachichthys*, *Hoplostethus*, many *Scorpænidæ*. But in fishes inhabiting depths of 1000 and more fathoms, the whole muciferous system is dilated; it is especially the surface of the skull which is occupied by large cavities (*Macruridæ*, deep-sea *Ophidiidæ*), and the whole body seems to be covered with a layer of mucus. These cavities collapse and shrink in specimens which have been preserved in spirit for some time, but a re-immersion in water for a short time generally suffices to show the immense quantity of mucus secreted by them. The physiological use of this secretion is unknown; it has been observed to have phosphorescent properties in perfectly fresh specimens.

The colours of Deep-sea fishes are extremely simple, their bodies being either black or silvery; in a few only are some filaments or the fin-rays of a bright scarlet colour. Among the black forms albinoes are not scarce.

The organ of sight is the first to be affected by a sojourn in deep water. Even in fishes which habitually live at a depth of only 80 fathoms, we find the eye of a proportionally larger size than in their representatives at the surface. In such fishes the eyes increase in size with the depth inhabited by them, down to the depth of 200 fathoms, the large eyes being necessary to collect as many rays of light as possible. Beyond that depth small-eyed fishes as well as large-eyed occur, the former having their want of vision compensated for by tentacular organs of touch, whilst the latter have no such accessory organs, and evidently see only by the aid of phosphorescence. In the greatest depths blind fishes occur with rudimentary eyes and without special organs of touch.

Many fishes of the deep sea are provided with more or less numerous, round, shining, mother-of-pearl-coloured bodies, imbedded in the skin. These so-called phosphorescent or luminous organs are either larger bodies of an oval or irregularly elliptical shape placed on the head. in the vicinity of the eye, or smaller round globular bodies arranged symmetrically in series along the side of the body and tail, especially near the abdominal profile, less frequently along the back. The former have not yet been anatomically examined. The number of pairs of the latter is in direct relation to that of the segments of the vertebral column, the muscular system, etc. (metameres); and two kinds may be distinguished differing from each other in their anatomical structure. The organs of one kind consist of an anterior, biconvex, lens-like body, which is transparent during life, simple or composed of rods (*Chauliodus*); and of a posterior chamber which is filled with a transparent fluid, and coated with a dark membrane composed of hexagonal cells, or of rods arranged as in a retina. This structure is found in *Astronesthes, Stomias, Chauliodus,* etc. In the other kind the organ shows throughout a simply glandular structure, but apparently without an efferent duct (*Gonostoma, Scopelus, Maurolicus, Argyropelecus*). Branches of the spinal nerves run to each organ, and are distributed over the retina-like membrane or the glandular follicles. The former kind of organs are considered by some naturalists true organs of vision (accessory eyes), the function of the latter being left unexplained by them.

Although, thus, these organs morphologically differ from each other, there is no doubt that the functions of all have some relation to the peculiar conditions of light under which the fishes provided with them live; these fishes being either deep-sea forms or nocturnal pelagic kinds. There are three possible hypotheses as to the function of these organs:—

1. All the different kinds of organs are sensory, or, in other words, accessory eyes.

2. Only the organs with a lenticular body are sensory, and those with a glandular structure produce and emit phosphorescent light.

3. All are producers of light.

There are very serious objections to adopting the first view. *Scopelus* and *Argyropelecus* possess not only perfectly developed, but even large eyes, specially adapted for a nocturnal life; and therefore accessory organs of vision must appear to be quite superfluous to them. On the other hand, in Deep-sea fishes without external eyes, which would seem to especially require these metameric organs of sense, they are invariably absent. And, finally, it is quite inconceivable that the glandular structures should have the faculty of conveying impressions of light to the nervous centre. The second supposition seems therefore to be nearer the truth; and is supported by the fact that the glandular organs of Scopeli have actually been observed to gleam with phosphorescent light, and by the obvious morphological similarity of the organs with a lenticular body and retina-like membrane to an organ of vision. We are, moreover, justified, from an *à priori* consideration, in supposing that in depths to which no sunlight descends, and which are illuminated by phosphorescent light only, peculiar organs of vision would have been developed. On the other hand, this supposition is opposed by the fact that many fishes which dwell in those abyssal depths are provided with large ordinary eyes (as the *Trachypteri*, the majority of *Macruridæ*), and, therefore, that the ordinary organ of vision is quite sufficient for seeing by phosphorescent light. Thus, whilst we must admit that those compound organs may prove to be organs of sense, we maintain at the same time that their morphological nature is not opposed to the belief that they too, like the glandular organs, are producers of light. It may be produced at the bottom of the posterior chamber, and emitted through the lenticular body in particular directions, with the same effect as light is sent through the convex glass of a "bull's eye." This hypothesis seems to be less bold than the other, which would require us to believe that vertebrate animals, with a nervous centre specialised for the reception of the impressions of the higher senses, should receive them through the spinal chord.

[See *Ussow*, "Ueber den Bau der sogenannten augenaehnlichen Flecken einiger Knochenfische." St. Petersburg, Bullet. 1879.]

Whenever we find in a fish long delicate filaments, developed in connection with the fins or the extremity of the tail, we may conclude that it is an inhabitant of still water and of quiet habits. Many deep-sea fishes (*Trachypteridæ*, *Macruridæ*, *Ophidiidæ*, *Bathypterois*) are provided with such filamentous prolongations, the development of which is perfectly in accordance with their sojourn in the absolutely quiet waters of abyssal depths.

Some of the raptatorial Deep-sea fishes have a stomach so distensible and capacious that it can receive a fish of twice or thrice the bulk of the destroyer (*Melanocetus*, *Chiasmodus*, *Saccopharynx*). Deglutition is performed in them not by means of the muscles of the pharynx, as in other fishes, but by the independent and alternate action of the jaws, as in Snakes. These fishes cannot be said to swallow their food, but rather draw themselves over their victim, in the fashion of an *Actinia*.

Before the voyage of H.M.S. "Challenger," scarcely thirty Deep-sea fishes were known. This number is now much increased by the discovery of many new species and genera; but, singularly, no new types of families were discovered: nothing but what might have been expected from our previous knowledge of this group of fishes. Modifications of certain organs, perfectly novel, and of the greatest interest, were found, as we shall see in the "Systematic Part;" but the most important results of this voyage are that the general character of the abyssal fish-fauna, the abundance of fishes, and the exact depths to which fishes may descend, have been ascertained.

However, the statements of the depths at which the fishes collected by the "Challenger" were taken cannot be received without some critical examination of each individual species. No precaution was taken to keep the mouth of the dredge closed during its descent or ascent, and therefore it is quite within the limits of probability that sometimes fishes were accidentally enclosed within the dredge, whilst it was traversing the surface strata. And this has happened more than once; for it is quite certain that common surface fishes like *Sternoptyx* and *Astronesthes*, never ranged to a depth of 2500 fathoms. On the other hand, the majority of the fishes obtained offer sufficient evidence from their own organisation that they live on the bottom, and are unable to support themselves in the water at a certain distance from the bottom or surface; and, consequently, that they actually were obtained at the depth to which the dredge descended.

As far as the observations go at present, no distinct bathymetrical regions, which would be characterised by peculiar forms, can be defined. The depths from 200 to

600 fathoms are inhabited by numerous forms, still strongly reminding us of surface types. To this fauna belong the few Chondropterygians of the deep sea, a Sebastes and Setarches, a Beryx and Polymixia, a Cottus, etc.; but they are associated with many others which descend to the greatest depths. And before anything like a division into bathymetrical zones can be attempted, the observations of the "Challenger" expedition must be confirmed and supplemented by other series of similar systematic observations. One of the most startling conclusions at which we would have to arrive from the "Challenger" observations is, that some of the species of Deep-sea fishes would range from a depth of some 300 fathoms down to one of 2000 fathoms; or, in other words, that a fish which has once attained in its organisation to that modification by which it is enabled to exist under the pressure of half a ton, can easily accommodate itself to one of two tons or more,—a conclusion which is not in accordance with anatomical facts, and which must be confirmed by other observations before we can adopt it. But if the vertical range of Deep-sea fishes is actually as it appears from the "Challenger" lists, then there is no more distinct vertical than horizontal distribution of Deep-sea fishes.

The greatest depth reached hitherto by a dredge in which fishes were enclosed is 2900 fathoms. But the specimens thus obtained belong to a species (*Gonostoma microdon*), which seems to be extremely abundant in upper strata of the Atlantic and Pacific, and were therefore most likely caught by the dredge in its ascent. The next greatest depth, viz., 2750 fathoms, must be accepted as one at which fishes undoubtedly do live; the fish obtained from this depth of the Atlantic, *Bathyophis ferox*, showing by its whole habit that it is a form living on the bottom of the ocean.

The fish-fauna of the deep sea is composed chiefly of forms or modifications of forms which we find represented at the surface in the cold and temperate zones, or which appear as nocturnal pelagic forms. The Chondropterygians are few in number, not descending to a depth of more than 600 fathoms. The Acanthopterygians, which form the majority of the coast and surface faunas, are also scantily represented; genera identical with surface types are confined to the same inconsiderable depths as the Chondropterygians, whilst those Acanthopterygians which are so much specialised for the life in the deep sea as to deserve generic separation, range from 200 to 2400 fathoms. Three distinct families of Acanthopterygians belong to the deep-sea fauna, viz. *Trachypteridæ*, *Lophotidæ*, and *Notacanthidæ;* they respectively consist of three, one, or two genera only.

Gadidæ, *Ophidiidæ*, and *Macruridæ* are very numerous, ranging through all depths; they constitute about one-fourth of the whole deep-sea fauna.

Of *Physostomi*, the families of *Sternoptychidæ*, *Scopelidæ*, *Stomiatidæ*, *Salmonidæ*, *Bathythrissidæ*, *Alepocephalidæ*, *Halosauridæ*, and *Murænidæ* are represented. Of these the *Scopeloids* are the most numerous, constituting nearly another fourth of the fauna. *Salmonidæ* are scarce, with three small genera only. *Bathythrissidæ* include one species only, which is probably confined in its vertical as well as horizontal range; it occurs at a depth of about 350 fathoms in the sea of Japan. The *Alepocephalidæ* and *Halosauridæ*, known before the "Challenger" expedition from isolated examples only, prove to be true, widely-spread, deep-sea types. Eels are well represented, and seem to descend to the greatest depths.

Myxine has been obtained from a depth of 345 fathoms.

It will be useful to append a complete list of Deep-sea fishes, with the depths as ascertained by the dredgings of the "Challenger:"—

List of Deep-sea Fishes.

	Fathoms.
CHONDROPTERYGIANS—	
Raja	565
Scyllium	400
Centroscyllium	245
Centrophorus	345-500
ACANTHOPTERYGIANS—	
Pomatomus	(? down to) 200
Sebastes	275
Setarches	215
Beryx	345
Melamphaes	(? beyond) 200
Polymixia	345
Nealotus	
Nesiarchus	
Aphanopus	
Euoxymetopon	
Lepidopus	345
Gempylus	
Anomalops	
Antigonia	
Diretmus	
Cottus	565
Bathydraco	1260
Oneirodes	
Melanocetus johnsonii	1850
" bispinosus	360
Himantolophus	
Chaunax	215
Ceratias	2400
Halieutichthys	
Dibranchus	360
Trachypteridæ	
Lophotes	
Notacanthus rissoanus	1875
" bonapartii	400

ANACANTHINI—	Fathoms.
Melanonus	1975
Halargyreus	
Lotella marginata	120-345
Physiculus	345
Uraleptus	
Læmonema	
Haloporphyrus australis	55-70
„ lepidion	345-600
„ rostratus	600-1375
Chiasmodus niger	1500
Sirembo grandis	1875
„ macrops	375
„ messieri	345
„ ocellatus	350
„ brachysoma	350
Acanthonus armatus	1075
Typhlonus nasus	2440
Aphyonus gelatinosus	1400
Rhinonus ater	2150
Bathynectes laticeps	2500
„ compressus	1075-2500
„ gracilis	1400
Pteridium	
Macrurus (12 species)	120-700
Coryphænoides norvegicus	
„ serratus	
„ nasutus	345-565
„ villosus	345
„ rudis	500-650
„ æqualis	600
„ crassiceps	520-650
„ microlepis	215
„ murrayi	1100
„ serrulatus	700
„ filicauda	1800-2650
„ variabilis	1375-2425
„ affinis	1900

	Fathoms.
Coryphænoides carinatus	500
„ longifilis	565
„ altipinnis	565-1875
„ asper	500-1875
„ leptolepis	350-2050
„ sclerorhynchus	1090
„ denticulatus	275-520
Malacocephalus	350
Bathygadus cottoides	520-700
multifilis	500
Sternoptychidæ—	
Argyropelecus	1127 [?]
Sternoptyx	0-2500 [?]
Polyipnus	255
Gonostoma denudatum	
„ microdon	500-2900 [?]
„ elongatum	360-800
„ gracile	345-2425
Chauliodus	565-2560
Scopelidæ—	
Bathysaurus ferox	1100
„ mollis	1875-2385
Bathypterois longifilis	520-630
„ longipes	2650
„ quadrifilis	500-770
„ longicauda	2550
Chlorophthalmus agassizii	215
„ nigripinnis	120
„ gracilis	1100-1425
Scopelus engraulis	255
„ antarcticus	1950
„ mizolepis	800
„ dumerilii	215
„ macrolepidotus	520-630
„ crassiceps	675-1550
„ macrostoma	2350-2425
„ microps	1375
Odontostomus hyalinus	

	Fathoms.
Odontostomus humeralis . .	500
Nannobrachium nigrum . .	500
Ipnops murrayi . . .	1600-2150
Paralepis	
Sudis	
Plagyodus	
STOMIATIDÆ—	
Astronesthes niger . . .	2500 [?]
Stomias boa . . .	450-1800
„ barbatus . . .	
„ ferox . . .	
Echiostoma barbatum . .	
„ micripnus . .	2150
„ microdon . .	2440
Malacosteus niger . . .	
„ indicus . . .	500
Bathyophis ferox . . .	2750
SALMONIDÆ—	
Argentina . . .	
Microstoma	
Bathylagus antarcticus . .	1950
„ atlanticus . .	2040
BATHYTHRISSIDÆ—	
Bathythrissa dorsalis . .	345
ALEPOCEPHALIDÆ—	
Alepocephalus rostratus . .	
„ niger . .	1400
Platytroctes apus . . .	1500
Bathytroctes microlepis . .	1090
„ rostratus . .	675
„ macrolepis . .	2150
Xenodermichthys . . .	345
HALOSAURIDÆ—	
Halosaurus owenii . . .	
„ affinis . . .	565
„ macrochir . .	1090-1375
„ mediorostris . .	700
„ rostratus . .	2750

MURÆNIDÆ—	Fathoms.
Nemichthys scolopacea . .	
" infans . . .	500-2500
Cyema atrum . .	1500-1800
Saccopharynx . .	
Synaphobranchus pinatus . .	345-1200
" bathybius . .	1875-2050
" brevidorsalis .	1075-1375
" affinis . .	345
Nettastoma parviceps .	345
CYCLOSTOMATA—	
Myxine australis . .	345

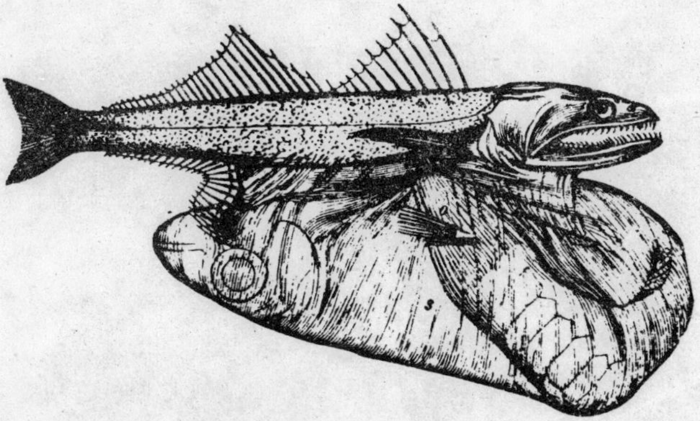

Fig. 111.—*Chiasmodus niger;* obtained in the North Atlantic at a depth of 1500 fathoms; the specimen has swallowed a large Scopelus (*s*); *o*, ventral fin.